PUBLIC AND THIRD SECTOR LEADERSHIP: EXPERIENCE SPEAKS

PUBLIC AND THIRD SECTOR LEADERSHIP: EXPERIENCE SPEAKS

BRIAN HOWIESON
University of Dundee, Dundee, UK

JULIE HODGES
Durham University, Durham, UK

Emerald

United Kingdom – North America – Japan
India – Malaysia – China

Emerald Group Publishing Limited
Howard House, Wagon Lane, Bingley BD16 1WA, UK

First edition 2014

Second edition 2016

Copyright © 2016 Emerald Group Publishing Limited

Reprints and permissions service
Contact: permissions@emeraldinsight.com

British Library Cataloguing in Publication Data
A catalogue record for this book is available from the British Library

ISBN: 978-1-78635-216-3

Printed and bound by CPI Group (UK) Ltd, Croydon, CR0 4YY

ISOQAR certified
Management System,
awarded to Emerald
for adherence to
Environmental
standard
ISO 14001:2004.

Certificate Number 1985
ISO 14001

INVESTOR IN PEOPLE

Contents

List of Figures

List of Tables

About the Authors

Brian Howieson (PhD, MPhil, MBA, BSc, FRSA) is Director of MBA Programmes at the Graduate School of Natural Resources Law, Policy, and Management at the University of Dundee. He joined the University of Dundee in 2013 after completing a 4-year Foundation for Management Education/Economic and Social Research Council Senior Fellowship at Stirling Management School, the University of Stirling. Prior to this, he had a 25+ year career with the Royal Air Force (UK Ministry of Defence — Defence Fellow (2002)) and the Royal College of Physicians and Surgeons.

Julie Hodges (PhD, MA, BA, PGCert) is Director of Global MBA Programmes at Durham University Business School and a senior fellow of the Foundation for Management Education. Prior to joining academia, Julie worked for 20 years in a variety of management and leadership roles in companies across the globe, including the British Council, Vertex and PricewaterhouseCoopers. Julie has worked extensively in the academic and business world in the field of organisational change and development. She is an experienced facilitator of individuals, groups and businesses facing change. Her areas of teaching and research expertise include leadership and implementing and sustaining change in organisations. Julie is the author of 'Sustaining change in organizations,' due to be published in Winter 2014.

About the Contributors

Jane Ashcroft joined Anchor in 1999 from BUPA, which had acquired Care First plc where she was Personnel Director. She was previously HR Manager and Company Secretary with Bromford Housing Group, and before that Assistant Secretary with Midlands Electricity plc. Jane chairs the English Community Care Association — the largest representative body for providers of adult social care and is a Trustee of The Silverline, a helpline for older people. She was appointed Chief Executive of Anchor on 9 March 2010. Jane is a Fellow of the Institute of Chartered Secretaries, a Member of the Chartered Institute of Personnel and Development, and a Non-Executive Director of Dignity plc.

Balbir Bhogal is the Deputy Director of Informatics in a large acute Teaching hospital. He has spent the last twenty years in a variety of different roles within the acute care setting. These have ranged from research and audit roles to the operational management of administration services. Balbir has spent the last few years within informatics leading a number of technology-enabled change programmes.

Gary Bishop is the Founder and Managing Director of Justlife, a Charity and Social Enterprise, which supports vulnerable people who are homeless and live in temporary accommodation. Gary and his wife Hannah started Justlife in Manchester when a friend of theirs was placed in Bed and Breakfast accommodation after leaving prison and died shortly after. Justlife now provides health and social care services to hundreds of people every week who find themselves living in similar circumstances in Manchester. Recently returning to his home town of Brighton, Gary has helped Justlife to launch a support programme for homeless people who are leaving hospital. He hopes to develop more integrated health and social care services to those who are often forgotten. Gary previously worked for The Salvation Army and has provided coaching, training and consultancy to a wide range of leaders and organisations across the sectors. He has three young children, is a novice marathon runner, and a keen supporter of Manchester City.

Carlton Brand has worked in local government since 2004 and joined Wiltshire Council in 2007. As Corporate Director, he led the transition to the new unitary Council — merging four district councils with the county based on a radical idea of localism through community area working. As part of the on-going transformation programme, he led the introduction of systems thinking (lean) from his manufacturing background to transform service performance for customers and communities whilst radically reducing costs. He has developed a new organisation model for the council, which is based on hubs and campuses, working with partners such as the police and health around the community areas. Carlton is passionate about developing future leaders and has led the development of a coaching and mentoring programme across the council in order to develop leaders and enable managers to share their skills and experience. He is an accredited executive coach and leadership mentor and a Chartered Manager and Fellow of the Chartered Management Institute. For the first twenty years of his career, Carlton worked for Ford Motor Company: first as a design engineer in product development and latterly as a senior manager leading large teams of engineers on the concept, design, development and launch into manufacturing of major new model programmes such as the Ford Focus. He worked widely across Europe, the United States and Japan in many Ford and supplier engineering and manufacturing facilities. Carlton runs his own executive coaching practice, www.leadershipmentor.co.uk. He holds doctoral and masters degrees in Engineering and Management and a Bachelors degree in Business Studies. His biography appears in Who's Who.

Sue Bruce is Chief Executive of City of Edinburgh Council having been previously Chief Executive at Aberdeen City Council and East Dunbartonshire Council. Sue Bruce holds an M.Phil. Politics/Government and LLB (Scots Law) from the University of Strathclyde, a Diploma in Youth and Community Studies from Jordanhill College of Education and Certificate in Strategic Public Sector Negotiation from the John F. Kennedy School of Government, Harvard University. She is an Elected Fellow of the RSA (FRSA). In May 2010 and again in May 2011, Sue received the Prince's Business Ambassador Award from HRH The Prince Charles; in October 2010 received the Scottish Public Sector Leader of the Year Award; and in November 2013, she was named Chief Executive of the Year in the HR NETWORK National Awards.

Alison Clare is a freelance project, programme and change manager with 25 years experience implementing business change and IT applications across both the public and private sector. An ex-Oracle employee, she has delivered change projects in the NHS since 2006, specifically at Royal Liverpool and more recently at Leeds Teaching Hospital rolling out the electronic patient record programme of work. Since completing an MBA in 2007, she has been researching change and sustaining change. Alison is currently completing her PhD from Durham University and also lectures on a part-time basis on business transformation and benefits management.

Bernard Collier is a Trustee at the National Private Tenants Organisation (NTPTO), which campaigns for professionally managed, secure, decent and affordable private rented homes in sustainable communities. Prior to this he was Chief Executive at Voluntary Action Westminster. Bernard has also been a Trustee at the National Association for Voluntary and Community Action and a Director at Paddington Integration Project. He is an enthusiastic, entrepreneurial leader with expertise in transforming and managing 'Not for Profit' organisations. Bernard has considerable experience of strategically influencing the operating environment for social action on a national, regional and local level. He is passionate about the unique contribution that community innovation and enterprise can make in improving people's lives.

David Cook has 20 years experience of leadership in charities and social enterprises, encompassing the arts, heritage and social care sectors. He is Chief Executive of Wasps Artists' Studios, an arts social enterprise which specialises in developing and managing affordable workspace for the cultural and creative industries sectors across Scotland, regenerating redundant buildings and rejuvenating failing neighbourhoods. Wasps is one of the largest organisations of its kind in the Europe, supporting almost 1000 creative people each year at 17 urban, rural and island locations. David has raised almost £20 million of capital funding in the last decade to invest in improving the organisation's services and reach across the country, driving its rapid growth and seeing turnover double every 4−5 years. He also played an instrumental role in forming the Scottish Artists Union, now an affiliated Trades Union with more than 1000 members. David also chaired the Investment Panel for the Scottish Government's Scottish Investment Fund, which invested £30 million into social enterprises across the country. He currently sits on the Scottish Government Third Sector Business Support Stakeholder Group, is a trustee of the National Federation of Artist Studio Providers, and chairs NVA, a leading environmental arts company. David recently became a Fellow of the Royal Institution of Chartered Surveyors.

John Cooper was commissioned into The King's Own Scottish Borderers (KOSB) in 1975. In his early career, he served in Zimbabwe, NW Europe and the United States. He Commanded 1st Battalion The King's Own Scottish Borderers in South Armagh, Belfast and Edinburgh, 12th Mechanized Brigade in Bosnia, the United Kingdom and Canada and 1st (United Kingdom) Armoured Division in Germany and Southern Iraq. He then became Director General Training Support responsible for all collective training organisations for the British Army around the world. He was the Deputy Commanding General of Combined Forces Command, Afghanistan in 2004 and Deputy Commanding General of Multi-National Forces Iraq in 2008−2009. He left the Army in the rank of Lieutenant General in 2009 and is now Chief Operating Officer of the Royal College of Physicians and Surgeons of Glasgow. He is a Companion of the Order of the Bath and holds the Distinguished Service Order and MBE. He is married to Judy and has two adult children.

Alison Elliot, as well as being the Convener of the Scottish Council for Voluntary Organisations, is also a Trustee of Community Service Volunteers. Her volunteering has mainly taken place within the church. She was the Church of Scotland's spokesperson on political matters at the time of the Scottish referendum on devolution. In 2004, she was the first woman to be Moderator of the Church of Scotland's General Assembly and also moderated the General Assembly of the Conference of

European Churches in 2009. Her career was in academic psychology and she taught and carried out research into children's language development in the University of Lancaster and then the University of Edinburgh. She is currently Associate Director of the Centre for Theology and Public Issues in Edinburgh University's School of Divinity.

Mike Finlayson is Chief Executive of Forth Sector, a social enterprise in Edinburgh. His early career was in retail management, managing department stores for a national chain. Later he moved into business development and venture capital. Mike became involved with social enterprise as retail advisor to an international NGO and as co-founder of the United Kingdom's first ethical supermarket chain. He has led a number of organisations, sometimes through very difficult times.

Nick Gargan joined Avon and Somerset Constabulary as Chief Constable in March 2013, at a time of significant change and upheaval for the organisation. He was appointed by Sue Mountstevens, the first Police and Crime Commissioner for Avon and Somerset. Nick's policing career began in 1988 when he joined Leicestershire Constabulary under the Graduate Entry Scheme: fresh from a degree in French and Politics at the University of Leicester. He attended the Accelerated Promotion Course and worked in Uniform and Detective roles across the City of Leicester. In 1995 he was seconded to the National Criminal Intelligence Service, working in Interpol and then in the British Embassy in Paris. He worked extensively on the investigation into the death of Diana, Princess of Wales, eventually giving evidence at the Inquest into her death and the death of Mr Dodi Al Fayed. Nick returned to Leicestershire in 1998 and rose through the ranks to become Chief Superintendent. In April 2006 he joined Thames Valley Police as Assistant Chief Constable and led the roll-out of Neighbourhood Policing across the force. Nick moved to the National Policing Improvement Agency at the beginning of 2010 and became its Chief Executive in the September of that year. He led the organisation throughout the period of its closure as its functions were divided between the Home Office, the College of Policing and The Serious Organised Crime Agency. He is the National Police Business Area Lead for Finance and Resources and recently accepted an invitation to become a Companion of the Chartered Management Institute (CCMI). He was awarded the Queen's Police Medal in the New Year's Honours List 2012. Nick's interests include running, cycling and opera. He is also a season-ticket holder at Leicester City Football Club.

Amanda Giles was commissioned as an officer in the Royal Air Force in 1980 and enjoyed a varied career spanning 33 years. Initially employed in air traffic control and airport management specialisations, she moved across to leadership development and education management roles by way of an MSc in Defence Leadership with Cranfield University. Amanda spent several years designing and directing strategic leadership programmes for senior MOD leaders at the Leadership and Management Division of the Defence Academy. Latterly, she transferred to the Royal Air Force Leadership Centre where she was responsible for overseeing the leadership curriculum for all RAF staff and command programmes from airman initial entrant level up to senior officers. Amanda is currently the Head of the Centre for Staff and Educational Development (CSED) at the University of East Anglia and continues to research, write and advise on leadership development matters. Her particular areas of interest include Ethical Leadership, Spiritual Leadership and comparative approaches to Just War Theory.

Peter Gray is the Royal Aeronautical Society Senior Research Fellow in air power studies at the University of Birmingham. He had a full career in the Royal Air Force spending his last three years as Director of the Defence Leadership and Management Centre where he designed and delivered programmes for senior officers and officials. He has lectured worldwide on leadership issues as well as on air power.

Paul Grice is Clerk and Chief Executive of the Scottish Parliament. He leads the Scottish Parliamentary Service which is responsible for delivering all services to the Parliament and its Members. The Parliament employs around 450 staff and has an annual budget of around £75 million. He graduated in 1984 from Stirling University and joined the Civil Service through the 'Fast Stream' in 1985. He worked for the Department of Transport and then the Department of the Environment on Bus Deregulation, Railways Policy and Local Government Finance, subsequently Private Secretary to Virginia Bottomley MP. Paul joined the Scottish Office in 1992 working on Housing and Urban Regeneration Policy, and then headed up the Management of Change Unit. He joined the Constitution Group in May 1997 with responsibility for the Referendum on establishing the Scottish Parliament: he managed the Scotland Act, which laid the new constitutional framework. He was appointed Director of Implementation for the Scottish Parliament in 1999 and set up parliamentary organisation and associated support systems. He was appointed Clerk and Chief Executive of the Parliament in summer 1999 and a member of the University Court at Stirling in 2006 and chair of the Finance and Research Committee from 2008 to 2012. He is also Secretary to Scotland's Futures Forum and an Honorary Fellow of RIAS. Paul was appointed to Economic and Social Research Council (ESRC) in 2009 (chair of Audit Committee since 2010) and appointed to the Bank of Scotland Foundation in 2011 and the Edinburgh International Festival Council in 2013.

Mike Grigor joined the Co-operative Bank in 2010 to set up and grow their new Charities and Social Enterprise Team to provide a full banking relationship for larger Charities and Social Enterprises throughout Scotland, while working closely with the key sector bodies. Prior to this he worked for 25 years in banking with the Bank of Scotland (now part of Lloyds Banking Group), in a range of managerial positions within Retail Banking, Financial Planning, Business Card Sales and Project Management. Prior to leaving the Bank, Mike led Business Development across the United Kingdom for the Banks Community Banking Team, focusing on the Charity Sector. Mike is a founding Director of JESSICA (Scotland) Trust and

Resilient Scotland — a £15 million Lottery funded trust set up to implement social investment activity to support the development of Scotland's communities who are most in need.

Edel Harris joined Cornerstone as Chief Executive in May 2008 having previously been Deputy Chief Executive of Aberdeen Foyer. Cornerstone is one of Scotland's largest charitable organisations providing a wide range of health and social care services to people with disabilities and other support needs. With a turnover in excess of £31 million and employing over 1700 people, Cornerstone is a sizeable business. Cornerstone's aim is to enable the people it supports to enjoy a valued life. Edel's background is in health promotion. She has a first class honours degree in Health and Social Care. Edel worked for NHS Grampian for many years and has significant experience in leading a commercial social enterprise and in developing new social care services. Edel is currently Chairperson of the Life Changes Trust and The Fragile X Society. She is also Vice President of Aberdeen and Grampian Chamber of Commerce and a former Chair of the Scottish Government's Scottish Investment Fund. Edel lives in Stonehaven, Aberdeenshire, with her husband and has two grown up sons. She enjoys swimming, spending time with her family, and is an avid football fan.

Douglas Howieson is Head of Land Management for the Forestry Commission in North England — an area that stretches coast to coast and from Scotland down to Yorkshire and Northern Lancashire. This area has an annual timber harvest of 500,000 tonnes per year and a replanting programme that needs 2.7 million young trees. He has worked for the Forestry Commission for 26 years in Scotland but mainly in England, in Wiltshire and Somerset, East Anglia, the Midlands, the Lake District and in Northumberland. He achieved full membership of the Institute of Chartered Foresters in 1998. Douglas is married to Barbara and has three sons. He is a keen fun runner and will do his 8th Great North Run in 2014.

Neil Hunter is Principal Reporter and the Chief Executive of the Scottish Children's Reporter Administration. He has held that post since April 2011. Neil has held previous jointly appointed service delivery, operational management and strategic posts across Social Work and Health Care Services in Glasgow/Greater Glasgow and Clyde for 20 years, including leadership of the Addictions Partnership for the City of Glasgow. Neil's work experience with children and young people goes back to the early 1990s when he was involved in the management of support services for young homeless people in Glasgow and later established one of Scotland's first substance misuse services for children and young people in Springburn, North Glasgow.

Jeff Hurst has been the Chief Executive Officer of Newcastle upon Tyne YMCA since 2008. He began his career with the Armed Forces, where he spent 22 years in a variety of roles including teaching and training recruits at the Royal Military Academy Sandhurst and teaching at the Royal School of Artillery. He left the army to become an independent Training and Development Consultant. He then spent four years as the Regional Manager for Fairbridge young people's charity. Jeff took over his current role at Newcastle YMCA at the start of the recession and since then has doubled the turnover and tripled the workforce, which has included a rescue merger of a failing charity. Since leaving the army Jeff has achieved a number of qualifications (LLB Hons, MBA) by distance learning, while working full time and raising 3 children.

Elizabeth Ireland has been a salaried GP in Kintyre since 2009. She has worked in a part-time capacity in the practice whilst taking on other roles within the NHS in Scotland. She was part of the first cohort of 'Delivering the Future' — Scotland's national strategic clinical leadership programme. From 2008 until 2010 and for another year from 2012, she was the national clinical lead for Palliative and End of Life Care for the Scottish Government, developing and implementing the actions that flowed from Living and Dying Well. She was appointed Chair of National Services Scotland Health Board in May 2013. Her academic appointment at the University of Stirling enabled her to develop thinking and practice in knowledge translation. She has an honorary chair with the University of Stirling.

Sue Johnson is the Chief Executive at County Durham and Darlington Fire and Rescue Service. Susan is the first woman and non-uniformed chief executive to lead a Fire and Rescue Service in the United Kingdom. In her role, Susan oversees a budget of over £30 million and almost 700 employees and is responsible for the delivery of emergency response, legislative fire safety and community safety to over half a million residents throughout the County Durham and Darlington area. Susan holds a first class honours degree in Business Studies and an MBA from Durham University. Susan previously held the position of Chief Executive of the Northern Business Forum and Executive Director Business Development for the Regional Development Agency, Yorkshire Forward. Susan was awarded the OBE for services to New Deal in the North East in 2000 and an Honorary Fellowship of the University of Sunderland in recognition of her services to businesses in the region.

Mike Jones was formerly the Director of the Foundation for Management Education an Educational Charity which instigated many initiatives for furthering the development of postgraduate management education within UK University Business Schools. He continues to service the many FME Fellows, who are all Academic practitioners as Dean of Fellows of the FME Fellowship Network Society. His views on Management and Business Education are widely sought by politicians, the media and academia. Following an early role as a professional classical musician, Mike's industrial career spans both mainstream corporate management at Board level together with side trips into Business School academia, including a spell as Dean of the Business School at the University of East London. He is a Trustee of the Lubbock Trust at Balliol College, Oxford. In more recent years, he was Director General of the Association of MBAs, the professional organisation for holders of the MBA degree where he was responsible at Board level for the total operation of a global membership organisation, covering strategy, marketing and finance as well as publicity and PR. Industrial appointments include two lengthy periods of Personnel Directorships, Consultancy with Price Waterhouse and a seven-year spell as Group Management Development Manager of Pilkington plc and Managing Director of its subsidiary leadership business, Lakeside Training and Development Ltd. In semi-retirement, Mike continues to work in a consultancy role within the International Business School community. He is an Advisory Board member at a number of the UK leading University Business Schools and has held Visiting Fellowships/Professorial appointments at both Aston Business School and Lancaster University School of Management. Educated at the Duke of York's Royal Military School, Dover and Salford University, Mike holds a Doctorate of Business Administration, a Masters degree in Management and is a Chartered Fellow of the Chartered Institute of Personnel and Development. He is a Liveryman and Court Assistant of the Worshipful Company of Marketors and a Freeman of the City of London. Married to Christine, a busy medic and with a grown up family — long gone, Mike lives on the Wirral.

John Jupp joined the Royal Air Force in 1979 as a pilot on completion of his degree in Philosophy and Mathematics at Kings College, London. He flew the Phantom and Tornado F3 in many parts of the world in operations and on exercise becoming an instrument rating examiner and weapons instructor, and commanding 111(F) Squadron. On the ground, he investigated aircraft accidents, was part of the team developing Typhoon avionics, and the operational fleet manager for the Tornado F3. He was also responsible for the preparation and deployment of all RAF operations during the fireman's strike and the second Gulf War before being promoted to Group Captain and setting up the RAF Leadership Centre in 2003. He then took over all generic education and training in the RAF, including leadership, until 2010. He attended Staff College with the Royal Navy, has a MA in Defence Studies. Since 2010 he has been an independent Leadership Consultant while also working as a RAF Reservist delivering strategic leadership programs to senior officers. He is studying for a PhD in leadership and has edited three books on the subject. John is married with four daughters.

Andy Kerr is a motivated and experienced professional with an interesting career history, from local government to Scottish Government, taking in on the way the setting up of various businesses, working as a consultant and working at senior levels in the private, public and third sectors. Currently he is employed as CEO of Sense Scotland — a charity and social enterprise working across Scotland employing over a 1000 people — where he is responsible for providing strategic leadership. Andy served as the Member of the Scottish Parliament for East Kilbride from 1999 until 2011, and in that time was the Convenor of the Transport and Environment Committee, Finance and Public Services Minster and latterly Health Minister, during which time the NHS achieved the lowest waiting times in the history of the NHS in Scotland and the first ban on smoking in public places in the United Kingdom was introduced. Andy is married to Susan and has three teenage daughters and enjoys football, of the Scottish League One variety, as well as running and is a recent convert to cycling.

John Lauder, after working in academic and national libraries, took a change of career in 2005 and joined Sustrans Scotland. Since then the organisation has grown substantially, both operationally and in terms of the role it plays nationally. Sustrans mission is to enable people to travel by foot, bicycle or public transport for more of the journeys they make every day. Sustrans currently has a staff of 40 and an annual budget of £11 million. It is the United Kingdom's leading sustainable transport charity, encouraging people to travel in ways that benefit their health and environment. John was born in Coldstream, Berwickshire where the cycling habit took hold.

Sophia Looney is the Director of Policy, Equalities and Performance at Lambeth Council. Her career started as a youth worker in Kent. While developing a county-wide approach to detached youth work, she was responsible for leading and developing interesting ways of encouraging youth workers to understand and measure the outcomes of their work with young people. She went on to work in economic development, before moving to the Audit Commission. While an operational inspector and performance specialist, Sophia also led the Commission's operational work nationally in relation to Asylum Seekers, and drove equalities work regionally. In 2007 she returned to a local authority, taking on her current role in Lambeth. There she has focused on business improvement and drives the strategic and policy support for the council's transformation. With her team, she has led the development of the innovative cooperative council initiative, and is now responsible for its implementation.

Rory MacLeod trained initially as a teacher and found a direction in youth and community work following an eye opening postgraduate experience. He has worked for 35 years in a wide range of settings and roles, including area officer, principal officer and head of service within local authority structures. Rory has led in national Community and Learning Development (CLD) agencies and a range of committees. He has also had roles as a lecturer, examiner, trainer and public speaker. Currently he is heading up the Standards Council for CLD for Scotland. In his spare time Rory works with others to establish a range of new community initiatives, including the environment and woodland trust, and children's charity activities. He is also active in the children's justice system and has been a radio producer and broadcaster for nearly 30 years.

Stephen Mann is the Chief Executive of Police Mutual, the United Kingdom's largest affinity friendly society and a not-for-profit financial services firm with over 200,000 members. A lawyer originally, Stephen has previously been an Executive Director at Aviva UK where he held positions as Strategy Director and Business Services Director. He has also been a non-executive Director at the UK Supervisory Board of ALICO and Chair of York Cares, the employee volunteering charity.

Fiona Mackenzie has been self-employed since October 2013 when she began a port-folio career. She is experienced both as an Executive and as a Non-Executive Director, and has had a career long interest in quality improvement and in govern-ance. Currently she is a Non-Executive Director of the Scottish Futures Trust, an Honorary Professor at the University of Stirling, and a part-time crofter. Fiona was the Chief Executive of NHS Forth Valley for 12 years and has been an NHS Chief Executive for a total of 17 years. She began her career as a Graduate Trainee having graduated from St. Andrews University with an honours degree in History. She worked in Grampian, Lothian, Lanarkshire and Highland before her appointment in Forth Valley. She was also a Non-Executive Director of NHS Education Scotland until August 2013. She holds an Executive MBA from the University of Hull, awarded in 2002, and is a career long member of the Institute of Healthcare Management, which awarded her Companionship in 2009. Her appointment at the University of Stirling dates from 2010.

Chris Mould splits his time between The Trussell Trust and the Shaftesbury Partnership. As Executive Chairman of The Trussell Trust, Chris leads a growing, award winning Christian charity that develops community-based projects tackling poverty and social exclusion. These include the rapidly expanding Foodbank Network — a social franchise that has launched 350 food banks across the United Kingdom in the last eight years. The UK Foodbank Network provided three days emergency food to 346,992 people in 2012–2013. To build on pioneering work by the Trussell Trust in Bulgaria, Chris founded and chairs the Foundation for Social Change and Inclusion, a Bulgarian organisation working with Roma people and young state care leavers in the EU's poorest member state. Chris is a partner at The Shaftesbury Partnership, a social business whose mission is to create trailblazing social reforms that empower communities by tackling disadvantage and creating opportunity. These include Nurse First and Franchising Works, which Chris chairs. Before focusing on the voluntary and social sectors, Chris spent over twenty years in senior public sector management where he held both Chief Executive and Chairman roles at local and national level. He was Chief Executive of Salisbury Healthcare NHS Trust for ten years and the founding Chairman of Healthwork UK (now Skills for Health). He then became Chief Executive of a new non-departmental public body reporting to the Home Secretary and responsible for police training across England and Wales. Chris has led over fifteen start-ups and mergers and has substantial experience in professional development, skills and employment. Chris read Modern History at Magdalen College, Oxford, and has an MSc in Social Policy from the London School of Economics. He has been a com-mitted Christian since his teens and worships at St Paul's Church, Salisbury. Chris is married to Angela and they have four daughters.

Roger Mullin is Honorary Professor at The University of Stirling, a director of a research company, and currently contracted by the Scottish Government to support the implementation of college reform, including assisting in eight large scale mer-gers. Over the last 30 years, he has been involved in a wide range of education, capacity building and research projects both at home and oversees. This has included 27 international assignments for United Nations agencies and governments. He has particular interests in organisational culture change and applied decision theory.

Verene Nicolas supports teams and individuals working with local communities and people in poverty. She facilitates individual, organisational and community renewal by teaching the skills and principles of collaborative leadership. These skills include: how to speak the truth with care; giving and receiving feedback; and resolving conflict and facilitating collaborative decision-making. Verene is working with the Church of Scotland's Priority Area teams and the Planning Department of Papua's Provincial Government in Indonesia. She teaches on the Training for Transformation course in South Africa and is actively involved in two local initiatives in Govan (South West Glasgow) where she lives. For several years, Verene has coordinated the master's degree in human ecology delivered in partnership by the Centre for Human Ecology and Strathclyde University's Geography and Sociology Department.

Steven Paterson is the Depute Director of the Centre for Excellence for Looked After Children in Scotland (CELCIS), which is committed to improving the well-being and protection of some of the most vulnerable and disadvantaged children in society. Steven is an experienced leader and manager working for 27 years in the voluntary and public sector, employed in senior management and leadership roles within two national organisations since 1998. His recent roles in leadership include the position of Assistant Director at the Scottish Institute for Residential Child Care (SIRCC) from 2005. Prior to this, he held the position of Assistant Director at Who Cares? Scotland (1996–2005). Steven has led two major transformation programmes, including the transition from SIRCC to CELCIS and the transition of Criminal Justice Social Work Development Sector (CJSWDS) in its recent relocation to the University of Strathclyde. Steven specialises in leadership, development and delivery of organisational change and transition programmes.

Michael Russell is the Cabinet Secretary for Education and Lifelong Learning in the Scottish Government, a position he has held since December 2009. He was previously Minister for Culture, External Affairs and the Constitution and before that Minister for the Environment. He is a writer and broadcaster having worked for a range of Scottish media outlets over many years as well as in his own production company and was also SNP Chief Executive from 1994 to 1999. Educated at The Marr College, Troon and Edinburgh University he has lived in rural Argyll for more than 20 years and in 2011 became MSP for the Argyll and Bute Constituency.

Pam Schwarz was Chief Executive of Mosscare Housing in Manchester, England, from 1997 to 2010. Pam joined Mosscare in 1973 as its first employee. Since retirement, Pam has joined the Council of Management of the Victoria Baths Trust,

Longsight, Manchester and has continued to serve on the governing body of Claremont Primary School, Moss Side, Manchester.

Martin Stepek has a diverse portfolio career covering business, literature, politics, mental well-being and Scottish–Polish relationships. From 1981 Martin was co-owner, and from 1987 to 2002, a director of the Scotland Top 500 business J. Stepek Ltd — which is famous for their ground breaking cult TV adverts with retailers Glens, Hutchison and Robertson's. Martin co-founded the Scottish Family Business Association in 2006 to bring global best practices for family businesses to Scotland. In 2011 he won the prestigious UK Family Business Ties lifetime award for services to family businesses. Martin teaches mindfulness, a set of mental well-being and training practices, approved by the NHS as a treatment for depression and anxiety, and a method by which emotional intelligence and compassion is cultivated.

Graham Sunderland is a Consultant Colorectal Surgeon and Clinical Director for General Surgery in Greater Glasgow and Clyde Health Board. He is intimately involved in the development of the new South Glasgow Hospital, currently under construction. This will see the amalgamation of three existing hospitals onto one campus and the unification of separate surgical services into a single entity in 2015. Graham is a member of the Patient Safety Board of the Royal College of Surgeons of Edinburgh and is part of the NOTSS Faculty. He is Chairman of the Joint Surgical Colleges Fellowship Examination Board in General Surgery. He has a long-standing interest in surgical education and Training and is a faculty member for the Diploma in Medical Education. He has been a member of the Reserve Forces since 1988 and has served on Operational Tours in Iraq and Afghanistan. He is currently the Officer Commanding, Clinical Squadron of 205 Scottish Field Hospital and has achieved the City and Guilds Institute Membership award in Leadership and Management. He is a member of the Faculty of Medical Leadership and Management.

Elaine Tait has an MBA from Durham University Business School and has held a number of management posts in the NHS in the North of England and Scotland and in the higher education and commercial sectors across the United Kingdom. She has worked in planning and quality improvement at a national and regional level, supporting two Chief Medical Officers. Elaine gained much of her management expertise in a busy district general hospital. She is currently the Chief Executive Officer of the Royal College of Physicians of Edinburgh which is an international organisation devoted to raising the standards of patient care through training and professional support for physicians.

Matthew Taylor has been Chief Executive of the RSA since November 2006. During this time the Society has substantially increased its output of research and innovation, has provided new routes to support charitable initiatives of its 26,000 Fellows — including crowd funding — and has developed a global profile as a platform for ideas. Prior to this appointment, Matthew was Chief Adviser on Political Strategy to the Prime Minister. Previous roles include Labour Party Director of Policy and Deputy General Secretary and Chief Executive of the IPPR, the United Kingdom's leading left of centre think tank. Matthew is a regular media performer having appeared several times on the Today Programme, The Daily Politics and Newsnight. He had written and presented several Radio 4 documentaries and is a panellist on the programme Moral Maze. He has written for newspapers including the *FT* and *Observer* and journals including *Management Today* and the *Municipal Journal*. He has posted over a thousand times on his RSA blog site and tweets as RSAMatthew.

Richard Taylor joined Imperial Cancer Research Fund (ICRF) in April 1998 as Head of Retail. Prior to joining the Charity, Richard enjoyed a career in commercial retail where his last post was as Retail Director for the Early Learning Centre. In 2004, Richard was appointed Executive Director of Fundraising and Marketing at Cancer Research UK and is responsible for generating the funds required to enable the charity to reach their ambitious goals. Cancer Research UK is the largest independent funder of cancer research in the world and in 2012−2013 directly contributed £351 million towards its scientific research programme. Alongside his commitments to Cancer Research UK, he is also involved in activities across the 3rd sector. As a Trustee of the Institute of Fundraising (IOF), Richard works to improve fundraising standards across the United Kingdom and to augment this he is a board member of the regulatory Fundraising Standards Board (FRSB), which oversees public complaints against charities. Richard lives in Kent with his wife and they have four sons.

Sara Thornton leads the largest non-metropolitan force in England and has done so for seven years. She is a Vice President of the Association of Chief Police Officers and Director of the Police National Assessment Centre which selects all candidates for fast track and chief officer. She has previously served in the Metropolitan Police but has spent thirteen years as a chief officer in Thames Valley Police and is very proud of the achievements of the force in cutting crime and developing a modern approach to policing. Sara is passionate about the need to professionalise the service and has led many initiatives aimed at building relationships with higher education and integrating evidence-based practice into the craft of policing.

Debra Tyler has been the Chief Executive of the Directory of Social Change since 2001. She is Founder Chair and Trustee of the Small Charities Coalition/Charity Trustee Networks and a Governor of White Knights Primary School. She is a member of the Charity Commission's SORP Committee. She is a Fellow of the Royal Society for the encouragement of Arts, Manufactures and Commerce. She is a member of the Royal Institution and Liberty. She was appointed a Special Ambassador for Girl guiding UK as a result of her work with the Commonwealth Chief Commissioners and is a member of the Advisory Panel for the MSc in Voluntary Sector Management at Cass Business School, City University, where she gives an annual lecture on leadership. She is a Licensed Practitioner of NLP. She is a member of the advisory panel of Winston's Wish, a charity specialising in services for bereaved children. She has worked in both the private and voluntary sectors carrying out a range of roles at all levels, including campaigning, policy development, sales, product development, media relations and training. She also spent some 14 years as a voluntary Trade Union Officer. She spent a year working with Youth at Risk, an organisation that works to rehabilitate young people who suffer severe social disadvantages. She was the first female Programme Director of the Runge Effective Leadership programme, one of the United Kingdom's leading programmes for senior managers. She is an internationally published author of several books covering topics such as leadership, management, communication skills, personal development and time management. Recent publications include 'It's Tough at the Top' for Chief Executives and 'The Pleasure and the Pain' for anyone working with people. She has spent many years working with the media, doing TV, radio, newspaper, magazine and internet features and interviews. She was a regular columnist for a major national newspaper on work-based issues and writes a regular column for *Third Sector* magazine. She delivers around 50 keynote speeches every year to the voluntary, private and public sector — on topics ranging from the relationship between the state and charities, leadership, and topical issues affecting the voluntary sector. She comes from five generations of military service, has a BSc (Hons) in Psychology, a Certificate in Natural Sciences, and a British bulldog called Mabel.

Acknowledgements

In completing this book, it is wholly appropriate that we record our thanks to the many people who have been instrumental in this book reaching completion from conception.

First, we must thank our many colleagues and friends who helped source and recommend authors who were willing to contribute to this book.

Second, this book would not be possible without the contribution of the said authors. We are most aware of how busy these people are; therefore, we place on record our immense and unreserved gratitude for the time and effort that they committed in completing their material. Put simply, without them, this book would not have been possible.

Third, Mr Ian Milne and his staffs at the Sibbald Library, The Royal College of Physicians of Edinburgh, for the use of an excellent library and *quiet space* for our various editorial meetings.

Fourth, Ms Kim Eggleton (who 'got' this project immediately) and Ms Juliet Harrison at Emerald Group Publishing.

Finally, we thank our families for their enduring patience and support especially:

Brian would like to thank TT, Christie, Lors, Shweetles, and Shreya and
Julie would like to thank Mick and Elliot.

Foreword

This book takes a different approach to most other books on leadership focusing as it does on the experiences of those who lead in the vibrant but often neglected Public and Third sectors. It is relatively easy to identify successful leaders; it is rather more complicated to describe what constitutes good leadership. This book gives the reader some shining examples as a way of sharing that experience.

The contributors to this book working in the two distinct sectors may well be natural leaders but they all encounter a wide variety of challenges to their leadership as they lead their organisation's growth and development. The Chairman of a voluntary organisation will be leading in a different way to the CEO of a public sector organisation be it hospital, local council, or even a university but they will all be deciding on courses of action and gaining consensus using that indefinable quality of character that creates confidence and inspires others to follow and/or to agree. The chapters in this book are their reflections as they take the reader on a journey of discovery with illustrative examples of their approaches to common goals.

This book and its contents have been put together by two experienced business practitioners who have graduated from the Foundation for Management Education (FME) Fellowship programme to become Business School academics. As such, they have experienced the 'world of work' in the public and services sectors and now translate that experience into their teaching and research to combine theory with reflection on real experience, always maintaining the FME ethos of Relevance and Rigour. For them, producing this book has been a long standing ambition, recognising as they do the absence in the literature of compelling insights and practical examples of good leadership in the public and third sectors. They have put together a timely and much needed book; in reality, a study of successful leaders within these sectors, which is an excellent starting point for the reader in search of continuous improvement. This is a balanced and relevant contribution to the leadership literature and I commend it to you.

Professor Mike Jones
Director
Foundation for Management Education

Preface

This book is a valuable guide both to key ideas from management research and to how those ideas are reflected in the practical experience of managers in the public and third sector. As a current third sector leader who has worked in Whitehall and also now chairs the board of a private company, I like the way it helps the reader think about whether the most important aspect of leadership is the specificity of the sector in which it operates or the generic skills demanded from every senior managerial post.

The truth is that every leadership situation we face is both completely unique and of its moment and also similar to a million other leadership situations. Reading the book's contributions there is so much all leaders will recognise, yet we all feel our particular approach is personal to us.

A recurrent theme, identified by the authors, is a rejection of command and control forms of leadership in favour of models based more on persuasion, collaboration and distributed authority and responsibility. Leadership is not merely about transmitting orders; it is about co-designing a mission, winning buy-in to that mission and a continuous process of aligning and realigning the organisation to that mission in a fast changing context. Interestingly, but perhaps not surprisingly, the task of mission definition and of ensuring the organisation is both ethically and organisationally aligned seems to be given slightly greater emphasis by third sector leaders, who may feel they have more scope to shape their organisations. The emphasis from the public sector is more on adaptation and engagement — not so much defining purpose as holding on to it in an environment where it can all too easily feel that leaders, let alone those they lead, are mere cogs in a machine.

At the risk of abusing my role as preface writer, there are two themes in the book which I want to suggest stop slightly short of the conclusions to which they intriguingly point. This is not a critique but a suggestion of what we might ask next.

While just about everyone recognises complexity and change as core characteristics of today's world there is still a sense in most of this book's first-hand accounts that leaders can and should communicate consistency and coherence. On one level this is, of course, correct: it is a part of the leader's role — whatever their own doubts and resentments — to convince colleagues that those within the organisation can strongly shape its destiny. But perhaps leaders need to acknowledge more fully that complexity is not contingent on context but inherent in their task.

The key idea behind the concept of 'clumsy leadership' (Grint, 2010; Thompson, 2008) is not merely that there are fundamentally different ways of thinking about and pursuing change in organisations (in the slightly adapted terms I use — 'the hierarchical', 'the solidaristic' and 'the individualistic'), nor that all three forms should be positively expressed to maximise the organisation's effectiveness, but that each mode is in tension with the others; indeed each partly gains its strength from its implicit critique of the others. Leaders search for a high functioning equilibrium yet when an organisation is firing on all cylinders, de-stabilisation comes from two sources: either one of the change modes will become dominant with the consequence that the others are likely to become at best underperforming and at worst actively subversive; or external factors will change the balance of power. As an example of the latter, in recent decades technology has generally moved from a force buttressing hierarchical authority to one which often undermines it and thus contributes to a more general decline of trust in hierarchical institutions.

The ineluctability of complexity is just one of the psychologically taxing aspects of modern leadership. Many of the voices in this book refer to the importance of emotional traits such as empathy and resilience. Yet, as Brian Howieson and Julie Hodges note, the contributors almost exclusively posit the formative stages of their leadership capacity in their experiences at work. While it is entirely understandable that people are protective of private information, as an account of personal development this is unconvincing. Not only does our style of leadership — how, for example, we cope with success and adversity — reflect personalities and predispositions largely formed in early life, but the very pursuit of leadership can be seen as a form of projection. Thus, as well as its publicly stated goals, the drive to lead will also involve the concealed attempt to treat wounds such as low self-esteem or a craving for dominance. Lacan mordantly described falling in love as 'giving something one doesn't have to someone who doesn't exist'. In psychodynamic terms the same is surely true of leadership.

To some degree we are all motivated by pain and lust, but as leaders it falls to us to mitigate the projection of our own needs and frailties on to our organisations. The emotional intelligence which several contributors say is essential is not something we can simply acquire and keep, like learning how to compose a spreadsheet. Just as the idea of clumsy leadership identifies inherent cultural contestation within organisations, psychological self-awareness lives with the fact that parts of our psyche are prone to attack other parts. Although most of the leaders in this book work in the human services sector, and all write about their own experience, there seems little appetite to connect the complexity and pathos of organisational leadership to the complexity and pathos of human subjectivity.

It has been said there is no greater falsehood than a truth half told. Recognising complexity and the importance of emotional resilience are challenging ideas for leaders but we must resist the temptation to simplify them or avoid their full implications: one of which must surely be that attending to psychological well-being is as essential to responsible leadership as physical well-being is to attaining sporting prowess.

In one way or another, the quality of public and third sector leadership in the twenty-first century will shape the life chances and experiences of all our citizens. This important book shows that much progress has been made in meeting contemporary challenges and forging the kind of leadership the world needs now. It also suggests there may be even deeper and even more exciting questions ahead.

Matthew Taylor
Chief Executive
RSA

References

Grint, K. (2010). *Wicked problems and clumsy solutions: The role of leadership.* Cranfield: Cranfield Univiersity.

Thompson, M. (2008). *Organising and disorganising.* Devon: Triarchy Press Ltd.

Chapter 1

Introduction

1.1. Overview

This book presents the reflections, in their own words, of leaders in the public and third sectors in the United Kingdom. The book is unique in that it provides an opportunity for the voices of individuals to be heard, who are in leadership positions in sectors, which are rarely considered in the literature. Each individual has contributed their personal opinions of what leadership means to them and their experience of it. They also reflect on the complex challenges which they are facing, and will face, as they grapple with profound changes in the economy, politics and society. The reflections serve as an illustration of the benefit of approaching leadership through the eyes of those practicing leadership.

We have divided the book into three areas. First, we provide an overview of the themes in the literature on leadership and we offer our views on what is relevant. Second, we provide an overview of the literature and the key challenges in each sector, followed by the individual reflections. Third, the implications for leadership in the public and third sector are drawn out in a conclusion — our contribution. This is a unique opportunity to hear from the men and women who have experience of leading public and third sector organisations, which we hope you will enjoy reading and which will provide you with an insight into the key challenges of leadership in these sectors.

1.2. Importance of Leadership

In 1978, the historian James Macgregor Burns wrote that leadership is one of the most observed and least understood phenomenon on earth. Since then, there has been an explosion of interest in leadership in academic research and in practice. Some writers have observed that leadership has taken over from management as the latest buzzword in public services, and have presented it as the solution to many intractable situations (Martin & Learmonth, 2012). Although some researchers caution that it needs to be good leadership, not just leadership for the sake of it. As Mourkogiannis and Fisher (2006, p. 149) say: *Leadership is the ultimate advantage, as when it is present, it makes all other advantages possible [while] poor leadership can turn even the best advantage into a disaster.*

The collapse of organisations such as Enron, Tyco, and WorldCom, and the financial sub-prime crises that started in 2007 and led to a Global financial crisis and the demise of companies such as Lehman Brothers and the nationalisation of UK banks, such as RBS and Northern Rock, have prompted speculation about the role and impact of bad leadership (Hodges, 2011). In particular, these high profile examples have blackened the credibility and ethical nature of leadership and raised questions related to the importance of leadership.

Rune Todnem By and Bernard Burnes (2013, p. 2) point out in the introduction to their edited book on *Organisational Change, Leadership and Ethics* that:

> Many leaders are arguably no more than very well-paid followers. Where is their courage, integrity, compassion, vision, contribution and ethical stance? Attending the same executive courses, utilizing the same executive mentors, networking during the same executive lunches they seem to become more and more alike — less and less leaders — all speaking the same language and very often outdated management and leadership blah blah. Many are scared of causing any upset or standing out from the crowd, as there is no guarantee that breaking the mould will have a positive impact on career progression. Therefore, let's do what is safe. Let's do what has proved successful for the career in the past. However, leadership is not about conforming or repeating the past, nor is it about playing it safe. It is about having the courage, values and beliefs to do what is right. What is right not just for the individual but for the majority of the stakeholders affected.

It used to be that a leader needed only to have charisma and be recognised by their peers and other key stakeholders, as having the willpower and credibility to lead. Now the spotlight is on leaders to demonstrate their leadership prowess, to have emotional intelligence, to be ethically aware; to show in thought and deed an understanding of the dynamics of how to enhance the value of their organisation; to be aware of opportunities and how to exploit them; and to be able to lead the people in their organisations through the complexity of change. This has added to the heightened awareness of leadership and why it matters. Several factors have come together to increase this interest and importance of leadership including:

- A need for leadership to solve complex problems in organisations (Mumford, Zaccaro, Harding, Jacobs, & Fleishman, 2000)
- A large number of leaders failing and more leaders being dismissed for failing to achieve objectives (Conger, Nadler, Strategy, & Governance, 2012)
- An increasing accountability being placed on leaders and the performance bar has been raised (Rus, van Knippenberg, & Wisse, 2012)

- Little leadership bench strength in organisations (Newhall, 2011)
- The need for leaders to sustain change and transformation (Hodges, 2014)

In order to address such issues, leadership must be a living entity inside an orga-nisation and continue to be evaluated and reviewed (Leavy & McKiernan, 2009) and the impact of its effectiveness considered. According to George (2010), the ulti-mate measure of effectiveness for leadership is the ability to sustain superior results over an extended period of time. Leadership is, however, a more widely pervasive phenomenon than this. Some researchers believe that the role of leadership is best seen not in terms of its economic impact but in how it shapes the organisational context, such as goals, members, incentives and culture (Hackman, 2010). Nohria and Khurana (2010) add to this saying that the scope and importance of leadership also need to be addressed, not only in terms of their impact on performance effectiveness but, and more importantly, in terms of their influence on the life of an organisation, such as meaning, morality and culture.

1.2.1. So, Why Is Leadership Important in the Public and Third Sectors?

For those bold enough to lead in this age of austerity, in either of the sectors, the challenges are immense. Seismic shifts have taken place in the public and third sectors. Political, economic, technological and social changes are driving profound transformation of organisational models, making predictability and stability elusive. The combined effects of the economic downturn and cutbacks in spending are hit-ting the public and third sectors hard. Organisations have to close or reduce services where demand remains high and financial resilience is reducing. The context is, therefore, extremely challenging, with many public and third sector organisations facing exceptional cuts in funding. A recent survey of charities found that more than 8 out of 10 said they thought the sector was facing a crisis (New Philanthropy Capital, 2013). Changes in funding and demand for services have led local authori-ties to work closely with third sector organisations, not just as funders but also as allies. This is a relationship which is expected to grow in the future as the third sector plays an increasing part in the delivery of public services. In addition, across both sectors, tough choices about priorities, survival and independence need to be made.

Given the government commitment to deficit reduction, it is certain that most parts of the public and third sectors will face reductions in spending for several more years. Even if the deficit is eradicated, there will then be a question of how to fund real spending increases at a rate faster than growth in the economy. The National Health Service, in particular, will find this length of constraint and the longer term need for slower rises in spending very problematic. Looking ahead, the situation is only likely to become worse, with the prospect of further cuts in public funding and further pressures on other sources of income, leading to continu-ing change.

Both sectors are entering a significant era of change. Although change is not, in itself, anything new, it is the increasing pace of change that is significant. This relentless pace of change is having an impact on leaders. Leaders in both sectors have to contend with a changing environment, especially as a result of economic drivers which have triggered the significant challenge of how to achieve more with less. The resources needed to cope with the increased demands are far less readily available in the public and third sector than the private sector. So public and third sector leaders have to manage with what they have got; however, these resources are being reduced. Yet they continue to face increasing demand with decreasing resources.

There are, however, some positive developments for the public and third sectors, in spite of the challenges they are facing. Perhaps because of the funding crisis, organisations in the sectors are working more closely in partnership. Leaders are developing the courage and techniques to define priorities and beginning to say explicitly what they have to stop doing and start doing differently.

1.3.   Why the Need for Another Book on Leadership?

There is a growing library of books on leadership. This literature can broadly be divided into populist and academic categories. The populist genre includes a huge commercial market in popular management books on leadership and a circuit of celebrity for those who write them. Populist books range from the hero-leader reflections and biographies to works by so-called gurus. The majority of books are written about well-known charismatic leaders, accompanied by convincing stories and snappy sound bites. These books follow a similar vein, in that they espouse the 'I did it my way' approach, and are often criticised for their lack of theoretical and methodological grounding. Such books provide an often longed for level of simplicity, yet there is no evidence that they enhance the learning and success of leadership.

In contrast, academic books on leadership which include student-orientated texts, critical monographs and research studies, tend to posit leadership as a complex phenomenon and are often couched in language that the practitioner finds impenetrable. They provide the theoretical grounding but frequently fail to relate it to practical examples in the business world.

1.3.1.   So Why the Need for Another Book on Leadership?

It is true that there are a multitude of books on how to lead. Many of these make excellent reference guides and provide valuable suggestions for leading people and organisations. Despite, however, the number of books on leadership, the literature is still lacking. We know little about leadership in the public and third sectors in the United Kingdom, especially from the leaders themselves. This gap in the literature poses a great opportunity, which this book seeks to address. The greater our understanding of leadership in different sectors, the more we will be able to appreciate leadership in different contexts. This book is about making sense of leadership in the public and third sectors.

1.4.   Audience

This book presents valuable insights about the experiences and perceptions of leadership, from leaders themselves, as well as what leadership means to them individually and collectively, as well as, the challenges they face now and are likely to face in future decades. Leaders and managers in the public or third sector, whether new or experienced, will find the book stimulating and useful for their own understanding and development. It also offers insights for human resource professionals, organisational consultants and organisational development practitioners who seek to work with and develop leaders. Academics and researchers who study and teach subjects in business and management, such as organisational behaviour, leadership, as well as change, will find the book a rich source of data for future inquiry, as well as, perhaps a confirmation or challenge to their own speculations about leadership. The book will also be of value to students studying business whether on an MBA programme or other business degree, as it will provide them with first-hand accounts of leadership and links with theoretical models and frameworks.

1.5.   Aim of This Book

The book has a specific focus on leadership in public and third sector organisations and is an attempt at bridging the gulf between academics and management practitioners. Our aim is to try and unearth current practitioner thinking in these sectors, in order to find out what leadership means to individuals who have experience of practicing in the public and third sectors. We also aim to compare theory and practice, where applicable.

1.6.   Unique Aspects

This book is unique in three aspects. First, leaders in the public and third sectors do not usually write about leadership. The literature on leadership is dominated by CEOs from the corporate sector. The world seldom hears from contemporary practitioners — the chief doers and shapers of leadership in the public and third sectors. Admittedly, they do make brief appearances now and again in the media. We are, however, rarely treated to deep insights into their leadership thinking, or to clues on how they distinguish valuable ideas from conventional wisdom. One reason, of course, is that they are usually too busy getting things done. To quote, one of our contributors Edel Harris: *Great leaders often are the ones we have never heard of.* Second, the book is authored and co-edited by two academics, who between them have over 40 years experience of working in the business world, in the public, third, and the private sectors, prior to joining academia. Third, the reflections in this book are written by leaders for leaders and aspiring leaders.

The contributors in this book are leaders of small and large organisations. The views they express are full of variety and reflect their own experiences. Despite the different contexts in which their organisations operate, the reflections they have contributed contain some common themes, which are outlined in Chapters 3 and 4, as well as in the concluding chapter, Chapter 5. The views and thoughts of leaders from the public and third sectors are a tremendous centre of power in society. How they think, how they prioritise, how they motivate people and, how they view the vectors of leadership, influence the progress and development of their sectors. As Europe and other parts of the globe trundles through recession, the socioeconomic impact of their thoughts and actions becomes all the greater. This is why a broad cross-sample of leaders have been identified for the book and asked to provide their candid views on leadership today and the challenges they face.

Behind the diversity of contributors and their reflections, a unity does emerge, which is a determination to deal with the challenges they are facing and a desire to achieve greater efficiency. The views and ideas shared in this book are not a fad, nor are they necessarily in vogue, but they are pragmatic. Clearly, today's leaders in the public and third sectors recognise that the challenges they face need to be addressed with interventions that are applicable to the circumstances in which their organisations are operating.

1.7. Format

This unique collection of reflections focuses on the experiences, perceptions, challenges and learning of leaders. This book has five chapters, including this introductory chapter. Chapter 2 reviews current leadership approaches including different definitions and concepts. Chapter 3 explores leadership in the public sector, while Chapter 4 focuses on leadership in the third sector. Each of these chapters (3 and 4) begins with an overview of the key theories and issues relevant to the sector. This is followed by the reflections of the leaders in the sector, outlining their experience and perception of leadership, what leadership means to them, the organisational challenges they face — particularly in times of austerity and change — and the leadership challenges for their sector. At the end of each of these sections there is a summary of the key overview of the themes and links, where relevant, to the applicable theory. The final chapter, Chapter 5, provides a summary of the key similarities and differences between the sectors, based on the reflections. Consideration is also given towards future research into leadership in the sectors.

References

Burns, J. M. (1978). *Leadership*. New York, NY: Harper and Row Publishers.

By, R. T., & Burnes, B. (Eds.). (2013). *Organisational change, leadership and ethics*. Oxon: Routledge.

Conger, J. A., Nadler, D. A., Strategy, B., & Governance, C. (2012). When CEOs step up to fail. *MIT Sloan Management Review*, *45*(3), 50–56.

George, B. (2010). The new 21st century leaders. Harvard Business Review (Guest edition), May 5.

Hackman, J. R. (2010). What is this thing called leadership? *Handbook of leadership theory and practice* (pp. 107–116). Boston, MA: Harvard Business School Publishing.

Hodges, J. (2011). The role of the CEO and leadership branding: Credibility not celebrity. In R. Burke, G. Martin, & C. G. Cooper (Eds.), Corporate reputation: Managing opportunities and threats. London: Gower Press.

Hodges, J. (2014). Sustaining change in organisations. London: Sage.

Leavy, B., & McKiernan, P. (2009). *Strategic leadership: Governance & renewal*. London: Palgrave Macmillan.

Martin, G., & Learmonth, M. (2012). A critical account of the rise and spread of leadership: The case of UK healthcare. *Social Science & Medicine*, *74*(3), 281–288.

Mourkogiannis, N., & Fisher, R. (2006). *Purpose: the starting point of great companies*. London: Palgrave Macmillan.

Mumford, M. D., Zaccaro, S. J., Harding, F. D., Jacobs, T. O., & Fleishman, E. A. (2000). Leadership skills for a changing world: Solving complex social problems. *The Leadership Quarterly*, *11*(1), 11–35.

New Philanthropy Capital. (2013). Money for good. Retrieved from http://www.thinknpc.org/publications/money-for-good-uk/. Accessed on March 3, 2013.

Newhall, S. (2011). Preparing our leaders for the future. *Strategic HR Review*, *11*(1), 5–12.

Nohria, N., & Khurana, R. (2010). Advancing leadership theory and practice. In N. Nohria & R. Khurana (Eds.), *Handbook of leadership theory and practice: A Harvard Business School centennial colloquium* (pp. 3–26). Cambridge, MA: Harvard Business Press.

Rus, D., van Knippenberg, D., & Wisse, B. (2012). Leader power and self-serving behavior: The moderating role of accountability. *The Leadership Quarterly*, *23*(1), 13–26.

Chapter 2

Current Approaches to Leadership

2.1. Introduction

Leadership is a subject that has generated interest among scholars and laypeople alike: the term connotes images of powerful, dynamic individuals who command victorious armies, direct corporate empires from atop gleaming skyscrapers, or shape the course of nations (Yukl, 2013, p. 17).

Field Marshal Bernard Law Montgomery (1st Viscount Montgomery of Alamein), Bill Gates (Chairman of Microsoft), and Abraham Lincoln (16th President of the United States) are good examples here. In fact, this 'great man approach' is probably a starting point for most people who are interested in leadership. The problem is that almost everyone who thinks, studies or writes about leadership interprets it differently.[1] Furthermore, although many specific definitions can be cited, most of the academic definitions (never mind the practitioner or lay view) depend on the theoretical orientation taken: besides influence, leadership has been defined in terms of traits, role relationships, occupation of an administrative position, group processes, personality, compliance, particular behaviours, persuasion, power, goal achievement, interaction, role differentiation, and/or a combination of two or more of these (Yukl, 2013, p. 18).

Although the phenomenon of leadership has been around since antiquity (Bass, 1990) [and quoted in House and Aditya (1997, p. 409)], the systematic social scientific study of leadership did not begin until the early 1930s with the focus of much of the research being an attempt to define and analyse leadership effectiveness. The resulting contributions have been cumulative and a great deal is now known about leadership phenomena. Researchers have attempted to discover what traits, abilities, behaviours, sources of power or aspects of the situation determine how well a leader has been able to influence his/her followers and, therefore, accomplish group objectives. In addition, the reasons why some people emerge as leaders and the determinants of the way the leader acts are other important

---

1. Finding out what makes the visionary hero, the super human or the great man (or woman) tick has become an obsession: the hope is that once these attributes are isolated, they can in turn be replicated, recruited against, and through training, be 'inculcated' in others.

questions that have been investigated.[2] Moreover, theorists and researchers usually define leadership according to their individual perspective, and the aspect of the phenomenon of most interest to them. For example, after a comprehensive review of the leadership literature, Stogdill (1974, p. 259) concluded that: *There are almost as many definitions of leadership, as there are persons who have attempted to define the concept.*

Northouse (2013, p. 5) offers the following definition of leadership: *Leadership is a process whereby an individual influences a group of individuals to achieve a common goal.* As editors of this book, we consider Sherman's (1995, pp. 91−92) definition of leadership to be instructive: *When you boil it all down, contemporary leadership seems to be a matter of aligning people towards common goals and empowering them to take the actions needed to reach them.* In short, leadership is a complex phenomenon that touches on many organisational, social and personal processes (Bolden, 2004). Leadership depends on a process of social influence, whereby people are inspired to work towards group goals, not through coercion, but through personal motivation. As Bolden (2004, p. 3) states: *Ultimately, however, the definition used is a matter of choice, informed by one's own predispositions, organisational situation and beliefs, but with an awareness of the underlying assumptions and implications of the particular approach.*

Campbell, Edgar, and Stonehouse (2011, p. 264) offer a chronological summary of theories of leadership and key authors to the start of the 21st century. This summary is shown in Table 2.1.

2.2.   What Are Leadership Approaches?

In terms of an objective overview, there are many different perspectives and lenses to look at leadership from and through; representative examples include:

- Bryman, Collinson, Grint, Jackson, and Uhl-Bien (2011) in their edited book, *The Sage Handbook of Leadership*, offer five perspectives on leadership deriving from disciplinary foci: overview perspectives; macro and sociological perspectives; political and philosophical perspectives; psychological perspectives; and emerging perspectives
- The International Leadership Association, who at their 2012 Annual Conference in Colorado, USA, discussed leadership from a variety of perspectives including:

---

2. There is a demand for this answer from both business (wanting to know the 'key predictors' of consolidated business-unit performance) and from academia (keen to find a way of measuring leadership).

Table 2.1: Chronological summary of theories of leadership and key authors to the start of the 21st century.

Theory	Key authors
Great man theory	Popularized in the 1840s by Thomas Carlyle
Trait theory	Stogdill 1974
	McCall and Lombardo 1983
	Bennis and Biederman 1998
Behaviourist theories	Merton 1957
	McGregor 1960
	Blake and Mouton 1961, 1964
	Pfeffer and Salancik 1975
Situational leadership	Lewin et al. 1939
	Maier 1963
	Likert 1967
	Hersey and Blanchard 1969
	Adair 1973
	Vroom and Yetton 1973
	House and Mitchell 1974
	Yukl 1989
Contingency theory	Tannenbaum and
	Schmitt 1958
	Fiedler 1967
	Hickson et al. 1971
	Adair 1973
	Fiedler and Garcia 1987
Transactional theory	Dansereau et al. 1975
	Graen and Cashman 1975
Transformational theory	Burns 1978
	Bass 1985, 1990
	Tichy and Devanna 1986
	Covey 1992
	Bass and Avolio 1994
	Hooper and Potter 1997
	Bass and Steidlmeier 1998
	Adair 2002
	Kouzes and Posner 2003

Source: Campbell et al. (2011), reproduced with permission of Palgrave Macmillan.

business leadership; leadership development; leadership education; public leadership; leadership scholarship; and youth leadership
- Grint (2005a) who considers leadership as a person, a result, a position and a process

- Gill (2012) who has specific chapters on leadership and vision, leadership and purpose, leadership and values, leadership and empowerment, leadership and engagement
- Yukl (2013) who conceptualises leadership as an individual process, a dyadic process, a group process and an organisational process. These levels can be viewed as a hierarchy, as depicted in Figure 2.1

Theories conceptualised at a higher level usually assume that related processes occur at lower levels, even though they are not explicitly described. For example, in a cohesive team — with high mutual trust and cooperation — some assumptions can be made about the likely pattern of dyadic leader–member relationships, and about each individual's values, attitudes and perceptions.

A helpful way to understand leadership is by exploring leadership thinking and theories using three conceptual viewpoints:

1. *Leadership model*: a leadership model contains theories or ideas on how to lead effectively and/or become a better leader (e.g. path-goal leadership)
2. *Leadership philosophy*: a leadership philosophy contains values-based ideas of how a leader should be and act and the sources of a leader's power (e.g. servant leadership)
3. *Leadership style*: a leadership style is a classification or description of the main ways in which real-life leaders behave (e.g. autocratic leadership)

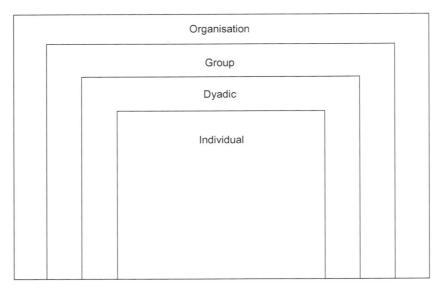

Figure 2.1: Levels of conceptualisation for leadership processes. *Source*: Yukl (2013, p. 30), reprinted by permission of Pearson Education, Inc.

Of the many major terms which refer to concepts or theories about leadership, we consider that these conceptual viewpoints (model, philosophy and style) together offer a useful structure by which to categorise and explore leadership.

It is also instructive, at this stage to revisit normative and descriptive approaches to leadership. For example, Leithwood et al. (2009, p. 1) consider distributed leadership as a normative perspective as 'distributing leadership' is a means for enhancing the effectiveness of, and engagement with, leadership processes. For such authors, the key question is how leadership should be distributed in order to have the most beneficial effect. Other authors including Spillane (2006) and Gronn (2002), however, take an explicitly descriptive approach, in which they argue that distributed leadership offers an analytical framework through which one can assess and articulate the manner in which leadership is (and is not) distributed throughout organisations.

It is not the purpose of this book to explain leadership models or styles in great detail. There are, literally, thousands of books and articles on these. For further reference of models and styles, the reader is directed to such work by Yukl (2013), Northouse (2013) and Schedlitzki and Edwards (2013).

In this section, and indeed, book, we will adopt the lens of the leadership philosophy in studying leadership. Leadership philosophies focus on what kind of leadership one should offer. A philosophy may underpin a model, and may also underpin a style. A philosophy also involves far more and deeper references to society, politics and civilisation than models or styles.

2.3.   Leadership Philosophies from 2000

Many leadership and organisational behaviour textbooks offer a chronological account as to how the theory of leadership has evolved since the Great Man theory popularised by Thomas Carlyle in the 1840s (see again Table 2.1). This chapter, however, will concentrate on the current approaches to leadership philosophies that have emerged, or are in vogue, since the start of this millennium. From the editors knowledge, pre-reading, database and literature searches of academic and practitioner sources, it would seem that the contemporary philosophies include (in alphabetical order): adaptive, authentic, distributed, ethical, informal, post-industrial, post-Newtonian, servant, shared, leadership 2.0, value-based and worldly.[3]

Table 2.2 shows the prevalence of current philosophies from the database *Business Source Premier* on 7 December 2012. This table shows the leadership philosophy, total number of 'entries' (for the period 2000—2012), ranking and hits/for each 2-year period years during the overall period 2000—2012.

---

3. This list is not exhaustive.

Table 2.2: Prevalence of current leadership philosophies from the database *Business Source Premier* on 7 December 2012.

Philosophy	Period: 2000–2012	% of total	Ranking	Year: 2000–2002	Year: 2003–2004	Year: 2005–2006	Year: 2007–2008	Year: 2009–2010	Year: 2011–2012
Adaptive	94	6.0	6	8	6	9	8	38	25
Authentic	246	14.5	4	7	29	38	62	49	61
Distributed	135	7.9	5	8	10	15	29	31	42
Ethical	507	29.9	1	54	60	66	71	140	116
Informal	52	3.0	8	3	5	9	11	9	15
Post-industrial	0	0.0	=12	0	0	0	0	0	0
Post-Newtonian	21	1.0	9	1	4	4	3	3	7
Servant	279	16.4	2	26	38	37	39	57	80
Shared	282	16.1	3	1	4	4	3	3	7
2.0	0	0.0	=12	0	0	0	0	0	0
Value-based	80	4.7	7	10	15	12	21	12	13
Worldly	1	0.0	=12	0	0	0	0	0	1
Total	1697	100.0		118	136	194	247	342	367

From Table 2.2, it is interesting to note the significant increase in entries (in reality, articles) in ethical leadership post-2008. In fact, there was an increase of 100% from 2007 to 2008 in the period 2009—2010 and close to it again in the period 2010—2012. This is also similar (although not quite as pronounced) in the change in adaptive leadership after the period 2007—2008.

More generally, there has also been an increase in adaptive, authentic, distributed, informal, servant and shared leadership during this overall period, 2000—2012.

In addition, and to corroborate further this ranking, Table 2.3 shows the results from two academic journals *Leadership* (Sage: UK Editorial)[4] and *Leadership Quarterly* (Elsevier: US Editorial)[5] in addition to the references offered by the *Chartered Institute of Personnel and Development* (CIPD) website.[6] For the interested reader, the *Wall Street Journal* and *FT.com* offer the following articles on these philosophies, which are shown in Tables 2.4 and 2.5.

From Table 2.2 and Table 2.3, it would seem sensible, then, to suggest that the most prevalent leadership philosophies, in the first part of this century, include (in alphabetical order) adaptive, authentic, distributed, ethical, servant and shared.

2.4. Inside Each Philosophy

For the 6 leadership philosophies, detailed above, we offer a brief overview of each one including: a working definition; the key author(s) (where applicable); a summary of the theory; and some suggested practical guidance. The philosophies will be introduced in alphabetical order. The reader is, however, reminded that there are many ways to study such philosophies. For example, Gary Yukl — in his book *Leadership in Organisations* — suggests that shared and distributed leadership are 'emerging' theories of leadership and that adaptive leadership is a sub-part of emergent processes in complexity theory. In addition, Northouse (2013, p. 4) [in quoting Fleishman et al. (1991)], states that in the last 60 years, 65 different classification systems have been developed to define the dimensions of leadership.

2.4.1. *Adaptive*

2.4.1.1. Working definition
In 1994, Ronald Heifetz introduced a theory of leadership aimed at clarifying two important distinctions: between technical and adaptive problems, and between leadership and authority. He also attempted to redefine leadership as an activity rather than a position of influence or a set of personal characteristics. In this respect, it is important to abandon the idea that 'leaders are born and not made'. It is suggested

---

4. http://lea.sagepub.com/
5. http://www.journals.elsevier.com/the-leadership-quarterly/
6. http://www.cipd.co.uk/

Table 2.3: Prevalence of current leadership philosophies in *Leadership*, *Leadership Quarterly* and the *Chartered Institute of Personnel and Development*.

Philosophy	Leadership[a]	% of total	Rank	Leadership quarterly[b]	% of total	Rank	CIPD[c]	% of total	Rank
Adaptive	5	2	7	180	8	=6	49	7	3
Authentic	31	15	=3	178	8	=6	13	2	=5
Distributed	51	25	=1	245	11	3	18	2	=5
Ethical	23	11	5	227	10	4	28	4	4
Informal	8	3	6	195	9	5	218	33	2
Post-industrial	0	0	=9	0	0	=8	0	0	
Post-Newtonian	0	0		2	0		0	0	=8
Shared	31	15	=3	578	27	1	326	49	1
Servant	51	25	=1	3	0	=9	15	2	=5
2.0	0	0	=9	25	1	8	0	0	=8
Value-based	2	1	8	540	25	2	0	0	=8
Worldly	0	0	=9	3	0	=9	0	0	=8
Total	202	100		2176	100		667		

[a] Accessed on 7 December 2012.
[b] Accessed on 7 December 2012.
[c] Accessed on 7 January 2013.

Table 2.4: Number of entries and examples of leadership philosophies in *Wall Street Journal*.

Philosophy	Entries	Representative article
Wall Street Journal[a]		
Ethical	1282	*Lockheed Martin, Home of today's second ethics-driven registration* by Tom Gara
Shared	59	*Seven steps for addressing post merger cultural issues* by Deloitte
Authentic	7	*Q&A: New Delhi's next archbishop: Right revd.* by Anil Couto
Distributed	19	*The nature of the firm in the digital economy* by Irving Wladawsky-Berger[b]
Adaptive	1	*Making succession planning for hedge funds effective*

[a]US edition (*www.wsj.com*), accessed on 7 January 2013.
[b]It is also interesting to note that 'shared' has more entries in this publication than 'distributed' Bolden (2011), in a review of the relevant literature, found that the proportion of publications on distributed leadership is significantly higher in the United Kingdom than in the United States and vice versa for publications on shared leadership.

Table 2.5: Number of entries and examples of leadership philosophies in *FT.com*.

Philosophy	Entries	Representative article
FT.com[a]		
Ethical	396	*Learning something different* by Lee Mrnjavac
Shared	1285	*Time to focus on the team, not the individual* by Khoi Tu
Authentic	159	*Would the real executive please stand up* by Anthony Goodman
Distributed	258	*A team of leaders* by Sue Cox
Adaptive	37	*View from Deauville: Leadership for the 21st century* by FT.com

[a]*FT.com* on 7 January 2013.

that this belief (that leaders are born) fosters both self-delusion and irresponsibility in those who see themselves as 'born leaders', and it can lead to inaction and dangerous forms of dependency in those who do not see themselves as leaders.

2.4.1.2. Key author

Ronald A. Heifetz is the King Hussein Bib Talal Senior Lecturer in Public Leadership and founder of the Center for Public Leadership at the John F. Kennedy School of Government, University. Known for his seminal work during the past two decades on the practice and teaching of leadership, his research focuses on how to build adaptive capacity in societies, businesses and non-profits. His book *Leadership Without Easy Answers* (1994) has been translated into many languages and is currently in its 13th printing. He also co-authored the best-selling book, *Leadership on the Line: Staying Alive through the Dangers of Leading* (Heifetz & Linksy, 2002). His third book, *The Practice of Adaptive Leadership: Tools and Tactics for Changing Your Organisation and the World* (Heifetz, Linksy, & Grashow, 2009) is a hands-on, practical guide, which contains stories, tools, diagrams, cases and worksheets to help managers develop their skills as leaders to enable them to take people outside their comfort zones and address the toughest challenges.

2.4.1.3. Theory

Technical and adaptive problems.   In his book, *Leadership without Easy Answers*, Heifetz presents a new theory of leadership in tackling complex, contemporary problems. Central to his theory is the distinction between routine technical problems which can be solved through expertise and adaptive problems, such as crime, poverty and educational reform, which require innovative approaches, including consideration of values. Five strategic principles of adaptive leadership are recommended: to identify the adaptive challenges; to keep the levels of distress with a tolerable range for doing adaptive work; to give the work back to people, but at a rate that they can stand; to focus attention on ripening issues and not on stress-reducing distractions; and to protect voices of leadership without authority (Heifetz, 1994, p. 128). Yukl (2013) suggests that adaptive leadership is an emergent process that occurs when people with different knowledge, beliefs and preferences interact in an attempt to solve problems and resolve conflicts. The result of this process is the production of creative ideas and new conceptions that can facilitate the resolution of conflict and an adaptive resolution to a threat or opportunity.

Leadership and authority.   Most people often equate leadership with authority.[7] As Heifetz (1994, p. 49) comments: *We routinely call leaders those who achieve high positions of authority even though, on reflection, we readily acknowledge the frequent lack of leadership they provide.*

In Chapter 8 to *Leadership without Easy Answers*, Heifetz suggests that we see leadership too rarely exercised from high office. Of note, he goes on to suggest that the scarcity of leadership from people in authority, however, makes it all the more critical to the adaptive success of a polity that leadership be exercised by people without authority. In addition, as we are not used to distinguishing or understanding the difference between leadership and authority, the idea of

---

7. Howieson and Kahn (2002) argue that authority is completely different from leadership and indeed, management. There is always a place for authority (or a Nike says *Just do it*). That said, one should aim to lead and exercise authority only when the situation demands it.

leadership without authority is new, perplexing and actually very difficult for many people.

2.4.1.4. Practice

Technical and adaptive problems.   Traditional management strategies are useful in dealing with technical problems, but in situations where beliefs and values come into play, technical 'fixes' tend to exacerbate the problem. Adaptive challenges then involve a disparity between values and circumstances. The task of the leader is to close the gap. This may involve marshalling energy, resources and ingenuity to change the circumstances. But just as often it requires that people change their values. Heifetz (1994, p. 76) gives an excellent example where a physician can help the patient with a technical problem (e.g. antibiotics for certain infections). For more complex problems (e.g. obesity/diabetes), the problem definition is not clear cut, and technical fixes are not available. In this respect, the situation involves leadership (an adaptive problem) where the patient will need to be 'lead' to face and make the necessary adjustments to his/her lifestyle. Leadership, therefore, consists *not of answers or assured visions, but of taking action to clarify values.* Good leaders know how to stimulate and contain the forces of invention and change, and to shift the process from one stage to the next.

Leadership and authority.   Since we are not accustomed to distinguishing between leadership and authority, this category has received very little scholarly attention and is often perplexing to people (Grint, 2005a, 2005b; Howieson & Kahn, 2002). While we usually focus attention at the head of the table, leadership may more often emerge from the foot of the table. For example, many women who have been denied formal authority roles in society have developed strategies for leading without authority. One of the authors of this book recently spent time in Saudi Arabia delivering a leadership programme for women in the Middle East. Many of the women on the programme were actively engaged in leadership at various levels in organisations but few were in positions of influence and authority. The same is true for other traditionally disempowered groups. Leaders without authority *push us to clarify our values, face hard realities, and seize new possibilities, however frightening they may be.* Gandhi, perhaps the most celebrated example of this type of leadership, tried to force attention to a set of problems in India which the British colonial government refused to acknowledge (Heifetz, 1994, p. 189). He (Gandhi) identified many adaptive challenges and used various methods of creative defiance to get people to face them. Other examples include Nelson Mandela, Lech Walesa, Martin Luther King Jr. and Margaret Sanger.[8]

---

8. Closer to home, the reader is directed to the excellent case study, *Policing the Drumcree Demonstrations in Northern Ireland: Testing Leadership Theory in Practice* (Bennington & Turbitt, 2007).

2.4.2. *Authentic*

2.4.2.1. Working definition
The definition of authentic leadership differs from writer to writer; however, they all emphasise the importance of consistency in a leader's words, actions and values (Yukl, 2013, p. 339). Caza and Jackson (2011, p. 354) state that authentic leaders are defined as:

> Leaders who exhibit four behavioural tendencies: self awareness, which is accurate knowledge of one's strengths, weaknesses, and idiosyncratic qualities; relational transparency, which involves genuine representation of the self to others; balanced processing, which is the collection and use of relevant, objective information, particularly that which challenges one's prior beliefs; and an internalized moral perspective, which refers to self-regulation and self-determination, rather than acting in accordance with situational demands.

Given these four behavioural tendencies, Caza and Jackson (2011, p. 354) then quote Walumbwa, Avolio, Gardener, Wernsing, and Peterson (2008, p. 94) who provide the following definition of authentic leadership:

> A pattern of leader behaviour that draws upon and promotes both positive psychological capacities and a positive ethical climate, to foster greater self-awareness, an internalized moral perspective, balanced processing of information, and relational transparency on the part of leaders working with followers, fostering positive self-development.

2.4.2.2. Key author(s)
The idea of authentic leadership has received a lot of attention in recent years, and several scholars and authors have provided offerings of theory (Avolio, Gardener, Walumbwa, Luthans, & May, 2004; Gardener, Avolio, Luthans, May, & Walumbwa, 2005; Ilies, Morgeson, & Nahrgang, 2005; Shamir & Elam, 2005). Definition varies from writer to writer; that being said, authentic leadership involves consistency in a leader's words, actions and values. Additional aspects include positive leader values, leader self-awareness and a trusting relationship with followers. Luthans and Avolio (2003) are credited with the commencing the research programme in authentic leadership (Caza & Jackson, 2011). The term authentic leadership was also used by Bill George in his book, *Authentic Leadership: Rediscovering the Secrets to Creating Lasting Value* (George, 2004). He wrote this text in 2003, around the time of the Enron and WorldCom scandals. These corporate scandals and crimes provoked a backlash, prompting a strong wish — certainly presented and reflected in the media and by politicians — for leaders of substance: leaders that people could trust. Authentic leaders, in other words.

2.4.2.3. Theory
Since its formal introduction in 2003, authentic leadership has been the focus of significant theoretical attention. Caza and Jackson (2011) offer an excellent and most readable summary of extant theory in their book section, *Theoretical Claims*. They suggest that the most important influence on the development of authentic leadership theory most likely emerged from the post-charismatic critiques of trans-formation leadership. Authentic leadership theory makes distinctions between three types or levels of authenticity: an individual's personal authenticity; a leader's authenticity as a leader; and authentic leadership as a phenomenon in itself.[9] These three types of authenticity are argued to be hierarchically inclusive, such that one cannot be an authentic leader without being individually authentic and authentic leadership is not possible without the intervention of an authentic leader. Caza and Jackson (2011) focus, in detail, on antecedents, consequences and mechanisms of authentic leadership.

Yukl (2013) also suggests that authentic leaders have positive core values such as honesty, altruism, kindness, fairness, accountability and optimism. These core values motivate these leaders to do what is right and fair for followers, and to create a special type of relationship that includes high mutual trust, transparency (open and honest communication), guidance towards worthy shared objectives and emphasis on follower welfare and development. These leaders also have a high degree of self-acceptance which is similar to emotional maturity.

2.4.2.4. Practice
In simple terms, authentic leaders know and live their values and they win peo-ple's trust by being who they are, not pretending to be someone else or living up to others' expectations. The notion of being genuine equates to being honest and truthful. Nick Craig, co-author with Bill George and Andrew McLean of the book, *Finding Your True North* (George, McLean, & Craig, 2008) lists four ele-ments of authentic leadership: being true to yourself in the way you work; being motivated by a larger purpose; being prepared to make decisions that feel right, that fit your values — not decisions that are merely politically astute or designed to make you popular; and concentrating on achieving long-term sustainable results.

George, Sims, McLean, and Mayer (2007) published an article in the *Harvard Business Review* entitled, *Discovering Your Authentic Leadership*. This article focuses on people who find their own voice rather than emulating those perceived to be good leaders. George and his colleagues conducted the largest in-depth study ever undertaken on how people can become and remain authentic leaders. They inter-viewed 125 business leaders from different racial, religious, national and socioeco-nomic backgrounds. Their interviews showed that an individual does not have to be born with any particular characteristics or traits to lead. In addition, an individual

---

9. For further reference, the reader is directed to Yukl's (2013, pp. 339–340) treatment in chapter 13, *Ethical Leadership*.

does not have to be at the top of their organisation. Anyone can learn to be an authentic leader. The journey basically begins with leaders understanding their life stories. Authentic leaders frame their stories in ways that allow them to see themselves not as passive observers but as individuals who learn from their experiences. These leaders make time to examine their experiences and to reflect on them, and in doing so they grow as individuals and as leaders. Authentic leaders also work hard at developing self-awareness through persistent and often courageous self-exploration. Denial can be the greatest hurdle that leaders face in becoming self-aware, but authentic leaders ask for, and listen to, honest feedback. They also use formal and informal support networks to help them stay grounded and lead integrated lives.

George et al. (2007) argue further that achieving business results over a sustained period of time is the ultimate mark of authentic leadership. It may be possible to drive short-term outcomes without being authentic, but authentic leadership is the only way to create long-term results.

2.4.3. Distributed[10]

2.4.3.1. Working definition

In the academic literature, the definition of distributed leadership is contested; for example, Grint (2005a, 2005b) [and quoted in Thorpe, Gold, and Lawler (2011, p. 240)] argues that: *That a universally accepted definition of distributed leadership remains elusive.* Gronn (2000, p. 317) defines distributed leadership very simply as: *An emergent property of a group or a network of interacting individuals* and as *concretive action,* which he describes as producing an outcome that is greater than the sum of its parts. While Petrov (2006) [and quoted in Gill (2008)] describes distributed leadership in more depth as: *A model that is based on the idea that leadership of an organisation should not rest with a single individual, but should be shared or 'distributed' among those with the relevant skills.*

2.4.3.2. Key author(s)

Distributed leadership is now attracting significant attention from scholars and practitioners alike. As a result, there are many people contributing to, and writing about, this leadership philosophy. From our research, it would seem that the following come to the fore in terms of their writing: Peter Gronn, Kenneth Leithwood, John MacBeath and James Spillane.[11]

---

10. We are most grateful to Ms Linda Daisley and Mr Elliot Jackson (University of Stirling MBA students of 2013 and 2012, respectively) for their contributions to this section.
11. Of interest, these authors are all educational scholars. Distributed leadership is now the recognised leadership philosophy in the education sector in the United Kingdom.

2.4.3.3. Theory

Distributed leadership is not a new concept. Oduro (2004) notes that there are accounts of distributed leadership dating back to 1250 BC. Gronn (2002) cites Gibb (1954) as the first author to specifically include distributed leadership in his discussions on leadership. Gibb (1954) argued that leadership should be attributed to group aims and values rather than to the actions of one individual. Gronn (2002) also notes that the concept of distributed 'lay dormant' for many decades, only to be discussed by a few authors during the 1980s and 1990s. During the last decade, however, distributed leadership has been studied extensively by scholars and explored by practitioners. Bolden (2011) — having researched the increased interest in the subject — found that a search of the internet in March 2011, using the term distributed leadership, returned 187,000 hits with 9220 books referring to the topic. Bolden (2011) argues that whilst this is only a small fraction of the overall literature on 'leadership' (201 million web pages and nearly 6 million books on Google.co. uk), if considered alongside related literatures, such as 'shared', 'collective', 'collaborative', 'co-' and 'emergent' leadership, it represents a significant and growing body of material.

At present, contemporary approaches to leadership are changing. Indeed, many writers (e.g. Gratton, 2009; Howieson, 2013) now question the utility and applicability of hierarchical leadership, with the all-seeing, all-knowing 'heroic' chief executive at the top. In an environment, increasingly characterised by complexity, the question may be: where does leadership go next? (Jackson, 2012). Distributed leadership is one possible solution. It is of increasing interest to the public sector in the United Kingdom and the wider business world, perhaps borne out of what Gronn (2002) refers to as: *A growing disenchantment with solely individualistic notions of leadership, heroic or otherwise.*

In this regard, distributed leadership — in the context of organisational improvement and change — becomes a collective rather than an individual responsibility. It is the interactions between the leaders and their followers that matter as opposed to what each individual does.

Badaracco (2001) contends that distributed leadership has become a popular post-heroic representation of leadership, which has encouraged a shift in focus for the attributes and behaviours of individual leaders to a more systemic perspective whereby leadership is conceived of as a collective social process emerging through the interactions of multiple actors. Many writers (including Bennett, Wise, Woods, & Harvey, 2003; Harris, 2003) have also suggested that distributed leadership is related to such constructs as participation, empowerment, delegation and engagement. This view is supported by Pedler, Burgoyne, and Boydell (2003, p. 126) who say that: *Today's leadership needs to be decentralised and distributed to every part of the organisation so those on the periphery who are first to spot challenges can act on them instantly.*

Work undertaken by Bennett et al. (2003), and extensive research undertaken into distributed leadership by the National College for School Leadership identified three distinguishing features that seem to be shared by most authors. They found that distributed leadership: is the product of an interacting group or network of individuals, rather than the act of a single person; opens up the boundaries of leadership to those who would previously have been excluded from leadership activities; and embodies the belief that expertise should be distributed across the organisation, rather than being concentrated in the hands of a few people.

As much as it is important to understand what distributed leadership is, it is equally important to understand what it is not. Spillane and Diamond (2007) dispel four common 'myths of distributed leadership' as follows: distributed leadership is a blueprint for leadership and management; distributed leadership negates the role of the CEO; from a distributed perspective, everyone is a leader; and distributed leadership is only about collaborative situations.

Co-leadership (Heenan & Bennis, 1999), democratic leadership (Woods, 2004), collective leadership, shared leadership (Fletcher & Käufer, 2003; Pearce & Sims, 2000), devolved leadership (i.e. Kets de Vries, 1990) are all seen to represent forms of distributed leadership.

Perhaps then, and on reflection, we agree with Harris and Spillane (2008) in that to be truly successful and to achieve the impact that it promises, the concept of distributed leadership really needs to connect in a meaningful way with the experiences and aspirations of leadership practitioners.

2.4.3.4. Practice

Although Gronn (2002) and Spillane (2006) defined distributed leadership theoretically, it remains a challenging concept to operationalise in practice. In her article, *The time is right for fresh ideas* Gratton (2009) suggests that the recession has brought into stark perspective the role of the leader. Up to this point, the dominant norm was the 'command and control' leadership style, where the organisation is viewed as a hierarchy in which decisions are escalated to the top, and a CEO makes the decisions. Gratton suggests that many people are now questioning the wisdom of placing so much power in the hands of so few. At the same time, insights from research in the decision sciences as well as technological advances have shown that often the best decisions are made by an 'intelligent crowd', rather than one all-powerful individual.

Perhaps, however, the best form of distributed leadership, in practice, is used by the British Armed Forces and is called 'Mission Command' (Bungay, 2005; Grint, 2011; Ministry of Defence, 2011; Yardley & Kakabadse, 2007). Mission Command is not command and control — it is about leadership. The underlying requirement of Mission Command is the fundamental responsibility to act (or in certain circumstances, to decide not to act) within the framework of a commander's intentions. This requires a style of leadership which promotes decentralised command and control, freedom, and speed of action and initiative.

Mission Command is not micro-management; rather, it encourages initiative and freedom of action by minimising constraints. The subordinate is given the minimum of direction but has complete access to his/her superior to seek clarification, if required. The subordinate is, therefore, empowered and trusted. For his/her part, the superior commander must craft each mission with care and ensure that the unifying purpose is succinct and accurate and the subordinate is correctly resourced to achieve that which he/she has been tasked to accomplish. Mission Command imparts understanding to subordinates about the intentions of a higher commander and their place within his/her (the commander's) plan, enabling them to carry out missions with the maximum freedom of action and appropriate resources. It is predicated upon delegation of authority and agility in execution. Its essence relies on striking an appropriate balance between direction and delegation, dependent upon the training, personality and experience of the commander and subordinates concerned. It requires trust, shared awareness and common understanding (Ministry of Defence, 2011, 5-4).

The successful implementation of Mission Command requires that subordinates understand what effect they are being asked to achieve. Every mission is constructed in a common fashion: a mission verb (i.e. *to do* something); a series of prioritised tasks; and the unifying purpose — why the task is required in the bigger picture. The unifying purpose is critical since it allows the subordinate to remain flexible when the situation inevitably changes and understand what it is that needs to be done. Mission Command, therefore, requires: clearly defined language and structure to mission statements (derived from a detailed and logical planning process); mutual trust between superior and subordinate; sufficient resources; and an attitude of mind within the subordinate that seeks to exploit every opportunity to display initiative and exploit freedom of action.

In recognising the limitations of top-down models of leadership, and the limitations of leadership when the unit of analysis is a single individual, there are certain aspects of the Mission Command philosophy that are relevant to all levels and positions of leadership. By bringing this military-based philosophy into the non-military world, the aim is to maximise human creativity, initiative and diligence, allowing employees to feel empowered and to act confidently. Indeed, business managers have found that the principles that underpin Mission Command have provided ideas that can help resolve issues they currently face in the workplace (IDG — The Sandhurst Partnership, 2010).

Of note, Mission Command ensures that: everyone within the organisation feels united and are working towards a common goal; responsibility can be delegated to the lowest level; employees feel empowered to operate with minimal supervision; and there is a better understanding between staff and managers.

Mission Command concentrates on telling subordinates the 'what' and the 'why' but not the 'how' to achieve tasks and this has utility for all organisations (not just military) seeking to increase the efficiency of management. Mission Command is applicable to all organisations, which operate in complex and unpredictable environments. It requires the following principles for its success:

- Unity of effort: everyone in the organisation needs to understand where they are going and why
- Decentralisation: the organisation's control process and the managers' and/or leadership mindset must be one of decentralised control

- Mutual trust between superior and subordinate
- Mutual understanding: the entire team must understand the process, the aims and how those above, below, and laterally behave and operate. Communication and training are key factors
- Timely and effective decision-making

The main problem with the Mission Command philosophy is that it has, unquestionably, a military flavour to it. This can worry or scare people who do not work in military organisations. Successful adoption is not helped by such quotes as The King's Fund (2012, p. 7): *There is growing evidence that the NHS needs to break with the command and control, target-driven approach.* In this respect, command and control are about structures and not leadership. Bungay and McKinney (2005) suggest, therefore, the term 'Mission Leadership' and argue its utility in business. For example, Mission Leadership allows: an empowered subordinate; agility in the face of changing circumstances; endorsement of initiative and original thought; minimal interference and micro-management from above; and high probability of seizing the initiative from the opponent and increasing chances of success. Bungay and McKinney (2005) go on to state that there are two sides to Mission Leadership: behaviours and process. The behaviours involve senior people being disciplined enough to simplify the complexities of their strategy so that they become very clear about their intentions and objectives. Those lower in the organisation have to be ready to accept responsibility to operationalise and implement this strategy, use the freedom they are granted, and not to delegate it back upwards. The other side is the (alignment) process, which is a way of structuring people's thinking which enables them to ensure 100% clarity over the 'what' and the 'why' of the mission, work through the 'how' it implies, and make explicit the boundaries within which they will work. The set of processes enables an organisation to translate intentions into concrete activity. This is important because leaders need to be secure enough to create 'white space' in their leadership: making room for others to express themselves. This view is espoused further by The King's Fund (2011, p. 26):

> Leaders in the NHS need to be given room to lead. If politicians and the public really want better leadership and more innovation in the NHS, then its leaders, using sound evidence where service reconfiguration is involved, have to be given the room to lead, and political backing when they so do. Too often, leaders feel the need to be omnipresent, directing everything that happens and, therefore, stifling innovation and creativity.

'White space' does not, however, reflect a lack of leadership or structure as it might seem. On the contrary, strong leadership is what makes it possible. A leader has to shape that space in an on-going way to ensure that they allow room for people to develop themselves, to contribute and, critically, to learn to lead. Wilson (quoted in Bungay, 2005) singled out three critical factors which made a difference in implementing Mission Leadership at Diego, one of the world's leading consumer goods companies: (1) give empowerment meaning by making objectives clear, putting in place the right people and then trusting them; (2) give teamwork meaning and break down silos by making clear who can take decisions about what and what impact those decisions, or lack of them, will have on others and; (3) embedding the discipline of decision-making.

Mission leadership cuts through the noise of management fads and the many and competing leadership theories and practices to focus on the essentials which have distinguished high performance organisations throughout history. There is now a growing body of evidence that business organisations of the 21st century, which have the persistence to embed it in their daily practice may be no exception. Every organisation is unique, but Mission Leadership can deliver universally beneficial effects including:

- Faster implementation of change
- More empowered teams with reduced staff turnover
- Greater feeling of community and team spirit
- Increased resourcefulness and initiative
- More time for senior managers to anticipate
- Faster decisions
- An enduring competitive advantage

2.4.4. *Ethical*

2.4.4.1. Working definition

The moral goodness of leaders has been a topic of analysis for centuries (Ciulla & Forsyth, 2011, p. 229). In studying ethical leadership, we try to understand many of the ethical challenges that are presented to us in leadership positions. In this pursuit, Ciulla and Forsyth (2011, p. 229) remind us that, in doing so, we draw from the philosophical literature on ethics that spans back to the beginning of the written word and indeed use some of the tools of philosophy, such as logic and conceptual analysis. By doing this, we can, perhaps, predict and understand how me might act when such situations arise or are presented to us.

To many, ethical leadership is seen to equate to moral leadership, or leading with a sense of great fairness. To others, it provides a basis for more detailed explanation and application, frequently connected to the principles of social responsibility (including Corporate Social Responsibility), sustainability, equality, Fairtrade, environmental care and humanitarianism, to name just some.

These are all vast concepts, which make it very difficult, and perhaps impossible, to define ethical leadership precisely and absolutely. Ciulla and Forsyth (2011) discuss the many challenges associated with studying ethical leadership including: trust and self-interest; self-discipline and virtue; virtue ethics and leadership; power and privilege; power and expediency; caring; the moral challenge of happiness;

and 'getting all of it right'. Two other challenges arise: the shifting and variable meanings of ethical, and the cultural and religious nature of ethical interpretation.

The Center for Ethical Leadership at the University of Texas at Austin[12] offers the following definition of ethical leadership: *Ethical leadership is knowing your core values and having the courage to live them in all parts of your life in service of the common good.*

Ethical leadership has been defined in many ways. Northouse (2013, p. 424) states:

> Ethics has to do with what leaders do and who leaders are. It is concerned with the nature of leaders; behaviour, and with their virtuousness. In any decision-making situation, ethical issues are either implicitly or explicitly involved. The choicer leaders make and how they respond in a given circumstance are informed and directed by ethics.

Yukl (2013) also comments in this area when he offers values which are emphasised in theories of ethical leadership and include: integrity, altruism, humility, empathy and healing, personal growth, fairness and justice, and empowerment.

2.4.4.2. Key author(s)

On 25 January 2013, with 'ethics' as a keyword, there were 2941 books on the Amazon website alone. Table 2.2. reminds us again of an increasing amount of articles in this most important and relevant subject area. There are no key authors in this area. Most current leadership textbooks, however, have sections/chapters dedicated to this area. For further reference, the reader is directed to By and Burnes (2013), Northouse (2013), Yukl (2013) and (Ciulla & Forsyth, 2011) for more detailed analysis.

2.4.4.3. Theory

The demand for leaders to behave ethically seems to have increased markedly during the 21st century. As mentioned in Chapter 1, this has been driven greatly by global financial crisis, corporate frauds, environmental disasters which have been judged failures of ethical standards, not failures of skills, or resources, or technology, or strategy, or business acumen.

One significant problem in the theory is that 'ethical' can mean different things to different people, and to a great degree, is a changing and fluid notion. Moreover, what was ethical a generation ago may not be today. What is ethical today may be considered unethical in a few years time.

Northouse (2013) does tackle leadership ethics theory in the — surprisingly — last chapter of his book. He offers perspectives from Heifetz (1994) and Burns (1978). Heifetz's perspective is related to ethical leadership because it deals with values: the

---

12. www.utexas.edu/lbj/research/leadership

values of workers and the values of the organisations and communities in which they work. For Burns (1978) it is important for leaders to engage themselves with followers and help them (followers) in their personal struggles regarding conflicting values. The resulting connection raises the level of morality in both the leader and the follower.

2.4.4.4. Practice
Northouse (2013, p. 430) offers five principles of ethical leadership, the origins of which can be traced back to Aristotle. Although not inclusive, these principles provide a foundation for the development of sound ethical leadership: respect for others; service to others; the importance of fairness and justice; honesty; and the building of community in our practice.

2.4.5. *Servant*

2.4.5.1. Working definition
Servant leadership, which originated in the writings of Greenleaf (1970, 1972, 1977), has been of interest to leadership scholars for more than 40 years (Northouse, 2013).

The idea of servant leadership is basically simple: the leader serves the followers or a cause, which benefits the followers in some way. A leader who embodies servant leadership is not leading for reasons of status, wealth, popularity or lust for power. Instead, a servant-leader wants to make a positive difference to the benefit of all, or at least the majority of followers.

Servant leadership is both a leadership philosophy and set of leadership practices. Traditional leadership generally involves the accumulation and exercise of power by one at the 'top of the pyramid'. By comparison, the servant-leader shares power, puts the needs of others first and helps people develop and perform as highly as possible.

Greenleaf (1970, p. 15) provides the most frequently referenced definition:

> Servant leadership begins with the natural feeling that one wants to serve, to serve first. Then conscious choice brings one to aspire to lead ... The difference manifests itself in the care taken by the servant — first to make sure that other people's highest priority needs are being served. The best test is: do those served grow as persons; do they, while being served, become healthier, wiser, freer, more autonomous, more likely to become servants?

2.4.5.2. Key author
The key author is Robert K. Greenleaf who — in a 1970 essay entitled *The Servant as Leader* — proposed the concept of servant leadership:

> The servant-leader is servant first ... It begins with the natural feeling that one wants to serve, to serve first. Then conscious choice brings one to aspire to lead. That person is sharply different from one who is

leader first, perhaps because of the need to assuage an unusual power drive or to acquire material possessions ....

Greenleaf's essay launched the servant leadership movement in the United States. His ideas were subsequently developed into a book, *Servant Leadership* (Greenleaf, 1977).

2.4.5.3. Theory

Most of the academic and non-academic writing on the topic has been prescriptive, focusing on how servant leadership should actually be, rather than descriptive, focusing on what servant leadership actually is in practice (Van Dierendonk, 2011) [and quoted in Northouse (2013)]. Table 2.2 shows that in the last 10 years the amount of publications has increased year-on-year, which has helped to clarify this theory and to build upon its basic assumptions.

The work of Northouse (2013, pp. 223−232) is very helpful in this area. He has dedicated eight pages to 'Building a Theory About Servant Leadership'. In detail, he introduces a servant leadership model based on the work of Liden, Wayne, Zhao, and Henderson (2008) and Liden, Pannacio, Hu, and Meuser (2014). The model has three main components: antecedent conditions (context and culture, leader attributes and follower receptivity), servant-leader behaviours (conceptualising, emotional healing, putting followers first, helping followers grow and succeed, behaving ethically, empowering and creating value for the community) and leadership outcomes (follower performance and growth, organisational performance and societal impact).

2.4.5.4. Practice

Servant leadership in the workplace is about helping others to accomplish shared objectives by facilitating individual development, empowerment and collective work that is consistent with the health and long-term welfare of followers. Spears (2002) in an attempt to clarify servant leadership for practitioners, identified 10 characteristics in Greenleaf's (1977) writings that are central to the development of servant leadership:

1. Listening
2. Empathy
3. Healing
4. Awareness
5. Persuasion
6. Conceptualisation
7. Foresight
8. Stewardship
9. Commitment to the growth of people
10. Building community

Together, these characteristics comprise the first model or conceptualisation of servant leadership (Northouse, 2013).

Servant leadership has been used extensively in a variety of organisations and taught throughout the world in universities and colleges. Closer to home, 'Serve to Lead' is the motto of the Royal Military Academy Sandhurst (RMAS). RMAS is where all officers in the British Army are trained in the responsibilities of leading soldiers. With this motto in mind, it is the leader's role to serve his/her team, to get the best out of them, and to coach, guide, mentor and encourage. This is, in effect, the true role of the leader — servanthood.

2.4.6. *Shared*

2.4.6.1. Working definition
Representative definitions, particularly from a US-perspective, include:

- Yukl (1989): *Individual members of a team engaging in activities that influence the team and other team members*
- Pearce and Sims (2000): *Leadership that emanates from members of teams, and not simply from the appointed leader*
- Pearce and Conger (2002): *A dynamic, interactive influence process among individuals and groups for which the objective is to lead one another to the achievement of group or organisational goals or both*[13]
- Carson, Tesluk, and Marrone (2007): *An emergent team property that results from the distribution of leadership influence across multiple team members*
- Bergman, Rentsch, Small, Davenport, and Bergman (2012): *Shared leadership occurs when two or more members engage in the leadership of the team in an effort to influence and direct fellow members to maximize team effectiveness*

2.4.6.2. Key author(s)
There are many authors and scholars who write about shared leadership. Indeed, most textbooks, particularly those from the United States, have sections on the term.

2.4.6.3. Theory
It is not the purpose of this chapter to detail the differences academically, and in practitioner terms, between shared and distributed leadership. A couple of points are, however, worthy of note:

- Brookes (2008, p. 6) [and quoted in Thorpe et al. (2011)], in writing about 'collective leadership', notes two elements: 'horizontal' (shared between organisations) and vertical (distributed throughout the organisation). While the horizontal

---

13. They added that this influence process often involves peer, or lateral, influence and at other times involves upward or downward hierarchical influence.

dimension is named 'shared' and the vertical 'distributed', Brookes (2008) uses the same labels interchangeably.

• In a review of the relevant literature, Bolden (2011) found that the proportion of publications on distributed leadership is significantly higher in the United Kingdom than in the United States and vice versa for publications on shared leadership. In addition, he also found that distributed leadership appears to be the concept of preference within business, management and other areas of the social sciences and shared leadership within and nursing and medicine. His analysis suggests that together, these findings indicate that while the concept of distributed leadership has made substantial headway in the past decade, its popularity remains very much restricted to particular geographic (UK) and sector areas (business, management and other areas of the social sciences).

Moreover, and in light of Bolden's comments about the geographic preference for 'shared' leadership (US-preferred), the issue of context and culture must also be considered. From this brief analysis, it would appear, then, that there are significant difference between the UK and US models of leadership. Furthermore, it could be argued that much of the leadership taught in the United Kingdom is US-derived, often taken 'unadulterated' or 'customised' from American institutions into the United Kingdom. Finally, it is worth considering that the notion of distributed and/or shared leadership is part of the current zeitgeist, made all the more popular by the recent fall from grace of heroic leaders in the private sector. Nevertheless, there are limits to re-branding, to the efficacy and reach of distributed and/or shared leadership, and the willingness of staff to treat themselves as followers when everyone else is a leader.

Northouse (2013) deals with shared and distributed leadership within the concept of Team Leadership. Yukl (2013) considers it within employee empowerment programmes and within 'Emerging Conceptions of Organisational Leadership'. Yukl (2013, p. 290) states:

> Some different ways of conceptualising leadership have emerged in recent years and they are eliciting interest among scholars who believe that the current popular theories are too limited. Examples include shared leadership and distributed leadership, relational leadership and emerging processes in complexity theory. These approaches are still evolving and as yet, there is still little conclusive research on them.

Shared leadership is also commonly thought of as the 'serial emergence' of multiple leaders over the life of a team, stemming from interactions among team members in which at least one team member tries to influence other members or the team in general (Yukl, 2013). All definitions of shared leadership, like distributed leadership, all make the fundamental distinction from the more traditional notions of hierarchical leadership.

As Pearce, Manz, and Sims (2009, p. 234) summarise, all definitions of shared leadership consistently include a 'process of influence' that is 'built upon more than just downward influence on subordinates or followers by an appointed or elected leader'. Nearly all concepts of shared leadership entail the practice of: *Broadly sharing power and influence among a set of individuals rather than centralizing it in the hands of a single individual who acts in the clear role of a dominant superior.*

Of note, with the complexity and ambiguity of tasks that teams often experience, it is becoming more apparent that a single leader is unlikely to have all of the skills and traits to effectively perform the necessary leadership functions. Teamwork is becoming increasingly important in the workplace literature as many organisations recognise the benefits that teamwork can bring. Thus, organisations consider it important to investigate team effectiveness and the elements that increase this. Leaders have been pointed to as critical factors in team performance and effectiveness — some have even gone as far as to say they are the most important ingredient for team effectiveness. Additionally, problems associated with team leaders are often cited as the primary reason for failures of work involving teams.

Thus, shared leadership is becoming increasingly popular in teams, as multiple team members emerge as leaders, especially when they have the skills/knowledge/expertise that the team needs.

2.4.6.4. Practice
Further guidance in a UK context can be found in the case study *changing a traditional and competitive organisation into a collaborative enterprise.* In this case study, Turnbull James (2011) offers an example from a training programme for a major housing association. In the first instance, the specification was very traditional, namely *leader* development. But they began to realise as discussions evolved that they wanted something that would really shift the culture and how they do their business, rather than simply up-skill their managers. The purpose of the programme was to generate collaborative and shared leadership, to create an organisation in which collaborative and shared leadership were hallmarks of the organisation, to create more engagement with the organisation and to create the conditions for more innovation in the organisation. This purpose coalesced as the leadership top team realised that there was only a limited amount of change that they can personally direct.

References

Avolio, B. J., Gardener, W. L., Walumbwa, F. O., Luthans, F., & May, D. R. (2004). Unlocking the mask: A look at the process by which authentic leaders impact follower attitudes and behaviours. *The Leadership quarterly, 15*(6), 801−823.

Badaracco, J. L. (2001). We don't need another hero. *Harvard Business Review, 79*(8), 120−126.

Bass, B. (1990). *Bass and Stogdill's handbook of leadership: Theory, research and managerial implications* (3rd ed.). New York, NY: Free Press.

Bennett, N., Wise, C., Woods, P. A., & Harvey, J. A. (2003). *Distributed leadership.* Nottingham: National College of School Leadership.

Bennington, J., & Turbitt, I. (2007). Policing the Drumcree demonstrations in Northern Ireland: Testing leadership theory in practice. *Leadership, 7*(3), 371–395.

Bergman, J. Z., Rentsch, J. R., Small, E. E., Davenport, S.W., & Bergman, S. M. (2012). The shared leadership process in decision-making teams. *The Journal of Social Psychology, 152*(1), 17–42.

Bolden, R. (2004). What is leadership? Leadership South West Research Report 1. Centre for Leadership Studies, University of Exeter.

Bolden, R. (2011). Distributed leadership in organisations: A review of theory and research. *International Journal of Management Reviews, 13,* 251–269.

Brookes, S. (2008). *The public leadership challenge: Full research report.* ESRC Seminar Series End of Award Report. RES-451-25-4273. Swindon: ESRC.

Bryman, A., Collinson, D., Grint, K., Jackson, B., & Uhl-Bien, M. (2011). The Sage handbook of leadership. London: Sage.

Bungay, S. (2005). The road to mission command. *British Army Review, 137*(Summer), 22–29.

Bungay, S., & McKinney, D. (2005). Mission leadership – the missing link. *The Ashridge Journal,* (Autumn), 14–19.

Burns, J. M. (1978). *Leadership.* New York, NY: Harper and Row Publishers.

By, R. T., & Burnes, B. (Eds.). (2013). Organisational change, leadership and ethics. Oxon: Routledge.

Campbell, D., Edgar, D., & Stonehouse, G. (2011). *Business strategy: An introduction* (3rd ed.). Basingstoke: Palgrave Macmillan.

Carson, J., Tesluk, P., & Marrone, J. (2007). Shared leadership in teams: An investigating of antecedent conditions and performance. *Academy of Management Journal, 50,* 1217–1234.

Caza, A., & Jackson, B. (2011). Authentic leadership. In A. Bryman., D. Collinson, K. Grint, B. Jackson, & M. Uhl-Bien (Eds.), *The Sage handbook of leadership.* London: Sage.

Ciulla, J. B., & Forsyth, D. R. (2011). Leadership ethics. In A. Bryman., D. Collinson, K. Grint, B. Jackson, & M. Uhl-Bien (Eds.), *The Sage handbook of leadership.* London: Sage.

Fleishman, E. A., Mumford, M. D., Zacarro, S. J., Levin, K., Korotokin, A. L., & Hein, M. B. (1991). Taxonomic efforts in the description of leader behaviour: A synthesis and functional interpretation. *Leadership Quarterly, 2*(4), 245–287.

Fletcher, J. K., & Käufer, K. (2003). Shared leadership: Paradox and possibility. In C. L. Pearce & J. A. Conger (Eds.), *Shared leadership: Reframing the hows and whys of leadership.* Thousand Oaks, CA: Sage.

Gardener, W. L., Avolio, B. J., Luthans, F., May, D. R., & Walumbwa, F. O. (2005). Can you see the real me? A self-based model of authentic leader and follower development. *The Leadership Quarterly, 16*(3), 343–372.

George, B. (2004). *Authentic leadership: Rediscovering the secrets to creating lasting value.* San Francisco, CA: Jossey-Bass.

George, B., McLean, A., & Craig, N. (2008). *Finding your true North.* San Francisco, CA: Jossey-Bass.

George, B., Sims, P., McLean, A. N., & Mayer, D. (2007). Discovering your authentic leadership. *Harvard Business Review, 85*(2), 129–138.

Gibb, C. A. (1954). Leadership. In G. Lindzey (Ed.), *Handbook of social psychology* (Vol. 2, pp. 877–917). Reading, MA: Addison-Wesley.

Gill, J. (2008). *Gill distributed leadership model gives 'illusion' of consultation.* Retrieved from http://www.timeshighereducation.co.uk/401985.article

Gill, R. (2012). *Theory and practice of leadership.* London: Sage.

Gratton, L. (2009). The time is right for fresh ideas. Retrieved from FT.com. Accessed on 5 February.

Greenleaf, R. K. (1970). *The servant as leader.* Westfield, IN: The Greenleaf Center for Servant Leadership.

Greenleaf, R. K. (1972). *The institution as servant.* Westfield, IN: The Greenleaf Center for Servant Leadership.

Greenleaf, R. K. (1977). *Servant leadership: A journey into the nature of legitimate power and greatness.* New York, NY: Paulist Press.

Grint, K. (2005a). *Leadership: limits and possibilities.* Basingstoke: Palgrave Macmillan.

Grint, K. (2005b). Problems, problems, problems: The social construction of leadership. *Human Relations, 58*(11), 1467–1494.

Grint, K. (2011). A history of leadership. In A. Bryman, D. Collinson, K. Grint, B. Jackson, & M. Uhl-Bien (Eds.), *The Sage handbook of leadership.* London: Sage.

Gronn, P. (2000). Distributed properties: A new architecture for leadership. *Educational Management Administration & Leadership, 28*, 317–338.

Gronn, P. (2002). Distributed leadership as a unit of analysis. *Leadership Quarterly, 13*(4), 423–451.

Harris, A. (2003). Teacher leadership and school improvement. In A. Harris, C. Day, M. Hopkins, M. Hadfield, A. Hargreaves, & C. Chapman (Eds.), *Effective leadership for school improvement.* London: Routledge.

Harris, A., & Spillane, J. (2008). Distributed leadership through the looking glass. *Management in Education, 22*, 31–34.

Heenan, D., & Bennis, W. (1999). *Co-leaders: The power of great partnerships.* Hoboken, NJ: Wiley.

Heifetz, R. A. (1994). *Leadership without easy answers.* Cambridge, MA: Harvard University Press.

Heifetz, R. A., & Linksy, M. (2002). *Leadership on the line.* Boston, MA: Harvard University Press.

Heifetz, R. A., Linksy, M., & Grashow, A. (2009). *The practice of adaptive leadership.* Boston, MA: Harvard University Press.

House, R. J., & Aditya, R. N. (1997). The social scientific study of leadership: Quo vadis? *Journal of Management, 23*(3), 409–473.

Howieson, W. B. (2013). Mission command: A leadership philosophy for the NHS. *Intentional Journal of Clinical Leadership, 17*, 109.

Howieson, W. B., & Kahn, H. (2002). Leadership, management, and command. The Officer's Trinity. In P. W. Gray & S. Cox (Eds.), *Air power leadership: Theory and practice.* Norwich: HMSO.

IDG — The Sandhurst Partnership. (2010). *What is mission command?* Retrieved from http://www.inspirationaldevelopment.com. Accessed on 11 May 2010.

Ilies, R., Morgeson, F. P., & Nahrgang, J. D. (2005). Authentic leadership and eudaemonic well-being: Understanding leader-follower outcomes. *The Leadership Quarterly, 16*(3), 373–394.

Jackson, E. (2012). *The contribution of a change in leadership philosophy in a public body in Scotland.* Unpublished MBA dissertation, The University of Stirling.

Kets de Vries, M. F. R. (1990). The organizational fool: Balancing a leader's hubris. *Human Relations, 43*(8), 751–770.

Leithwood, K., Mascall, B., Strauss, T., Sacks, R., Memon, N., & Yashkina, A. (2009). Distributing leadership to make schools smarter: Taking ego out of the system. In K. Leithwood, B. Mascall, & T. Strauss (Eds.), *Distributed leadership according to the evidence*. London: Routledge.

Liden, R. C., Pannacio, A., Hu, J., & Meuser, J. D. (2014). Servant leadership: Antecedents, consequences, and contextual moderators. In D. V. Day (Ed.), *The Oxford handbook of leadership and organisations*. Oxford, England: Oxford University Press.

Liden, R. C., Wayne, S. J., Zhao, H., & Henderson, D. (2008). Servant leadership: Development of a multidimensional measure and multi-level assessment. *Leadership Quarterly, 19*, 161–177.

Luthans, F., & Avolio, B. J. (2003). Authentic leadership development. In K. S. Cameron, J. E. Dutton, & R. E. Quinn (Eds.), *Positive organisational scholarship: foundations of a new discipline* (pp. 241–258). San Francisco, CA: Berret-Koehler Publishers.

Ministry of Defence. (2011). Joint Doctrine Publication 0-01 (JDP 0-01). British Defence Doctrine (4th ed.).

Northouse, P. G. (2013). *Leadership: Theory and practice* (6th ed.). London: Sage.

Oduro, G. K. T. (2004). Distributed leadership in schools: What English head teachers say about the 'pull' and 'push' factors. Paper presented at the British Educational Research Association Annual Conference, University of Manchester, 16–18 September.

Pearce, C. L., & Conger, J. A. (2002). *Shared leadership: Reframing the hows and whys of leadership*. New York, NY: Sage.

Pearce, C. L., Manz, C. C., & Sims, H. P. Jr. (2009). Where do we go from here? Is shared leadership the key to team success? *Organizational Dynamics, 38*(3), 234–238.

Pearce, C. L., & Sims, H. P. Jr. (2000). Shared leadership: Toward a multi-level theory of leadership. *Advances in the Interdisciplinary Studies of Work Teams, 7*, 115–139.

Pedler, M., Burgoyne, J., & Boydell, T. (2003). *A manager's guide to leadership*. Maidenhead: McGraw-Hill.

Schedlitzki, D., & Edwards, G. (2013). *Studying leadership traditional and critical approaches*. London: Sage.

Shamir, B., & Elam, G. (2005). A life stories approach to authentic leadership development. *The Leadership Quarterly, 16*(3), 395–417.

Sherman, S. (1995). How tomorrow's best leaders are learning their stuff. *Fortune, 132*(11), 90–102.

Spears, L. C. (2002). Tracing the past, present, and future of servant leadership. In L. C. Spears & M. Lawrence (Eds.), *Focus on leadership: Servant leadership for the 21st Century* (pp. 11–24). New York, NY: Palgrave Macmillan.

Spillane, J. P. (2006). *Distributed leadership*. San Francisco, CA: Jossey-Bass.

Spillane, J. P., & Diamond, J. B. (2007). Taking a distributed perspective. In J. P. Spillane & J. B. Diamond (Eds.), *Distributed leadership in practice* (pp. 1–15). New York, NY: Teachers College Press.

Stogdill, R. M. (1974). *Handbook of leadership: A survey of the literature*. New York, NY: Free Press.

The Kings Fund. (2011). The future of leadership and management in the NHS. *No more heroes*. Retrieved from http://www.kingsfund.org.uk/applications/dynamic/?searchstring = leadership&searchtopic = &searchauthor = &filter = &id = 20250&sort = date&x = 0&y = 0

The Kings Fund. (2012). *Leadership and engagement for improvement in the NHS: Together we can*. Retrieved from http://www.kingsfund.org.uk

Thorpe, R., Gold, J., & Lawler, J. (2011). Locating distributed leadership. *International Journal of Management Reviews, 13*, 239–250.

Turnbull James, K. (2011). *Leadership in context: Lessons from new leadership theory and current leadership development practice.* Retrieved from www.kingsfund.org.uk/leadership commission

Van Dierendonk, D. (2011). Servant leadership: A review and synthesis. *Journal of Management, 37*(4), 1228–1261.

Walumbwa, F. O., Avolio, B., Gardener, W. L., Wernsing, T. S., & Peterson, S. J. (2008). Authentic leadership: Development and validation of a theory-based measure. *Journal of Management, 34*(1), 89–126.

Woods, P. (2004). Democratic leadership: Drawing distinctions with distributed leadership. *International Journal of Leadership in Education, 7*, 3–26.

Yardley, I., & Kakabadse, A. (2007). Understanding mission command: A model for developing competitive advantage. *Strategic Change, 16*(2), 69–78.

Yukl, G. (1989). *Leadership in organisations* (2nd ed.). Harlow: Pearson Education.

Yukl, G. (2013). *Leadership in organisations* (8th ed.). Upper Saddle River, NJ: Pearson Education.

Chapter 3

The Public Sector

3.1. Introduction

In writing this chapter, it was actually very difficult knowing where to start. For example, the public sector in the United Kingdom is large, complex, complicated, and when we consider the organisations which are part of this sector, most sophisticated. A quick search of the Office for National Statistics website[1] on Monday 8 July 2013 revealed that at Quarter 1 (2013), 19.2% of all people in employment in the United Kingdom were employed in the public sector which represents 5.7 million people.[2] Of note, and as of this date, the largest three employers in this sector were: National Health Service (NHS) (1.6 million); Education (1.5 million); and Public Administration (1.1 million). In addition, the breadth and depth of organisations are vast: the gov.uk website (www.gov.uk/government/organisations) reveals that there are 24 ministerial departments, 20 non-ministerial departments, 334 agencies and other public bodies, and 12 public corporations in the public sector today.

This chapter is, however, not about the public sector in the United Kingdom today *per se*. It is about its leaders and leadership. For further public sector-specific literature, the reader is directed to many of the texts available currently including: Stevenson (2013); Flynn (2012); Starling (2010); Brookes and Grint (2010); and Raffell, Leisink, and Middlebrookes (2009). Rather, and before getting to the contributors' reflections, we hope in this chapter to: try briefly to understand what the sector is at present in the United Kingdom; detail some of the many challenges ahead in the sector; and describe, again briefly, the current leadership thinking in this sector. It is hoped that this approach will offer a back-drop to the reflections by contributors from throughout the sector. After the reflections, we will analyse and conclude, where possible, on the key themes which emerge.

---

1. www.ons.gov.uk
2. Although this is indeed a significant number, the percentage of the UK population now working in the public sector is at its lowest since 1999.

3.2. Sector, Service or Good?

3.2.1. Public Sector

At the basic level, we consider that public sector organisations are organisations that are owned and controlled by the government or local government. These organisations aim to provide public services, often free at the point of delivery, for example, the NHS. In his Introduction to 'Public Sector Management', Flynn (2012, pp. 2−4) offers several definitions of the public sector in the United Kingdom. He states:

> It could be seen as part of the assets of the economy and society that is owned by the state. Or it could be those services that are provided collectively and funded in whole or in part from taxation. Or that part of the labour market in which people work for a public body, not a private company.

Flynn goes on to say that although these definitions are sensible, the boundaries between what is public and what is private in the United Kingdom are becoming ever more 'fuzzy' and perhaps blurred by each day. Indeed, and although outside the scope of this chapter (and book), Forth Sector Development Limited (2012, p. 5) develops this theme further (the blurring of boundaries) by stating:

> The demarcation lines between sectors are weakening. As public sector funding declines or disappears, the third sector is adopting business practices. While the public sector, especially in England, is creating quasi-third sector organisations in the form of social enterprises and co-operatives, or simply privatising services.

3.2.2. Public Service

Public service is a service which is provided by government to people living within its jurisdiction, either directly through the public sector, or by financing private provision of services. The term 'service' is associated with a social consensus that certain services should be available to all, regardless of income.

3.2.3. Public Good

In economics, a public good is a good that is both non-excludable and non-rivalrous in that individuals cannot be effectively excluded from use and where use by one individual does not reduce availability to others. Examples of public goods include defence, flood prevention and control systems, and lighting. Public goods that are available everywhere are sometimes referred to as goods. The opposite of a public good is a *private good*, which does not possess these properties. A bottle of Rioja, for example, is a private good; its owner can exclude others from using it, and once it has been consumed, it cannot be used again.

The economic concept of public goods should not be confused with the expression *the public good*, which is usually an application of a collective ethical notion of 'the good' in political decision-making.[3] Another common confusion is that public goods are goods provided by the sector. Although it is often the case that government is involved in producing public goods, this is not necessarily the case. Public goods may be naturally available. In addition, they may be produced by private individuals and firms, by non-state collective action, or they may not be produced at all.

Continuing this theme, Flynn (2012, p. 10) suggests that there are four elements to the definition of what is public and what is private:

- Public goods: they produce externalities or benefits that accrue to people other than those who benefit directly (for example, education). Also, people cannot be excluded
- How services are financed: services are public services if they are paid for mainly through taxation rather than by direct payments by individual customers
- Who owns the facilities and by whom the service providers are employed. Traditionally, for example, public services were provided by public employees using publicly owned assets. Again, such a distinction is not absolute
- Lack of direct connection between ability to pay and access to the service and the fact that there is not always a direct benefit from attracting customers that makes management in the public sector distinct

Although this sector, as previously stated, is becoming increasingly blurred, Flynn (2012) notes that it does, however, have a moderately distinct shape. It includes services that are provided as public goods, that are wholly or partly funded by taxation, and that are managed through governance arrangements which involve some degree of public accountability and political control or influence. The sector also includes the whole process of collecting taxes to pay for those services and all the transfer payments to individuals and companies. In addition, there is also the continuity issue, as Flynn (2012, p. 2) points out:

> The shape of the institutions may have changed, the layers of management above the schools, prisons, hospitals, benefits offices may have

---

3. Forth Sector Development Limited (2012, p. 4) states that pursuing public good builds social capital. In its crudest form, public good is about working together for the good of society at large; sometimes called 'the commonweal'.

expanded, shrunk, split up, merged and reorganised but at the 'front end', the interface with citizens, there is a degree of continuity.

At present then:

- There has been an increasing momentum in public sector reform in the United Kingdom since 1997 as part of the wider modernising government agenda (HMSO, 1999) [and quoted in Brookes & Grint, 2010, p. 1]
- The boundaries between public, private, and third sectors in the United Kingdom are changing continually
- The relative size of the public sector has ebbed and flowed over the last 30 years as a result of political and fiscal choices — this is expected to continue
- The process of devolution has resulted in differences in policies, in institutional forms and policy, and management processes in the constituent parts of the United Kingdom, although in certain areas (i.e. defence), it remains centralised[4]
- Governments (central, devolved and local) reorganise structures very frequently
- The public sector represents a significant part of the national economy that was, until 2010, growing

Looking ahead, Flynn (2012, p. 28) discusses briefly the 'Hollow State'. In detail, he suggests that some theorists, as a result of changes to scale, structure and function, now doubt the existence of the state and offer that it needs to be defined in new ways. For example: Jessop (2002) who talks about the hollow state, where the state has contracted out many of its activities and withdrawn from others and so it is a hollow replica of its formal self; and Moran (2003) and King (2009) who discuss the transition from the welfare state to the regulatory state where the state has shrunk to a set of regulators of activities previously carried out by the state and now done by private companies.

Whatever the case, the public sector, whichever lens it is looked through, or interpreted from, and although changing, in terms of regulation or the interaction between the government and the private sector and third sectors, remains significant and a vital part of the United Kingdom, its economy and its *DNA*.

3.3.   Challenges Ahead

It would seem, that even from a cursory look at the sector, that significant challenges are present, and will continue to be present in the years ahead,

---

4. In the United Kingdom, devolved Government was created using simple majority referenda in 1997. One year later, the Scottish Parliament, the National Assembly for Wales, and the Northern Ireland Assembly were established by law. England was left un-devolved. The newly created Scottish Parliament and National Assemblies have powers to make primary legislation in certain 'devolved' areas of public policy; for example, health.

including: continual demands to modernise; higher expectations on the part of the general public and consumers who expect public services to keep up with private ones; a greater focus on connectedness; increased opportunities, and requirements, for partnership working both across the public sector and with private and third sector organisations; more personalisation of services; pressures to harness new technology and deliver government services electronically; and to deliver improved services through a motivated workforce in an age of austerity.

But perhaps the main challenge facing the public sector in the United Kingdom today is that of leadership from the sector itself and of the sector by its leaders. As an aside, it is interesting to note that Leavy and McKiernan (2009) argue the case for leadership being considered as a strategic variable in its own right. In this respect then, perhaps we are witnessing a move away from the paradigm on New Public Management (NPM) that seems to have dominated this sector for over 20 years. Before looking specifically at leadership in this sector — or New Public Leadership (NPL) as Brookes and Grint (2010) call it — it is, perhaps, important to understand the background to, and history of, NPM.

3.3.1. NPM: A Brief History

NPM denotes broadly government policies, since the 1980s, that aimed to modernise and render more effective the public sector. The basic hypothesis holds that the 'market-oriented management' of the public sector will lead to greater cost-efficiency for governments, without having negative side effects on other objectives and considerations. Ferlie, Ashburner, Fitzgerald, and Pettigrew (1996) describe 'New Public Management in Action' as involving the introduction into public services of the '3 Ms': markets, managers and measurement. Defined in this way, NPM has been a significant driver in public management policy around the world, from the early 1980s to at least the early 2000s.

NPM, compared to other public management theories such as organisational theory, is oriented towards outcomes and efficiency through better management of the public budget. It is considered to be achieved by applying competition, as it is known in the private sector, to organisations in the public sector, emphasising economic and leadership principles. In addition, Gudelis and Guogis (2011, p. 3) describe NPM as:

> The business sector's gift to public administration. It calls for a qualitative dynamic, in clear contrast to the traditional public administration model, typically characterized by a lack of flexibility and focused on process and procedure rather than goals and results. Among the primary aims of NPM reforms are the reduction of expenses to public administration and increased effectiveness and quality in the work of civil servants.

NPM addresses beneficiaries of public services much like customers, and conversely citizens as shareholders.

Moving towards the present, Gill (2012) suggests that by 2010, leadership in the public sector was still an intractable issue. But now it faced an additional, unavoidable challenge — a prolonged period of scarce resources. According to the Executive Director of the Institute for Government and former Permanent Secretary in two UK ministries, Lord Bichard [and quoted in Gill (2012, p. 52)] — in addressing public sector 'needs' — what will be required will be:

- Less risk-averse and more innovative organisations
- More engagement between leaders and the front line
- Better management of risk
- Valuing, recognising and promoting successful innovators
- Removing process-based targets that stifle people's creativity
- Attacking energy-sapping and needless paper, reports and meetings
- Developing genuine collaborations with partner organisations and measuring their (collaborations) success in terms of outcomes
- Emphasising the skills of influencing, negotiating, building trust and sustaining coalitions
- Exercising caution over further restructuring that consumes energy and has marginal benefits

Of note, as we continue to witness an increase in virtual working, team working and matrix management, traditional forms of authority, hierarchy and command may not reflect accurately the reality of public sector management. What we know about organisations is that the speed of external change, whether operational, strategic or technological, is now rapid (Dunning, 2008; Lüscher & Lewis, 2008; Ojasalo, 2008) [and quoted in Thorpe, Gold, and Lawler (2011)]. This (change) produces an imperative within organisations for them to be able to respond ever more quickly and adaptively.[5] New organisational forms have included flatter structures, matrix structures, and ever more widely linked network structures, all of which reflect, in their varying ways, the limitations of top-down models of management and the limitations of leadership. Where organisations have become increasingly project- or knowledge-based (Lindkvist, 2004), where they involve professional work (Vermak & Weggeman, 1999) or where innovation occurs through knowledge of intensive exchange processes within networks (Hallikas, Karkkainen, & Lampela, 2009), leadership is now moving to a form that is able to cope with collective endeavour, where individuals can contribute to the establishment and development of a common purpose/vision (Thorpe et al., 2011, p. 240).

In view of this, it is, perhaps, not surprising that Stephen Brookes and Keith Grint — in their aptly entitled book, *The New Public Leadership*

---

5. It is interesting to note that many organisations are recognising this in their 'strap lines'. For example, the Royal Air Force uses 'Agile, Adaptable, Capable' (see www.raf.uk).

Challenge — suggest that time is now ripe to move beyond NPM and more towards NPL. In this regard, Brookes and Grint (2010) argue that the need to lead within these complex networks requires a new way of thinking about leadership. Whilst aspects of management will, and should, remain the real challenge for the public sector, according to Brookes and Grint (2010) is to advance a stronger theory of public leadership that emphasises its 'collective' nature. This theme is also echoed by Leavy and McKiernan (2009, p. 41) in their discussion of the importance of a leadership culture, as opposed to a managerial culture, in progressive organisations:

> A managerial culture sees organisation as a commercial machine, contractual in nature, instrumental in purpose, hierarchical, centralised in decision-making, and self-regulating in operation. A leadership culture, however, sees organisation as strategic in its own right, a living system, communitarian in nature, moral in purpose, networked in structure, decentralised in decision-making, and self-reviewing in operation.

At this stage, it is instructive to introduce the notion of tame and wicked problems which are noted by Grint (2005, p. 1473):

- A *Tame Problem* may be complicated but is resolvable through unilinear acts because there is a point where the problem is resolved and it is likely to have occurred before. In other words, there is only a limited degree of uncertainty and thus it is associated with Management. The manager's role, therefore, is to provide the appropriate *processes* to solve the problem
- A *Wicked Problem* is complex, rather than just complicated, it is often intractable, there is no unilinear solution, moreover, there is no 'stopping' point, it is novel, any apparent 'solution' often generates other 'problems', and there is no 'right' or 'wrong' answer, but there are better or worse alternatives

In this respect, Brookes and Grint (2010, p. 11) suggest that NPM, in essence, is about dealing with tame problems and NPL is about dealing with wicked problems.

More generally, the importance of NPL seems to be supported by research dating back to 2001 by The Performance and Innovation Unit of the UK Cabinet Office. Some key findings of this research are still worthy of note today:

- Managers roles are also changing: over recent years there has been a growth of virtual teams and the majority of managers (70%) say that increasingly, they are required to manage cross-functional and virtual teams
- As matrix organisations become more popular, the majority of respondents (74%) say those management roles in their organisation are increasingly about influencing people over whom they have no line management responsibility

- Too little attention is paid to the growing importance of leadership across organisational boundaries, or to learning between different sectors
- There is little shared understanding of the qualities required for effective leadership in today's public services
- Fundamental to improved leadership is a clearer shared understanding of what leadership behaviours work in delivering today's public services
- Across the public sector, there is a need for better development of leaders, with greater emphasis on learning across sectors

The last words in this section are left to Brookes and Grint (2010, p. 2) who suggest that in presenting a public leadership challenge, the key question is *How and why do public leaders engage collectively through partnership activity in the delivery of public services?*

3.4. Leadership Thinking within This Sector

3.4.1. *State of Play*

At the grand strategic level,[6] Raffell et al. (2009, p. 1), in the introduction to their book, *Public Sector Leadership: International Challenges and Perspectives*, offer what is actually a most profound statement:

> The need for public sector leadership is greater than ever before. There are many substantive and process challenges today and they are new, complex and dynamic. Challenges — such as those posed by global warming, the credit crisis in the world's financial system and threats to public health and security — span and interconnect boundaries, crossing levels of government, sectors, communities and nations. As a result, the importance of effective public sector leadership is multiplied, impacting millions of people. Thus, there is both a broader recognition of the need and higher expectations for effective public sector leadership.

In light of this statement, it is worrying that the literature, scholarship, theory and practice in this sector (with a particular emphasis on leadership) seem so limited.

At the general level, the leadership literature and guidance is vast (e.g. a Google search on leadership on Friday 12 July 2013, with the word 'leadership' revealed

---

6. Within the North Atlantic Treaty Organisation, there are four levels currently accepted as providing a framework for command and analysis: the grand strategic, the military strategic, the operational and the tactical. In simple terms, the grand strategic can be understood to represent the inter-state or country (geo-political) level.

410,000,000 results; in addition, on the same date, there were in excess of 72,000 books available on Amazon.co.uk). In more detail, it is actually very difficult to find a book that 'majors' on the public sector in the United Kingdom with a detailed focus on leadership. Brookes and Grint (2010) lead the way with their most readable text, *The New Public Leadership Challenge*.

It is, however, not just a UK problem. Raffell et al. (2009, p. 3) comment on similar problems in the United States: The New York Public Library has a million volumes on leadership but not one book on public sector leadership. Van Wart (2003, p. 17) in his review of public sector leadership offered a more analytical conclusion: *[The] literature on leadership with a public-sector focus is a fraction of that in the private sector.*

Hitherto, it would seem that both the public and third sectors tend to gravitate towards private sector leadership models for leadership solutions. Whether these models have, in fact, served the private sector is still very much open to conjecture.[7]

3.4.2. Classification

Looking at the available literature, it would seem that public sector leadership (if indeed a term exists) is more specific and context-based than that of general leadership. Some scholars have tried to classify the available literature. In trying to classify the material, Van Wart and Dicke (2008) [and quoted in Raffell et al. (2009, p. 3)] outline several types of public sector leadership in, perhaps, a US-context: organisational, political and movement (such as the role of Martin Luther King in the civil rights movement). Morse, Busset, and Kinghorn's (2007) categorisation, again from a US-context, includes: political leadership (elected or high appointees, top governmental leaders); organisational leadership (formal leadership within public organisations, from line supervisors up); and public value leadership — beyond government and into governance focusing on 'solving problems' and including 'on-the-ground-leadership'.

3.4.3. Theory

In terms of approach, Lawler (2008, p. 27), in his criticism of individuality in leadership, comments:

> The focus of much of the leadership individualises leadership, that is, implies leadership as resting with one individual who is expected to

---

7. In this respect, the reader is directed to Antonacopoulou (2010). This issue is somewhat critical of some university teaching, particularly from leadership models, and approaches, developed from the private sector.

influence other individuals/groups ... leaders are seen variously as visionary, heroic, transformational, transactional, charismatic, inspirational, flexible, sensitive, innovative, but the enduring theme is that leadership is individualised.

This view is echoed elsewhere. In writing about distributed leadership, Thorpe et al. (2011) offer:

Distributed leadership is the very antithesis to the preoccupation of most Western writers about leadership, with the position reified in single individuals — usually those at the top of an organisation (Harris, 2009) ... Where organisations have become increasingly project- or knowledge-based (Lindkvist, 2004), where they involve professional work (Vermak & Weggeman, 1999) or where innovation occurs through knowledge of intensive exchange processes within networks (Hallikas et al., 2009), leadership is now moving to a form that is able to cope with collective endeavour, where individuals can contribute to the establishment and development of a common purpose (a common vision).

In a similar vein, Raffell et al. (2009) continue by citing Crosby and Kiedrowski (2006, p. 1) who state that, in general, the field of leadership has now moved from a focus on leadership that is, from individuals as leaders, to the relationship between leaders and followers (or constituents, colleagues, collaborators).[8]

Bekkers, Edelenbos, and Steijn (2011) discuss the importance of leadership and boundary spanning: in this respect, leadership has been perceived as one of the cornerstones of innovation, because it plays an important role in changing the *status quo*.

There is now a clear recognition that the potential for leadership is broader than has been thought hitherto. In essence, the single authoritarian leader (the 'individual'), seeming to be dominant in our culture, is not well suited to the demands for leadership and change (Holzer, 2008). Leadership, then, seems to be about making it possible for everyone in the institution or within a network of institutions to contribute. Gill (2012, p. 51) also echoes these views in that a unique leadership challenge in the public sector appears to be the shift away from traditional technical or operational roles on the one hand and from advisory roles on the other to more collaborative, networked leadership roles. These leadership roles (collaboration) carry high levels of accountability yet less authority, implying the need for greater political awareness, more collaborative and engaging leadership behaviour, and exceptional influencing skills. In the *Proceedings of the*

8. For further reference, the reader is directed to Kellerman (2008).

European Conference on Management, Leadership & Governance, Worrall (2009, pp. 274–282) states:

> In a new era of collaboration, public service leaders in the 21st century need to be able to work collaboratively across the whole public service system horizontally across organisational and sector boundaries, but also vertically across national, regional and local levels of governance.

In this respect, then, it would seem that leadership is now much more about using one's personal power (influence) than one's position power (authority).[9]

In his most readable chapter, 'What Do We Expect of Public Leaders' Lord Turnbull (2012, p. 121) [and quoted in Brookes and Grint (2010)] offers personal reflections on the role of public leadership, which includes:

- Valuing diversity, including diversity of thought
- Improving performance
- Maintaining optimism and energy
- Setting a tone of openness
- Setting a consistent course
- An ability to take decisions
- Encouragement of partnership and sharing
- Developing successors
- Treating others as you would like to be treated yourself

More generally, Leslie and Canwell (2010) suggest that the term 'leadership' is best defined through activities or decisions rather than through looking purely at positional power or traits. Leadership, they argue, should be tied into the successful delivery of results and, importantly, requires multiple actors across an organisation or system. Thus, leadership is not about an individual in a senior role, it is about many people across an organisation involved in leadership activities for which core capabilities are required. Leslie and Canwell (2010) state that senior public sector leaders will need to demonstrate four key leadership capabilities:

- Developing the insights necessary for successful change within complex systems
- Building the cognitive skills to manage effectively in demanding environments
- Demonstrating the emotional intelligence to motivate their people
- Building leadership at all levels of the organisation, by developing capability and ensuring that overly complex structures do not impede the ability of individuals across the organisation to exercise leadership

---

9. For a further explanation of this theme, the reader is directed to Howieson and Kahn (2002), Grint (2005) and Brookes and Grint (2010).

It would seem, then, that with budgets being radically reduced while citizen expectations continue to rise, public sector leaders will be challenged to demonstrate a set of capabilities that will be unfamiliar to the current leadership of most public sector organisations at both central and local levels.

Trevor and Kilduff (2012) argue that a collective or network leadership strategy is most suitable for the information age. Future organisations will necessarily rely upon knowledge-intensive networks of highly connected and autonomous talent, empowered to rapidly converge on singular intersections of common interest without guidance from above. Such coordination will not be achieved through centralised command and control, but through network leadership, in effect, self-direction in the interests of a common purpose and guided by shared values.

3.4.4.   Looking Ahead

In terms of future research directions, Raffell et al. (2009, p. 9) stress:

- More systemic research examining organisational leadership as a process will provide a more detailed perspective of how effective leadership functions
- Understanding the applicability of organisational leadership in other sectors to the public sector
- Leadership in the public sector emphasises internal efforts, a more extensive view is required, which is aimed at external, multi-party collaboration dedicated to serving collective interests
- Few international/comparative works on public sector leadership are included in recent textbooks or anthologies — a more global view on leadership is required

Bekkers et al. (2011, p. 27), in relation to networks or the milieu of innovation, suggest that more attention should be paid to a type of leadership, which can be understood in terms of 'boundary-spanning' and 'brokerage'. Leifer and Delbecq (1978, pp. 40—41) define boundary-spanners as people who operate at the periphery or boundary of an organisation, performing organisationally relevant tasks, relating the organisation with elements outside it. This is important because these managers stimulate interactions between people at the intersections of different organisations in an informal area where (diverging) perspectives, values and information meet, leading to innovation.

Brookes and Grint (2010, pp. 7—11) also discuss the development for an NPL framework, which will include:

- A form of collective leadership. If we are faced in the public sector with complex (wicked) problems that require a collective response, public leadership should require a collective leadership style in which the responsibility for leaders is distributed throughout each organisation and shared across other organisations and institutions

- Context. Within the public domain, leadership could take place within 4 contexts: community; political; organisational; and individual. These 4 suggested forms of public leadership (domains) are likely to have differing styles and reflect differing accountability and governance requirements
- Type and scale of problem. Public leaders need to tackle uncertainty. There is a tendency for leaders to focus on 'known' problems and known solutions and develop expertise in relation to critical incidents and thus crisis management
- Collaborative advantage. Leaders will engage collectively if there is a 'mutual benefit' to each member and when the whole is considered to be greater than the sum of the parts
- Performance and public value. A focus should be more on publicly valued outcomes represented by social goals as opposed to quantitative targets set by central government
- Reflecting trust. If the creation and demonstration of public value is the key outcome of effective public leadership then the development of trust and legitimacy by public leaders must, therefore, represent one of the key determinants of a new public leadership framework

In the Epilogue to their book (Brookes & Grint, 2010, pp. 343–344), *Reform, Realisation and Restoration, Public Leadership and Innovation in Government* Stephen Brookes argues that an NPL challenge should be set for 2011 and beyond through the purpose, process, praxis and public value of public leadership. In his writing, he offers detailed analysis of each and the reader is directed to this material. In summary, however, he suggests:

- Purpose: the 'purpose' of public leadership is to set out clearly what it is that public leaders seek to attain through clearly stated intentions and aims
- Process: the 'process' of public leadership represents the sequence of leadership actions that are required to transform the purpose of public leadership into practice and how activities are coordinated
- Praxis: the 'praxis' of public leadership represents the actual practice of particular public leadership styles at all levels
- Public value: 'public value' as the outcome of effective public leadership requires an alignment between the social goals identified by the stakeholders, the trust and legitimacy which leaders secure in the delivery of these goals and the extent to which organisational capability matches the stated purpose to practice through the process of public leadership

3.5.   The Reflections

Included below are the individual reflections from people who hold, or have held, leadership positions in the public sector in the United Kingdom. These authors do not speak for their organisation or indeed, the public sector at large; in addition, they do not speak to the public sector leadership agenda. That being said, we consider that their material offers a most interesting and insightful snapshot into the leadership realities at the coalface by people who hold a variety of positions in the UK public sector.

We have sourced authors from a variety of sub-sectors. In addition, their views and thoughts range from the tactical level of analysis through the operational level to the strategic level of analysis of some of the most significant and complex organisations in the United Kingdom today.

In terms of editing, we have deliberately followed a light touch; other than asking the authors to ground their material on their experience of leadership, their perception of leadership, what leadership means to them, the leadership challenges for the United Kingdom and Europe particularly in times of change/recession, and the leadership challenges for their sector in this decade, in light of the challenges described above, what is written is generally what we, as book authors and editors, received.

Within the rapidly changing business context of the public sector in the United Kingdom, the focus of this research is on understanding further the leadership challenges in this decade. Indeed, the opportunity to use the insights of this group enables leading edge research, providing first-hand knowledge, and understanding and interpretation of the unique role of leadership within its contemporary context.

As stated previously, the public sector is broad in context. It is, therefore, outside the scope of this book to include all sub-sectors and organisations that make up the public sector in the United Kingdom. We have, however, material from authors who are employed in the NHS, the Scottish Parliament, the British Armed Forces, the Police and Fire Services, local authorities, the Scottish Government, and the Forestry Commission.

We do judge, with some conviction, that they all have 'a story to tell'.

3.5.1.   National Health Service

Balbir Bhogal

I have worked in a large acute teaching hospital for more than 20 years and I have experienced leadership through many organisational re-structures during this time period. I have also been a leader of many different types of teams in the organisation mainly administrative and clerical throughout my career. My current experience of leadership can be split into two key components of my role:

- First, the provision of professional leadership to informatics[10] staff. Within this element of the role, I am responsible for setting direction and providing standards for the professional delivery of a service. The informatics function has a wide reaching remit and within this, there are a number of professional groups that interact. My responsibility for leadership within this element of my role is to ensure that the staffs within this function understand the professional standards that they are required to work to and I need to ensure that I can evidence through competency and capability. Within this remit, there is the need to ensure that the profession aligns with needs of the organisation and can use its skill to support the delivery of high quality health care
- Second, to ensure that I have embodied the vision and goals of the organisation and act as a role model ensuring that all parts of the organisation are empowered and engaged. I have gained this experience of leadership through the management of many operational teams and also through the delivery of strategic organisational goals. I work closely with the senior management team and have a clear understanding of where the organisation wants to go. Within my leadership role, I need to ensure that this vision and these values are cascaded through the organisation so that teams are empowered in moving the organisation forward

Leadership is a critical component of a successful organisation. Without strong leadership, organisations can often lose their sense of purpose, become distracted and eventually become ineffective. Having said that, it is easier to define poor leadership and the impact of it than it is to observe effective leadership. I say this because often an individual's leadership style is commented upon over a period of time after you see a pattern of behaviour — we often use the word leadership as an entity and forget that it is a product of behaviours, situations and internal and external conditions. When we talk about leadership, we tend to focus on people and their personal characteristics. My perception is that leadership is 'a way of working' and that it requires behaviours to be demonstrated rather than just personality. We often associate leadership with the top of an organisation and although this is critical in setting direction and moving the organisation forward, we need to see signs of leadership behaviour at all levels in an organisation. Without this type of behaviour, organisations become static, fail to resolve problems and seldom demonstrate innovation.

---

10. Informatics is a branch of information science that focuses on the study of information processing and particularly as respect to systems integration and human interactions with machine and data.

Effective leadership breathes life into an organisation. It allows the organisation to consider what its purpose is and how it might then fulfil that purpose. Effective leadership assumes control but allows for engagement and empowerment. Leaders are required to make decisions and then stand by them as they need to be seen to follow through on actions. If leaders are seen to change their minds or not follow through, then this can weaken the whole vision of the organisation.

In times of change and recession, organisations tend to not want to innovate as the *status quo* becomes the comfort zone. Leaders often feel restricted themselves because the external environment almost places a restriction on the options for innovations. Leadership almost becomes harder because the environment becomes a distraction. This often requires leaders to step back and redefine the purpose of the organisation and reset the strategic direction. Leadership becomes a challenge where leaders feel that they do not have the time and headspace to respond to change. Money is often associated with change as the initial investment acts a catalyst to enable improvement programmes to get underway and create the opportunity for 'out of the box' thinking. Therefore, in times of recession, leadership becomes strained because the ability to allow organisations to innovate in this way becomes financially prohibitive. This has a direct impact on the level of empowerment and engagement that a leader can secure from the team.

The leadership challenges within the NHS have been particularly difficult. Whilst there has been a recognition from all parts of the NHS for the need to 'deliver more for less', in practice, given that the cost base of many NHS organisations is predominantly pay (60–70%) of the total, this inevitably forces organisations to consider reduction in workforce. In many other sectors, technological advancement has been seen as the solution to a redesigned workforce but the track record of successful IT in health care has yet to be proven. It is accepted that technology will be the key for the future to deliver this efficiency, but this needs to be done through business process refinement and management of change in a sensitive way.

The key leadership challenge in informatics is ensuring that the organisation embraces the business change associated with the technology. Often when new technology is deployed, it creates greater disruption in the first instance. Informatics leaders need to ensure that stakeholder engagement and clinical commitment supports them in delivering the change for the organisation. The external pressures on the NHS have almost disempowered leaders across the service. The ability to create a vision for organisations is currently limited due to confined financial constraints within which the NHS is expected to deliver.

Alison Clare

Leading change projects in the health care sector over the last 6 years has been a challenging experience. Transforming a large acute hospital in Liverpool by turning patient notes into computerised medical records, requires not only knowledge of the health care sector but more importantly, project planning and negotiation skills which have been adapted from previous work in the private sector in utilities, insurance, construction and manufacturing. This previous experience has provided me with a rich learning bed that I can apply to my role as a business change project manager in the NHS.

Specialising in business change leadership is about listening to ideas and adapting those ideas into a strategy and providing focus and direction so that everyone can be part of embedding the change process. A critical tenant of leadership is setting the example and involving people, leaving no one out of the loop, and communicating clearly to everyone. When leading change programmes, it is important for the leader to ensure that everyone understands why the change is important, and what the outcomes and benefits will be. Once implemented, a strong leader will then demonstrate the new ways of working in order to sustain the change.

Leading is about having the ability to listen and learn from everyone but be willing to apply good solid arguments to support or disregard suggestions. Leadership is about persuasion to encourage buy-in rather than traditional command and control.

A large scale programme of work to transform the NHS from paper-based to computerised medical records has been underway in various forms for the last decade. Removing paper and installing computerised records will reduce costs by removing head count. Many trusts around the country have an army of staff moving hundreds of thousands of paper records around at any one time. Any project manager will tell you resistance is a common problem in a project but that combined with the tough economic climate makes it even more difficult to make large scale redundancy in the NHS. The NHS is one of the largest employers in the United Kingdom: it will need strong leadership to bring about such change in what is a substantially democratic organisation with strong union representation from both clinical and administration staff. Change of this nature requires a varied mix of skills and experience to ensure success.

In the private sector, leaders tend to have a variety of industrial experience. For example, a senior executive in banking might have come from a manufacturing background so the breadth of business experience is much wider. To be a strong leader requires leadership skills and the industry background should not matter to the NHS in the same way that it does not matter in the private sector. But the recruitment process for senior managers insists on candidates having NHS experience.

If senior managers do not come from a wider resource group, their skills-base will be insufficient to solve challenging problems thrown up by the IT and business transformation programme. This is the skills gap the NHS faces at the moment, being so specific as to exclude potential leaders because they lack NHS experience, narrows the field and prevents a wide range of leadership talents entering the pool of senior managers. In addition, the NHS is not goal-oriented in the same way as the private sector is. Most, if not all, private sector leaders are motivated partly by performance bonuses. In the NHS, there are few variable elements to the compensation package; this, on occasion, appears to create an attitude of turn up and get paid. And there is also evidence of a reluctance to address weak performance with ineffective staff remaining in post for the duration of their employment even if they are underperforming. There is an additional factor which is specific to the NHS where the organisation structure is skewed by a parallel clinical structure which often means a department head has to lead senior medics and surgeons who have superior schooling and academic qualifications. Because of their limited leadership skills and experience to draw from, the department heads find it very difficult to engage clinical staff in the change process. An obvious improvement to this situation would be to remove the insistence to have NHS experience, in the recruitment of senior managers, to minimise the impact of dominant clinicians, remove some of the tiers of management within the health service and eliminate ineffective managers. In addition, it will be important to widen salary bands so staff can progress without having to be promoted into different posts linking promotion to merit and performance. Professional qualifications should be mandatory and further training incorporated into personal development plans. Leadership skills, along with wider experience from outside the health care sector, should provide stronger, better educated, more capable managers with the skills to lead strategic change and reduce costs to make the health service efficient and lean.

Finally, the overall structure of the NHS is ripe for change. There are over 200 trusts in England, with multiple trusts often spread across the same city. For example, in Liverpool there are five acute trusts plus primary care and mental health. All of these have their own corporate services and duplicated management positions.[11] By merging trusts together into one large, rather than five small trusts, the NHS will be able to bring about large efficiency savings. Moreover, with new ex-private sector leaders in place, using the suggested recruitment strategy above, the teams will be better educated with experience from multiple industries that can be harnessed to overcome resistance to the change, which must happen to bring the NHS into the 21st century.

Elizabeth Ireland

My experience of leadership has developed from the variety of roles I have been fortunate to hold in the NHS in Scotland. This experience has included: as a GP (where we have both distributive models of leadership in large democratic practice and positional leadership models as senior partner); as

---

11. Unlike Newcastle where there is a single acute trust bringing all the hospitals together with only one corporate services department.

a Clinical Lead of a Managed Clinical Network (involving personal and collaborative leadership styles, influencing and engaging, demonstrating evidence
of delivery, impact and improvement); as a National Clinical Lead for the
Scottish Government (translating evidence into policy, ensuring stakeholder
engagement throughout, personal visibility, developing infrastructure to lead
local change, setting up developmental groups to continue the engagement of
thought leaders, maintaining momentum and strategic profile, and 'integration
for sustainability', which has involved developing a shared vision and shared
language); and as a Non-Executive, Vice Chair, Interim Chair, and now Chair
(ministerial appointment) of a major NHS Scotland Health Board, NHS
National Services Scotland, which has, and continues to involve strategic leadership, governance, responsibility and personal accountability.

My perception of leadership is that leaders should create opportunities to
galvanise the development of teams, organisations and strategy that address
key issues in a way that enables all that are involved to feel empowered,
enabled and supported. To do this, positional leaders need to develop values
and a culture that enables trust and respect, leading to a sustainable distributive model of leadership. Organisations can then deliver a service that is recog-
nisable to customers, of high quality, receptive to feedback and change, and
continuously improving.

For me, leadership is about: personal understanding and development; confidence in one's abilities and, of course, personal limitations; recognising conflict early, and addressing it, and, harnessing the passion that comes from it;
honing strategic understanding and inter-linkages to maximise impact; an ability to stretch beyond one's own professional background; and a need to deliver
service excellence. I am also mindful of the ability to influence through appropriate challenges and style, and being prepared to place one's head 'above the
parapet' if required.

I consider that there are many and significant challenges ahead. We must
be cognisant of the influence and role of the media, the ageing demographic,
the persistent health inequalities and the vast technological advances. A significant and perhaps the biggest challenge, however, will be in our inability to
understand and articulate the opportunities of these challenges. For example,
the use of IT in flexible working allowing the opportunity for people and
families to provide more care for elderly relatives.

Looking specifically at my sector, I consider that challenges will include:
demographic changes; financial challenges; the structural changes within
health and social care; the need to invest in communities and to disinvest in
Acute Care environments; and understanding the impact that possible Scottish
independence could have on health, well-being, care and its delivery.

Fiona Mackenzie

I have been in various formal leadership roles from my time at university to
being a Chief Executive since 1996. My experience is that it's a very practical

role and not the airy fairy strategic role I might have once thought. You do need to have a broad perspective in a Chief Executive role, but you will achieve nothing if it is all in your head and you can't make things actively happen. So much of it is about working with others to get things done — seldom, if ever, does a top-down diktat work.

I learnt a lot in my junior leadership roles about what effective leadership means to people. One of the best lessons was that what people think happens if they sit in their office remains a fantasy! Indeed, the reality of what is really going on is always found at the coalface and it is very important to speak to one's troops. The second big lesson is to work with good people and build your team to complement your strengths. The third is to have good information systems that help to tell you when you need to delve into detail. In my experience, the people I have admired the most do these things well.

Over time, especially in this sector, a significant amount of leadership activity takes place with other organisations, and that brings about a whole set of new experiences. I have found it very rewarding when you strike gold but hugely frustrating when it's pushing water uphill, which it can be for a while. In all joint working, there needs to be a collective benefit, not just a warm collaborative feeling.

I don't think leadership is that well understood. I always think it is very hard to define but you do know it when you see it. I perceive it as fascinating and it has drawn me to it. I can't think of many more interesting things than organisations and all the human dynamics that are involved in team working, hence my fascination with leadership. I used to think that the gurus had the answers and it was a case of selecting the model you believe in. Now I know it's all about us as people and, therefore, it's individual and bespoke. Leadership has some common features and skills but there is a lot of room for individuality. Realising that it is an *authentic*, not prescribed, thing is a great enabler.

Outside of formal organisations, I think most people assume that someone says something at the top and within a short period of time something happens at the front line. This could not be further from the truth, as very little works that way, and more ideas and success come from a different model which values the contribution many bring as leaders. I see it as very important in my organisation. Formal leadership roles of different types are obviously important but less formal leadership really needs to be nurtured if genuine improvement and continual progress is going to be achieved. I personally believe that this aspect needs just as much attention as looking to your formal leadership roles for progress.

For this reason, developing the right culture in an organisation is key and in health that culture should be built on commitment to the patients and the public at all times. Difficult choices should be faced within that context.

Having been a Chief Executive for so long, I do think I would find it hard not to have that ultimate responsibility for the way things go. At times, there are lonely aspects to it if you actually care about what you do. I think it's really important that it does matter to you, but at the same time you need perspective and I know I really have that even in the worst of times.

The economic environment is a huge challenge. The reality is so difficult, it's not easily amendable to the usual hurly burly of politics. We have lived through a golden period with inflated lifestyles and adjusting is very hard for people. The leadership challenge has to be to paint a picture of a new future balancing some of the downsides with possible upsides, like our food may actually be what we thought it was!

Politicians need to work differently to achieve this — it's a totally changing set of circumstances. As yet, the ability to adjust to working in a different way has not materialised at a political level, and I am not sure, as a population, we have made a shift in thinking ourselves.

Our challenges are a microcosm of the above. The on-going march of technology and science brings great possibilities and great financial pressures, coupled with this, the increasing population of elderly people pose real dilemmas. Given the corresponding reduction in the number of people in employment contributing to wealth and, indeed the need for caring roles, there is a circle that can't be squared. Politicians are still operating under the old rules and have been very slow to grasp this nettle. I believe that the choice to 'turn a blind eye' to these basic challenges around population growth and increased fiscal constraint is hard to defend. Unfortunately, the radical changes needed will now be implemented in a crisis-driven environment that could have been, whilst never avoided, minimised. The decisions that will have to be taken, therefore, will necessarily be poorer as they will be unplanned. I think we have a strong case to say that we have been badly let down.

We have the benefit of unified health systems, something we have not yet got maximum benefit from but are gradually uncovering. We are, in many ways, the envy of the world in this regard and we need to use this to best effect to make the best of the challenges ahead. Sector leaders are going to need great stamina and vision to deal with the future, but I suspect the climate will be more enabling, out of need unfortunately.

Graham Sunderland

Poor leadership leads to poor team performance — this is recognised in many walks of life and in organisations, big and small. The public inquiry into standards of heart surgery at Bristol Royal Infirmary, published in 1999, was the longest-running and widest-ranging investigation into medical standards in the United Kingdom at the time, and among other issues, identified significant failures in leadership as one reason why dedicated, caring professionals were involved in poor patient outcomes over a sustained period. As a consequence of this and other high profile failures, leadership in the NHS does not have a good reputation.

There are a number of leadership actions that we might expect to see which are particularly problematic in the NHS. The first area of concern is visibility:

leaders should be identifiable. In an informal survey conducted among my medical colleagues, none could name or point to an individual they considered their leader. All could name their Clinical Director but this, as the title implies, is a managerial role and not necessarily a leadership position, although the two disciplines are often confused and can be difficult to separate. For a medical leader trying to hold a full time clinical commitment and maintain visibility across a wide geographical area can be very challenging. There simply are not enough hours. Most medical leaders will be performing this role as additional work, and taking time away from their core activity is more and more difficult. As clinicians become more senior, and perhaps take an opportunity to reduce their clinical time, they find themselves more deeply involved in direct management activity, with even less time to visit the 'shop floor'. This issue needs to be addressed and could be if appropriate resources were allocated. Visibility needs to be recognised as a key action for leadership and structured into the activity of clinical leaders.

Leaders should keep their teams informed of progress and developments within the service. In health care, the measures employed to assess performance are rarely those that are relevant to the individual practitioner; for example, a great deal of effort goes into saving costs within the service and success is measured by funds saved. This has little impact on the individual doctor—patient interaction and is often perceived as a negative by clinicians who feel more money needs to be spent to improve the quality of the patient experience. Another measure might be the number of complaints experienced but some individuals may have none while others feel that a more positive outcome factor ought to be measured. There is a tendency to make what can be measured important and a good leader will know that not all the important things can be measured easily. Inconsequence, bringing good news stories and encouragement to the team can be a difficult balancing act.

The origins of the NHS, in the wake of the World War II, were quite military in many respects. At inception, medical staffs were accorded senior, authoritative positions by virtue of their profession and senior doctors automatically assumed a leadership role. This has changed. In the modern health service, the medical practitioner is much more part of a team in which the leadership role may shift, depending on the phase or nature of the patient's treatment. There is also a levelling of the old hierarchical structure. Previously, a senior, more experienced (older) consultant would automatically be accorded leader status. Today, there is a very flat structure where all consultants consider themselves equal and each one a leader in their own right. In a military environment, command and control are paramount and every soldier and officer knows who gives and takes orders and where to go for guidance. In the health service, consultants may discuss clinical care with colleagues but many of them will have a non-medical line manager which can lead to confusion when they seek guidance or leadership. It should be clearer to all concerned that when clinical lead or director appointments are made that this is a leadership role and, although there will be managerial issues, leadership behaviour will be sought and recognised.

To stay with the military analogy, reward and discipline are well understood in that environment and easily and regularly administered. Contrast with the health service where reward, notwithstanding the personal satisfaction that comes from good patient outcomes, may amount to no more than approval and rarely even that. There are financial rewards for meritorious performance and leadership behaviour, but these have been severely curtailed and remain under threat. Doctors have the most arcane disciplinary process, which allows little local sanction other than perhaps disapproval and is rarely administered by the empowered non-medical managers. Escalation of disciplinary action then rises to national (General Medical Council) level, which can include restriction of practice and suspension from the Medical Register. This extreme level of sanction can mean loss of employment and complete loss of income for the individual — as the NHS is a monopoly employer — and tends to be reserved for the most serious cases. A review of the process of reward and discipline within medicine would be most welcome. There is still the ability to reward locally but the options for local censure are very limited. It is perhaps time to consider this a role for medical leaders and the coming revalidation process may allow us to identify where problems are developing and to suggest methods which might enable these to be addressed.

Prior to the development of the NHS, physicians and surgeons were private, independent practitioners and an element of this remains today, where General Practitioners (in the community) retain this status. The idea that individual consultants have freedom to make their own clinical and management decisions remains strong and has led to the famous 'herding cats' concept as a description of trying to coordinate consultant activity. Leading such disparate groups, with often conflicting aims and aspirations, is enormously difficult and presents many challenges. There is huge competition for resources and in times of austerity and cutbacks, this can lead to a survival of the fittest mentality. Prioritising support is a key role for a leader but with the rather unfocussed nature of the NHS, it is difficult to choose a particular direction outside of one's special interest area. It would be helpful if the NHS was clear on what represents its core activity. For example, a good leader would attempt to make his team understand their common goal but in a working environment that has one group of doctors pursuing anti-obesity surgery, competing for resource with a group struggling to provide nourishment to intestinal failure patients, this can be hard. Amplify this to a national level where the health service is trying to provide fully comprehensive 'cradle to grave' care for all illness and many conditions which are not entertained as health issues in other parts of the world. If leaders could agree a medical agenda with politicians and the public, this might make achieving goals considerably easier. This is extraordinarily difficult to achieve as has been demonstrated by the Oregon studies[12,13] and while it may help leaders achieve targets, the benefit to individual patients or society is debatable.

The changes in the delivery of health care in response to demands to reduce waiting lists, bed stays and increases in efficiency have reduced opportunities for consultants to meet and for a leader to interact. Use of modern technologies such as mobile telephones and e-mail makes personal contact easier. Such contact has a tendency to assume an undeserved immediacy and can easily overwhelm. Leaders need good information management skills to control their own flow of information and disseminate appropriately. Face book© and LinkedIn© social networks allow like-minded groups to interact at their own pace and may have a role to play. Managers are rightly anxious about security issues and there are a number of policies around the use of social media by NHS employees. We can see how blogs such as Dr Rant[14] can reach many people quickly and media like Twitter can spread news and information much faster than conventional agencies. It may be that in the future medical teams will have their own health book secure medium with which they can share information.

There are few easily identifiable medical leaders. There are inspirational doctors who have made great strides forward in patient care through research and high quality practice. There are also individuals who lead doctors' organisations, such as the British Medical Association, but they can rarely be seen to unite clinicians and move them as a concerted group. Witness the poor efforts of the British Medical Association, who represent two thirds of doctors, to get a clear consensus on action over pension changes. The General Medical Council offers guidance to doctors and suggests standards of care and behaviour. It is, of course, a regulatory body and is not perceived as a leader, being seen as part of the punitive disciplinary process. The Medical Royal Colleges, who are taking an increasing role in education, are traditionally examining bodies. They may have a future role to play in revalidation, but are seen as remote from day-to-day practice and don't offer a leadership role to the working clinician.

Do doctors want to be lead? Are they prepared to demonstrate leadership behaviour or is the independent nature of medical practice too deeply entrenched? Much of the current problem stems from the increasing demands on clinicians' time. Increased patient throughput, more administration, less secretarial support and more demanding management have resulted in fewer opportunities to meet regularly. Despite modern communication technology, there is no substitute for face-to-face human contact and a sharing of values and aspirations if leadership is to be successful. There is a need for leadership but the common confusion between leadership and management sets up a

12. http://www.oregon.gov/oha/herc/Pages/Prioritization-Methodology.aspx
13. Thorne (1992).
14. http://www.drrant.net/

natural antipathy to any attempt to coordinate behaviour and leads consequently to an inherent resistance to the leadership process. The newly formed NHS Leadership Academy[15] aims to correct some of these misconceptions by introducing a Leadership Framework programme, and is attempting to reach down into the service and begin to change some of these deep-rooted concepts. This will take some time and the recently established, although unfortunately titled, Faculty of Medical Leadership and Management[16] seeks to engage with current leaders in an effort to raise the profile of some of the issues I have raised while, hopefully, not further confusing those different roles!

In short, there is room for cautious optimism. We need medical leadership and recognition is the first step to recovery. Those first steps have been taken and we can look forward to good leadership leading to better performing teams and good outcomes for patients. Perhaps in the future the cats will want to follow the leaders.

3.5.2. *The Scottish Parliament*

Paul Grice

Reflecting on my own experience of leadership for this book, I considered the question 'what has caused me to be the leader I am?' Looking back, my early experience of team sport had a strong influence. Indeed, my first experience of leadership came at age 10 when I was made vice-captain of the school cricket team. It was an early lesson in responsibility. It also taught me the value of contacts as the captain was my cousin!

Sports teams have clarity of purpose — to win the game. Within that, the importance of playing by the rules of fair play, the need to collaborate, and to back one another for the good of the team. But also the importance of individuals within a team. Embracing such talents, often mercurial, was an integral part of being successful. I confess that my childhood sporting experience gave me a taste for competing and a liking for winning!

My first boss on joining the Civil Service as a graduate trainee left a strong and lasting impression. She set high standards, was a little scary and told me that an empty in-tray was not acceptable. To get on, I should go looking for work: passivity was not the style of future leaders! That has stayed with me and it now manifests itself as a desire to push the organisation onwards and (hopefully) upwards.

Having joined the Civil Service, I was fortunate enough to get increasingly significant opportunities to lead teams. But my major break came with the opportunity to lead one of the three divisions within the Constitution Group.

---

15. http://www.leadershipacademy.nhs.uk/
16. http://www.fmlm.ac.uk/

This was a highly motivated, high-performing team operating in a very pressurised environment. It was a great crucible in which to develop organisational and communication skills and it was there I learned to set priorities and take decisions. The secret is to take whatever time is available, be it 5 minutes or 5 days, to gather as much information as possible then make your choice and be clear about it. An even bigger break came with the opportunity to become Clerk and Chief Executive of the Scottish Parliament. This gave me the unique opportunity to build a complex organisation from scratch and to lead it through its major early challenges as the Parliament itself developed. I think I was able to bring to bear focus, drive, direction, and a sense of optimism and belief that we could, indeed would, succeed in having a fully functional parliament ready for the first elections in May 1999.

I have developed a lot as a leader since then and I hope without losing my sense of enthusiasm and optimism. But I have become more reflective and more rounded with experience. Leadership must always be work in progress and an area I have looked, in particular, to develop my leadership skills is through non-executive work, in my case with a university, a research council and a charitable foundation. The experience has been enormously important to me by exposing me to other leaders from whom I can learn and by enabling me to see how other organisations tackle issues and what makes them successful.

In my view, leaders are largely made not born, though there are certain natural attributes which can make leadership easier. For example, it is hard to argue that a strong intellect is not an advantage. Though a well-trained intellect is more useful still, as is the ability to communicate effectively and with authority. And, as an extrovert, I can say that it certainly helps to be able to walk into new situations without any great anxiety. For most of us, however, leadership is a long-term incremental process where we develop our skills through experience, conscious self-development, education and training.

The other qualities which, in my view matter, are a sense of optimism. Leaders must convey hope and be able to create confidence. That said, leadership is often simply about refusing to quit, persevering even when the going gets tough. Another critical aspect of leadership is providing a sense of direction, even better a destination, for the organisation. For me, one of the most challenging aspects of leadership is getting the best out of people. Cheerleading success is important but just as key is turning around the performance of someone who is trying hard but sinking beneath the waves. Above all, leadership is about relationships within the organisation: supporting, encouraging, challenging and inspiring. And outside the organisation, they are about drawing on other people's knowledge, experience and ideas as well as promoting and encouraging interest in the organisation.

Leadership for me is the opportunity to do something with purpose and value. I believe in public service and its importance to society. I have rarely come across a public servant who does not see their role in those terms. The privilege of leadership is that it allows for more leverage, more impact.

Leadership obviously brings a degree of power and in some circumstances a lot of power. The use of power and leadership probably merits a chapter on its own — the vital point for me is that power must be used wisely. Indeed, the notion of 'soft power' in leadership is a guiding thought for me personally.

Leadership brings a sense of ownership and commitment both to the institution I lead and to the wider public service. Authenticity is another key aspect of leadership. And to be authentic, I believe you must sincerely believe in what you are doing. I have no doubt as to the importance of a parliament as the central voice in a democracy just as I have no doubt about the importance of democracy to society as a whole.

The fundamental challenge for the public sector is one of declining resources and rising demand for services and, therefore, a pressing need to identify priorities and make tough decisions. On any reasonable outlook, there is little prospect of significant additional resources for public spending over the medium term. The demand for public services will be driven over that time by underlying factors such as demographic change and social inequality as well as by rising expectations. The question, therefore, is how we get more from less, how we become more effective, how we focus on the right priorities.

The major specific challenge for myself and the Scottish Parliamentary Service is, of course, to prepare for possible different constitutional futures in the run up to and beyond the 2014 referendum. But my on-going focus will continue to be to support the Parliament as an institution, the Members individually in carrying out their parliamentary work, and the broad agenda of engagement with the public. There is inevitably some competition for resources within and between these broad objectives. And, as the Parliament is not an organisation with a manifesto for action in the same way as, say, a government, nor does it have an equivalent of a First Minister to enforce collective decision-making, decisions must be reached by a process of negotiation and persuasion. Without the power to direct, the need to influence becomes of paramount importance. This complexity is also reflected in my dual role as Clerk and Chief Executive. The first element reflects the role as chief advisor on parliamentary matters, including the procedures which underpin the operation of Parliament — it exists in the political space though clearly on a non-party basis. The latter is more of a classic business leader, including strategic planning, resource allocation and key service delivery. I feel the role also carries a responsibility for the long-term interests of the institution.

In concluding, I would observe that leading a parliamentary service has a great deal in common with leading any other public sector organisation. A unique feature of the Scottish Parliament is that our principal 'customers' — the Members of Parliament — are ultimately in control of the institution and yet, quite legitimately and understandably, they will not always have a single position on some of the key issues. This is particularly true around the referendum: in my view, one of the most important events in recent Scottish history. Leading the parliamentary service, therefore, requires an understanding of the political currents which flow in and around the Parliament as well as a willingness to use persuasion and influence as a means of achieving outcomes. And much of this is, of course, done under the intense spotlight of the media. All of this makes for an interesting, unpredictable and fascinating job.

3.5.3. *British Armed Forces*

John Cooper

I was a soldier for 36 years. At the most basic level, leading a team of 10 soldiers and at the most complex, commanding 25,000 troops on operations. Operational activity is the *raison d'être* of a military force and was the single largest factor in guiding and informing my philosophy and approach to leadership. Training and preparation are an important part of applying that leadership, but the true test only comes on operations, where events and consequences are real. Leadership in its rawest form is identical whether at platoon or divisional level, but there are many shades that need to be applied. Operations today are multi-agency and involve civilian, diplomatic, economic, international and host-nation players, each with their own agenda, culture and needs, which place varying and sometimes conflicting demands on leaders. The last decade of my military service was spent in a multi-agency environment in a UK Joint command[17] and a Combined international role.[18] I was lucky enough to be the Coalition Deputy Theatre Commander in Afghanistan (2004) and Iraq (2008−2009) where I witnessed the unifying and cohesive nature of US political/diplomatic/military/economic power applied within a Coalition by a unified civil-military leadership[19] that was empowered and resourced to take decisions and act.

The first principle of war is selection and maintenance of the aim; arguably, it is the first principle of life. Leaders need to set clear and achievable objectives and not be swayed from them unless the overall situation is changed radically. Recent history has several recent examples where a shifting aim led to failure or sub-optimal outcomes.[20] I expect leaders to use their teams and subordinates to advise them, but for the leader to take decisions and carry the load. *A problem shared is a problem doubled* was never more graphically illustrated to me than by a four-star NATO commander telling me in Banja Luka how difficult things were for him in Bosnia. In contrast, in Iraq and Afghanistan senior leadership carried that load in very difficult times and did

17. Joint means single nation Naval, Army and Air Force operations and can include national multi-agency involvement.
18. Combined means international, or alliance operations including Navy, Army and Air Force elements and can include international multi-agency involvement.
19. Ambassador Zalmay Kalilzad and Lieutenant General Dave Barno in Afghanistan and Ambassador Ryan Crocker and General David Petraeus in Iraq.
20. Including Vietnam and Southern Iraq and arguably in Afghanistan too.

not flinch; for example in Iraq in 2007, insurgent attacks peaked at almost 1600 per week before the campaign was turned around as Iraqi political and security conditions changed and matured.

Becoming a soldier does not automatically make a person an above average leader. It requires study and self-analysis. At every level of command I held, I insisted leadership was formally studied. A significant aid to leadership is the military structure that gives a leader an acknowledged moral and intellectual framework within which to work. There is a Military Covenant[21] with soldiers that states that in return for forgoing certain freedoms (including in conflict, the right to life) that the military will offer wider support in return, including looking after families. Whereas the rights of an individual are upheld throughout, the needs of the mission and the needs of the team may take priority. This culture — and its impact on leadership — is supported by doctrine, tactics and procedures, military law, experience and history. It is a truth-based leadership culture, which assists leaders and the led, particularly during difficult times.

In order to achieve the aim set by political, military or civilian leadership, it is essential that those charged with the task have Authority, Responsibility, Accountability and Resources (ARAR) placed in their hands. Where this does not happen, then success is much less likely. Effective leadership at the highest level must be given direction and empowered with ARAR. When leaders at the level of Crocker/Petraeus and Kalilzad/Barno spoke to Heads of Government, Chiefs of Defence and senior diplomats, it was clear that they held the ARAR of the United States and as a result, they achieved Effect. I am sorry to say that the same delegated approach was not applied by the UK Government, with a concomitant reduction in Effect.

The UK military arena has been as hard hit as any by the current recession. Force elements will be reduced by up to 20% and some capabilities will be lost. The Strategic Defence and Security Review was honest, in that it was based on affordability rather than on requirements, but whilst that honesty may solve today's budgetary problems, it is a possible hostage to fortune in terms of changing political and security threats over the horizon.

Challenges for the future are many and include being asked to do more or the same with less. Resources are finite and money is in short supply, thus keeping soldiers enthused and believing in what they are doing will be more challenging. The increased reliance on the use of Reserve Forces is a risk. An enduring medium scale operation, similar to Iraq and Afghanistan, is likely to have up to 25% of its force being made up of reserves after the first few roulements of six months. Increased alignment and training with Regular forces will help, but a shortage of resources may be telling. US Reserve Forces are

---

21. The Army's Values and Standards that form part of the Military Covenant state that all soldiers must display 'selfless commitment, respect for others, integrity, loyalty, discipline and courage'.

equipped with tanks, artillery and jet-fighters. UK Reserve forces have land rovers. The strategic risk is significant and the leadership challenge even more so.

Perhaps the biggest challenge after withdrawal from Afghanistan will be a loss of interest in the military and a reluctance to use them to good effect. The British public has been very supportive of its military, which has meant that leading troops on operations have been uncomplicated by lack of support at home. After 2014, interest may understandably wane and with that comes the risk of further budget and resource cuts which will make leading soldiers a much more challenging undertaking.

All of the above is bearable, as long the future does not undermine the military covenant with our people. Soldiers are robust, resilient and committed to their profession, but they do need to know that they are valued, supported and resourced.

Amanda Giles

My leadership journey has been predominantly influenced by over 33 years as an officer in the Royal Air Force. The military is, by nature and necessity, a hierarchy delineated by a robust rank structure and characterised by bureaucracy, rules, regulations and a shared ethos — 'how things are done around here'. That said, there is still room within a formal structure for individual agency; in fact, the strength of the military is founded on the ability of its members to make decisions independently and utilise their training and initiative to best effect. However, many of the approaches to leadership advocated within the military can be applied equally to non-military organisations and situations: leadership founded on trust and mutual respect between leaders and followers; shared goals and a sense of achievement when those goals are met or exceeded; and honest empowerment and acceptance of responsibility are universally important, no matter the context.

I perceive leadership to be a multi-layered series of relationships. It is a relationship between a leader and one or more followers; and we are all both leaders and followers depending on the situations we inhabit. Leadership is also a relationship between conflicting desires, limitations and opportunities which must be balanced in order to achieve an aim. A leader needs to know *who* he is — be self-aware; *what* is to be achieved; *how* he intends to achieve it; and, fundamentally, *why* it is worth his efforts and those of her/his followers. Leadership is messy. It is about people. It is not a science but an art.

Leadership, as an art, can be developed but not necessarily taught. The acquisition of leadership skills will be a lifelong work in progress which takes time and experience: the key to which is self-awareness. Only through knowing ourselves — our aims and aspirations, prejudices and perceptions, desires and drivers — can we begin to understand how we differ from other people and appreciate the richness of such diversity.

Self-awareness is the capacity to understand our own emotions and is one of the four dimensions of Emotional Intelligence (EQ).[22] The other three dimensions are: the abilities to self-manage those emotions; to recognise emotions in others; and to manage relationships between self and others as a consequence. This aptitude, to manage inter-personal relationships, is a fundamental leadership skill which can only be achieved successfully when relationships are based on mutual respect and trust.

A leader also needs to possess sufficient cognitive ability, commonly referred to as Intelligence Quotient (IQ) to be able to understand complex situations and solve challenging problems. She/he need not be a genius or necessarily a technical expert but she/he should be bright enough to be credible and capable.

EQ and IQ are essential capacities required to manage relationships, tasks and priorities, to competently juggle the often conflicting *who, what, how* and *why* leadership dimensions, yet these dimensions might also be considered elements of management process. A third intelligence that is required which provides action, with meaning and context, is Spiritual Intelligence (otherwise referred to as Spiritual Quotient — SQ). SQ is defined by Danah Zohar[23] as:

> The intelligence with which we solve and address problems of meaning and value, the intelligence with which we can place our actions and our lives in a wider, richer meaning-giving context, the intelligence with which we can assess that one course of action or one life path is more meaningful than another. The combination of EQ and IQ, afforded direction and significance by SQ, raises the craft of management to the art of leadership and enables it to become a meaningful act of service.

As my practical experience and understanding of leadership have grown and matured, I have come more and more to see leadership *as an act of individual or collective service* to a larger community. Within the military, this concept is reflected in the ethos of military service to the Sovereign, the Government and the community it protects. Members of Her Majesty's armed forces are servicemen or servicewomen. An officer has responsibility for, and owes service to, those under her/his command as well as to his/her superiors, as epitomised by the motto of the Royal Military Academy Sandhurst — *Serve to lead.* For a leader to serve those around her/him and to act as a catalyst to enable and empower the contribution and growth of others to achieve a shared, meaningful aim seems to me the best form of leadership.

---

22. Although there are many advocates of EQ theory, the most well-known is Daniel Goleman (1996).
23. Zohar and Marshall (2000).

Today's globalised society is interconnected more than ever before. The effects of the economic recession have been felt worldwide. Political instability quickly spreads (as evidenced by the Arab Spring) and all nations compete for increasingly scarce resources. We are inextricably linked by physical and virtual networks: telecommunications; the internet; political, religious and cultural ideologies; food, fuel and water storage and distribution systems; world commodity markets; banking and financial centres; and rail, road and air routes and transport infrastructure. This means that leaders, whether of nations, multinational corporations or a small company manufacturing widgets in Basingstoke, are affected and constrained by global influences. Globalisation also offers opportunities with access to wider markets, knowledge and rapidly evolving technology. Never before has it been so important to work together to combat mutual problems to achieve common aims and the equitable distribution of finite resources.

To operate successfully in this interconnected environment, leaders cannot afford to remain isolated but need to work collaboratively with customers, suppliers, partners and other stakeholders. Fundamental to building and maintaining strong relationships, particularly those outside of formal authority structures, is the ability to create rapport and respect between parties and to build trust within those relationships. Leaders will need to exert their influence outside formal hierarchical frameworks. Negotiation skills will come to the fore and short-term compromise, even sacrifice, may be required to achieve long-term success. Significantly, as we face a future marked by political and economic instability, and uncertainty associated with evolutional and transformational change, the need to nurture, establish and maintain cooperative and mutually supportive relationships may be the greatest challenge faced by leaders, today and tomorrow.

The UK military is just a microcosm of wider society and it too is subject to the trend towards inter-dependent operability, be it with other government departments, other nations' security forces or commercial partners. Increasingly, military operations will be conducted by coalition forces, in concert with non-military support agencies with increasing reliance on technological solutions. However, despite rapidly growing advances in technology, military operations — whether combat, peace-keeping, counter-insurgency or humanitarian relief — will remain an inherently human endeavour. It is people who work together to achieve an aim and people who matter.

Inter-national and intra-national conflicts cannot be solved by military intervention alone. They require diplomatic and economic solutions, with military forces being utilised in support of political aims such as nation-building and peace-making. To facilitate such ends, British military leaders must be skilled at working across organisational boundaries in partnership with assorted agencies. In an interconnected, interrelated world, the need for collaborative leadership skills within the military has never been greater. The challenge for HM Forces in this decade is to ensure that its people are fully empowered to operate independently and as members of a team, both within their own Service and with wider parties. Again, the establishment and maintenance of respect, rapport and mutual trust between parties are essential to the success of this endeavour.

At a time when budgets and force levels within the UK military have been drastically cut, yet the same operational output is envisaged, the ability and will of individual servicemen and servicewomen to achieve more than has been asked of them than before is directly related to the quality of the leader—follower relationships and the support provided by third parties. It is a multi-faceted challenging relationship which reflects the complex nature of humanity.

Peter Gray

Leadership in defence is a complex and emotive issue, both from within defence and especially in the wider community. All too often, the perception of leadership in defence is that it is a bit of a luxury because, at the end of the day, leaders at all levels just give orders. The alternative viewpoint is that those in defence have raised the art and possibly the science of leadership to new levels. In my experience, the reality falls somewhere in the middle. It is true that there are, as in any organisation, a plethora of rules and instructions which are usually called orders for historic reasons. But actually having to tell someone to do something or more usually not to do it, is a much rarer occurrence outside of actual combat. In any event, in most circumstances the military-speak term is command rather than leadership, an equally complex subject which involves the right to legal sanction to back up those orders.

Issues of leadership are further complicated by the levels at which it is exercised. Leadership at the strategic or executive levels is more demanding than at the lower levels not least because of the complexity, ambiguity and lack of immediate closure. The true leader at this level has to be at least comfortable with these situations and the best are often masters of their manipulation — at this point, the expression Machiavellian comes to mind! The senior leader is also characterised by the necessity of having to master a much broader constituency than the narrow tactical stovepipe from which they came. Again, there is a further complication in that part of the senior leader's role is to manage the interface with other organisations. A more junior leader may be required to push his or her own team to achieve targets and results often heedless of the good of the wider enterprise. A good strategic leader does not have this luxury and has to understand the vision, purpose and greater demands of the organisation as a whole. These may sound like management buzz words, but are not, they are the realities of senior leadership.

It is important in any consideration of leadership, at all levels, to embrace development and education. This may seem obvious to readers of a book such as this, but the realities of having to design and deliver meaningful programmes suggest otherwise. It is not too much of a caricature to suggest that willing contributors to leadership education are the ones that need it least; the converse is certainly true. There are a vast number of definitions of leadership, many including the Defence Leadership and Management Centre description used when the author was Director, emphasise the visionary nature of leadership. Equally, they point out that there is no prescribed style of leadership. In these circumstances, the process of education is just that. It is immediately complex and a 'wicked' problem that does not lend itself to linear or training solutions. Genuine engagement in these processes is not only challenging, but also can be a seriously uncomfortable experience. A typical defence mechanism in these situations is bravado and superficiality. In cases where leadership education is elective, such participants are likely to give the programme a poor reputation, which could be detrimental to its survival.

One of the key leadership challenges in the United Kingdom and in Europe, in times of austerity, is to maintain the standards and levels of leadership education and development. It is all too easy for programmes that do not have an immediate balance sheet benefit to be cut. In many cases, the bean-counter wielding the axe had previously found the course, or development opportunity, particularly challenging. A significant challenge beyond this is that change, budget cuts and wider austerity all have serious implications for the people in the organisation. All too often, organisations proclaim that their people are their greatest asset when what they actually mean is that they are either a liability or a readily disposable commodity. The mechanisms for shedding people are supposedly easier in the commercial sector where they can be bought out, but they are certainly all too prevalent in the public arena.

In all walks of life, there are technological challenges. Many of us are all too well aware of this and long for the nostalgia of a fountain pen while forgetting the frustration of waiting for work to come back from the typing pool. As if the challenges of keeping pace with technological and software developments are not sufficiently demanding in their own right, the real leadership challenge in this arena is in the field of innovation. One needs not only to keep pace, but to be out in front of competitors. At first sight, this may sound like commercial-speak from the private sector but examination of the pace of weapons development, utilisation of space (and certainly in the cyber domain) shows that defence has its fair share of problems. These leadership problems are exacerbated in times of austerity by research and development often being the first to lose funding. Reliance on academia and industry sound like good plans, but these sectors are also operating in an era of austerity and see defence as a net provider. The highly structured bureaucracy of defence, and the costs of shedding senior personnel, means that the organisations are led by an older generation who are invariably more conservative than the younger and more technologically adept. Admitting one's shortcomings in this field for the greater benefit of the organisation is not easy.

Leadership in defence is more than telling people what to do and what not to do. It is as complex and demanding as it is in any walk of life. In times of change, recession and austerity the pressure for savings and cuts inevitably impact on people. The debate on these issues, and on the care of those affected, is often merely a conversation with a spread sheet with no more than a sideways glance. In these circumstances, leadership education is all the more important, but all too often, those at senior levels do not consider that such development is appropriate for their needs because their abilities ensured their promotion to their current levels without it in the past.

John Jupp

As I followed the path of my career, I learnt from the examples of leadership around me, both good and bad, mostly from my squadron commanders and station commanders. There were those who relied on their position and those who did and said things that made me think I must never be like that, but there were also those who truly inspired me. I learnt that I needed to be good at what I did to earn the respect of those around me, that honesty and integrity were important, and that my own standards and discipline must be beyond reproach. But I also learnt that those who inspired me the most were those who had the energy, the zest for both work and life and made both fun, not the pious. All these things helped me enormously as my leadership waxed through various ranks and roles as a staff officer, as a squadron executive, and squadron commander. Of course, as all good leaders should, I tried to analyse every leadership event that I could and listened to those about me to try to learn to do better. One of the things that, in retrospect, I think I never did well, especially as a senior staff officer and squadron commander, was to clarify properly the purpose of what we were doing and communicate that sufficiently to all my people. I was asked to set up and lead the RAF's Leadership Centre, an entity the organisation had not previously had. The success of this allowed it to grow into the Generic Education and Training Centre covering a wide remit across the entire Service, part of which became delivering leadership interventions to the very senior officers in the RAF. It was a role that, most unusually, I held for 8 years which taught me about the importance of continuity in leadership. The old expression that if you want to learn about something, teach it, is so true. The observations that follow come in part from my experience of leadership but mostly from my observations of it and thinking about it.

Everyone's view of leadership is coloured by their experience of it wherever it comes from. During our formative years this comes from our teachers and perhaps from our sports experience. Like so many others, I wish that I knew then what I know now, then we would have had a much better rugby side! Unlike so many other sectors, we were formally introduced to leadership at the start of our working life in the RAF at the Initial Officer Training course. There the only model then used was John Adair's 'Task, Team, Individual' three circles model. And we were given a chance to practice using it during exercises in the physical environment. However, looking back, the course was really much more about management and administration than it was about leadership *per se*, and on reflection this is not so bad a thing. As a junior officer, once my training was completed, management and administration was what I spent most of my time doing. But the spark of leadership had been lit within me and would continue to grow as my career progressed and leadership became more important.

There seems to be ever more calls for good or better leadership to solve the problems that any organisation gets into, calls that become ever more clamorous, especially in the difficult times. Leadership seems to have become the panacea to solve all problems. But leadership cannot change the circumstances within which we live. Leadership can contribute to those circumstances but it cannot change them outright. The Chief of the Air Staff cannot change the economic circumstances this country finds itself in but he can contribute towards it by his leadership of the RAF and how much it spends. Every leader at all levels needs to know the context within which they are working and the purpose their team is there for.

Leadership then becomes the relationship between the leader and his or her followers where the leader persuades the followers to do or not to do things. The interesting detail is how the leader chooses to project their character to persuade the followers. For me, it is always best to get the followers to take responsibility for the outcomes and for them to do their best endeavours to achieve the tasks they are given. They too need to know the circumstances within which they are working, the purpose of the team and the specific tasks they have to do. They must believe in their task. This all takes a great effort in communication by leaders, at all levels. Once the boundaries — within which the followers must stay — are understood the followers can be unleashed. This is delegation through the philosophy of Mission Command.[24] To do this, of course, the leader needs to: know themselves and their people and how to engage and influence them including across the generations; be good at what they do; able to handle the ambiguity that inevitably arises, especially at the higher levels of an organisation; and be agile and adaptable to changing circumstances. They need to think about the attributes for RAF leaders. The

---

24. Mission Command has four enduring tenets: timely decision-making; a clear understanding of the superior commander's intent; an ability on the part of the subordinate to meet the superior's remit; and the commander's determination to see the plan through to a successful conclusion. It has the following key elements:

- A commander ensures his or her subordinates understand his or her intentions, their own missions, and the strategic, operational and tactical context
- Subordinates are told what effect they are to achieve and the reason why it is necessary
- Subordinates are allocated sufficient resources to carry out their missions
- A commander uses the minimum of control so as not to limit unnecessarily his or her subordinate's freedom of action
- Subordinates decide for themselves how best to achieve their missions

attributes do not make leaders but they help the leadership in an organisation.[25]

There are many challenges which current leaders face. Across Europe we seem to be in a sustained period of low or no growth. From this stem many things. Leaders need to shape the expectations of everyone to fit these circumstances as public sector spending inevitably shrinks. Jealousies over real or perceived advantages of others within Europe will have to be faced. The EU will have to remember its original purpose. At the same time, world power and standing is moving away from Europe, as the economic and political power of China and India, in particular, is growing and changing the political landscape within which all leaders must work. We need to understand the new context within which we are working and think differently about what we do.

For leaders within the RAF, this will mean coming to terms with and understanding the simple question 'how do we do more with less?' It is difficult to predict exactly what this means but it is likely to include: leaner structures; innovative ways of working; the collapsing and regeneration of capability and understanding the risks that entails; working with different alliances; relying on other organisations to provide services for us, including civilian and commercial ones; understanding how to lead without authority; how to lead different types of group, such as Service personnel, Reservists, Civil Servants, Commercial teams; and understanding the *Whole Force Concept*. It will certainly require leaders to be flexible and agile and to lead change well. Leaders will need to know all the different types of people who make up their team and to lead the necessary changes in behaviour and attitude. Some may say that this is what leaders have always needed to do 'plus ca change, plus ca le meme chose'.

3.5.4.   *The Police Service*

Nick Gargan

Having joined the Police Service in 1988, I am not sure at what point I became a leader. I felt like a leader when I took control of events on a quiet street in the Highfields area of Leicester one dark Saturday evening after a pedestrian had been mown down and killed by a hit and run driver. But I had no formal control over anyone or anything at the time. Or maybe it was at the time of

---

25. The nine attributes for RAF leaders are: Warfighter; Courageous; Emotionally Intelligent; Willing to Take Risks; Flexible and Responsive; Able to Handle Ambiguity; Technologically Competent; Able to Lead Tomorrow's Recruit; Mentally Agile — Physically Robust; Politically and Globally Astute — Air Warfare Minded. They are allied to the four leadership objectives: embrace Mission Command as an everyday practice; realise the importance of employing the RAF leadership attributes through a variety of leadership styles; understand the leadership of change; andrealise the importance of, and promote, followership.

my promotion to Inspector? The force supplied me with a different coloured shirt as if to remind me that I was different now. Certainly by the time I became a Chief Constable at the National Policing Improvement Agency, responsible for looking after a staff of over 2000 as the organisation closed down, whilst ensuring we continued to deliver crucial services to policing, I felt I had a worthwhile leadership challenge. I feel a similar sense of challenge as the Chief Constable of Avon and Somerset Constabulary with responsibility for leading an organisation of almost 6000 people with a budget approaching £300 million per annum. My experience is that leadership is a great privilege and pleasure. Theodore Roosevelt's quote, comes to mind: *far and away the best prize that life has to offer is the chance to work hard at work worth doing.* And for me leadership is worth doing.

As I developed through the Police Service, I was very conscious of a false paradox that was presented between leadership and management. Leadership was romanticised where management was derided. The leader was a hero but the manager was a nit-picker. Yet actually, far too often in our sector leadership can be a misleading label, used by those who would rather pontificate than do their homework. But there is a lot more to leadership than the ability to motivate through rhetoric which was so often the sole tactic of the people I am describing. In my view, there are technical components to leadership which I will describe below. But the two biggest determinants of successful leadership in my view are: first, the quality of strategy — the leader's thinking, the plan, the mission; and second, the quality of the relationship between the leader and the led, at all levels in the organisation.

For me, leadership has a handful of indispensable ingredients. The first of these is *integrity*. If a leader lacks integrity, they lack authority and without authority they cannot properly lead. The second is *knowledge*. Leaders may not need a detailed knowledge of the business at the outset but they must develop it quickly. And if you do not know your business, how can you be expected to develop it and exploit opportunities? The third dimension from my perspective is *strategy*, indeed as indicated above, it is one of the two most important determinants of successful leadership. The ability to develop a strategy is fundamental to organisations and a clear strategy, even if imperfect, will be a reliable predictor of future organisational success. The fourth characteristic of leadership in this sector is *ambassadorship*. In a policing world that can be excessively introspective and frequently defensive and where leaders are often perceived to hold together in safety in numbers against an outside world that does not understand outward facing leadership shines out. Where police leadership is trusting, transparent and open, it commands the immediate respect of the communities we serve. The fifth component is an understanding of, and a commitment to, effective *organisational performance*. The idea of a high-performing policing organisation comes into and out fashion from time to time but ultimately, understanding what you are there to do and knowing whether you are doing it must be one of the basic tests of any leader. Finally, and also one of the two most important determinants mentioned above, for any leader is the *quality of the relationship* between the people leading the organisation and the people who actually do the work. It is the one area in which my conviction has strengthened most since I started to reflect on leadership several years ago.

I think that Britain and Europe face the challenge of modernising, connecting and, in the case of the Public Sector, shrinking simultaneously. This calls for a new skill set from a leadership cadre who, in most cases, learned how to lead in times of relative plenty. The confusing nature of this challenge is made worse by wide-spread re-thinking of the role of Government, particularly in the United Kingdom where Ministers demonstrate an increasing commitment to localism and smaller Government. Furthermore, as the internet develops, the ability for the United Kingdom and Europe to defend themselves effectively from external threats and from threats that cannot be authenticated will be an area of enormous challenge. Developing the skills to deal with this changing world will be a key challenge for leaders, and in the case of the European context it will be ever harder for Britain to be influential, as the number of young people studying languages continues to collapse.

Many of the sector's challenges reflect those of the United Kingdom and Europe more generally, especially the skills challenge for a leadership cadre that had grown into the leadership positions answering one set of questions only to see those questions change as they reached the top of their organisation. The emerging cyber threat and challenges of authentication will be felt as acutely in policing as anywhere else. But other threats are less novel. In a policing world that is organised vertically and in which the Chief Constable owns all the threat in his or her policing area, incentives to collaborate are sometimes difficult to find given its challenges. These challenges seem automatically to increase at a time when Governments demand economies of scale, yet devolve the power that may lead to them being achieved.

So, the future leadership challenges for policing will be a mixture of the old and the new. A community that demands protection from the most serious threats yet wants to see an officer on every street corner and leadership that is torn between the needs of the local community and those of the national government trying to find solutions where the best is sometimes the enemy of the good. New threats will continue to emerge whilst the old threats, be they from the burglar or the yob, will continue. And an ever more demanding public will see more and more areas in which it makes demands of the police, from child protection to mental health.

Sara Thornton

I am a Chief Constable and lead Thames Valley Police, a large public sector organisation, with over 9000 staff and a revenue budget of nearly £400 million. I have led the organisation for more than six years and it is both a privilege and a burden. It is a privilege because I am able to have a significant influence in the way my organisation delivers services but it is completely unrelenting.

I am on leave today, writing this article, and have dealt with my e-mails and taken three important phone calls.

So who would be a leader? I did not set out with the ambition of being a Chief Constable but I did work hard at every stage of my career and I have always wanted to grow the organisation ahead of wanting to grow my career. Many leaders talk about leadership for good and I hope that is what I practice. As a Chief Constable, I want my officers and staff to use their formidable powers to protect the public and to cut crime and so earn the confidence and trust of the people who live in the Thames Valley.

Leadership and management are sometimes discussed as if they were opposites, as if they were alternatives for an organisation. I strongly believe that to lead a police force effectively, both are necessary. As a leader, I need to set a clear vision and to establish the right values and a healthy culture but I also need to manage the plan, align the budget and ensure that systems are working. My job requires me to lead and manage, to be both transformational and transactional. I try to ensure that I do both simultaneously. For example, I might chair a budget discussion but I am ensuring that my values of service to the public and integrity are shot through the discussion.

Both leadership and management involve making decisions and making decisions can mean disappointing people. It can require the moral courage to choose a course which is not the most popular and which may be resented by staff or members of the public. Of course, I try to take people with me but it is just not always possible. Staff may lose their jobs, a member of the public will have to live with the consequence of a criminal caution as they seek employment, or a specialist unit cannot have the resources that they argue are essential. These decisions can be tough and I do take the responsibility personally. In all, I try to be the good king — wise and making decisions in the interests of everyone not in my own self-interest.

Leadership is essentially about having a relationship with followers and so the need to engage, to listen and to build trust is paramount. Spending time with officers and staff is always important and never urgent and so it can easily get bumped out of the diary. I do enjoy talking to people about the work that they do and understanding from a practical point of view the impact of new policies or changes in patterns of crime. But leadership is also about having relationships with the outside world to enable an outside-in perspective. It is sometimes said that leaders need to create meaning for an organisation and I think that I have a very important role in interpreting the world for my staff so that our vision and strategy meet the needs and expectations of the public. I need to be on top of my game: understanding the evidence base; professionally expert; and self-confident in my leadership as a result.

Few Chief Constables are female and it is implicit that my experience of leadership has taken place in a highly gendered workplace. The police service has transformed its attitude to women officers in the last 25 years but there is still room for improvement. But as a leader, I share responsibility for that improvement and while I would never see myself as a role model, I am aware that many of my colleagues look to me to set an example.

You should never let leadership go to your head. In a hierarchical organisation it is easy to become detached, to have a fan base rather than a management team and to unintentionally silence debate. Creating a team and a culture that allows team members to feedback, to bring bad news and to offer constructive dissent is essential. I sometimes talk about the importance of humility in leadership and I will always try to ensure that I see the issue from the perspective of the other. Ultimately, a leader is only as good as the team they lead.

All public sector leaders are managing the challenge of austerity. In policing, we are responding to a 20% reduction in our government grant and I have worked very hard with my chief officer team to ensure that, as far as possible, we cut budgets not services. While much of this work is intensely managerial, I do think that it presents opportunities to show leadership. For example, we are reducing the size and numbers of our buildings, with desk sharing and open plan offices for senior staff that have long enjoyed their own space. I have also taken the opportunity to work in an open plan office with my chief officer team, so I am walking the talk but also demonstrating an open, accessible and modern culture.

Policing is one of those things where most people have a view. Indeed, debates about the merits of policing have characterised its development since Sir Robert Peel founded the Metropolitan Police Service in 1829. Police forces are important institutions of the state and, for many, promise much in terms of protection from harm. In contrast, they are also regarded with wariness by others. Whether it is the health service, education, the media or commercial organisations I can see that people's relationships with all institutions is changing. We are all more wary, more critical, require more scrutiny and openness and do not trust professionals in the way we did 20 years ago.

Coupled with the development of crime as technological and international, these public expectations require a very different policing response. Policing has traditionally been craft-based, a reactive and tactical response to crime but that is no longer enough. The professional transformation of the service is underway with a focus on evidence and standards and significant changes to terms and conditions and career structures. There are opportunities to be grasped but our staffs tend to look backwards at what they have lost. My responsibility, then, as a chief officer is to look forward, lead transformational change and equip the organisation for the next thirty years.

3.5.5. The Fire Service

Sue Johnson

My first experience of leadership was my placement year in IBM, where I observed leadership rather than being a leader. I was very fortunate at that time to have a manager who was, from my perspective, a role model in how leadership should manifest itself. He was a very inclusive person. Definitely a people person and very engaged in the professional development of his staff. He was very good at recognising success and achievement. At this time, I thought that was what all leaders were like. My view changed when I started my first job at a very small company. The guy who founded it was a technical person and quite myopic about how he saw the business. The business was all about the technology, not the people. His was a very different leadership style. From then on, I realised that it was the person that made the style not the other way. You don't just fit a style to a person.

Later, when I became group marketing manager in another organisation, it was then that my employing organisation spent time and money investing in my development. That was my first real experience of leadership development. The structured learning environment was where I began to learn about leadership. That is when I began to reflect on my own leadership style, and where I wanted to take my part of the business, and how it fitted with the strategy.

Later in my career, I started a part-time MBA and sometime after that was approached about joining the North East Business Forum as Chief Executive. I had the title of Chief Executive and was working out of a stationary cupboard, with no staff. A key lesson for me was not to assume that a title gives you the position of a leader. Rather, it is what you do and how you do it that is important. I was responsible for bringing in the money to keep the business going. Essentially, I was in a business start-up position. As the Chief Executive, I was dealing with business leaders across the northeast of England, who were leading the economy of a region and their own businesses. I was fortunate to have time with people who had built their own business and were hugely respected regionally, nationally and internationally. However, I experienced that when you get some very powerful, highly intellectual people, who control their own destiny in their own business and you try and get them together to decide on a consensus, it was like a clash of the planets. There were some forceful character who were all very successful in their own right. From my own position, I was being asked to comment on things that I knew little about because I had Chief Executive as my title. This was the same situation when I moved to my current role — suddenly I was expected to know everything, within 24 hours of sitting at my desk. As a leader you have to call on every ounce of heuristic and acquire knowledge, experiences and interactions that you have to bring to bear on the situation that you find yourself in.

Moving to the Fire Service is the biggest leadership challenge I am ever going to have. The first day in the job I sat in the Chief Executive's chair and everyone expected me to know everything from the first morning in the job. That was a tipping point for me because of the weight of responsibility that was on me. Add to that the fact I am running an emergency service and the weight doubles. Add to that the fact that the people who work for me run into hazardous situations when everyone is running away and that triples the weight on my shoulders. It really took me by surprise about how I felt. I was ecstatic I got the job. I never expected to get it. I was thrilled I was coming in as Chief Executive but I was petrified due to self-doubt about whether or not I could do it.

It was also a huge shift in culture for me. I had never worked in an environment before where the union representation was so strong. I was not welcomed in the job at all. There were lots of negative comments; for example, the Fire Brigade Union objected outright to my appointment as they thought it was the worst thing to have happened to the fire service while my peers from other fire services also thought it was the wrong thing. For me as a leader, establishing credibility was paramount. Everyone was watching for the train to come off the tracks. I felt like I was in a gold fish bowl. Everyone was waiting for me to fail.

One of my biggest jobs as a leader is to develop those who come after me. The institution will be here much longer than any Chief Executive. So it is the Chief Executive's responsibility to make sure that there are leaders with clear values who have been developed and exhibit the right kind of behaviours. I am a leader who invests in the leadership of others.

Resilience is the number one skill you need as a leader. I have found resilience I did not even know I had. I have closed the door and cried, but then got on with it again. Emotional resilience combined with a belief in yourself that you are doing the right thing and that you are doing it for the right reasons are vital for a leader. For me, that is what I have seen in other good leaders. Doing it for the right reasons and in the right way.

I have also learnt to call on support when I need it. I have had a coach and mentor while being in this job and they have been absolutely marvellous. Without my coach in the first 2 years of this job I would not have lasted. I was going home thinking I would never break through this treacle. But being able to talk it through with my coach was absolutely invaluable. So call on your support as a leader when you need it. Just because you have leader in your title does not mean that you are on your own.

I have also learnt that taking time to invest in yourself is time well spent. Investing in yourself is not a selfish thing to do. You need it as a leader. You need time out to think. That will be a challenge going forward. In the public sector, senior teams are shrinking and the time they have to discuss and think ahead is very limited.

In terms of what leadership means to me, I define it in what one would see in the organisation as being different. In addition, it is very important to consider how one's staffs see you as the leader. For example, the fire service is traditionally hierarchical, militaristic, and has a very disciplined, very formulaic and task-orientated culture. In this respect, there was never any work done on medium-term financial planning or long-term strategic planning. I think what I have brought as a leader is business-like approach, although I am always corrected if I refer to the organisation as a business.

I have brought customer care to the service as well as productivity and value — all those business disciplines which make the business successful. But it has taken a long time. It took me a while to figure out that I was trying to educate and change the way that we worked as an organisation, but I was working with people who had no terms of reference at all of how it could be different. So the thing that I learnt about myself in that first 12−24 months was how much I had to paint a picture about the future, the opportunities, the behaviours expected and how we should interact with each other. I needed to spend much more time in articulating that and illustrating it.

Driving and delivering change is the biggest challenge. The fire and rescue service has hardly changed in the last 50 years. In the fire service, leaders are finding the deficit reduction very hard. Those who could exit and take retirement have done so. My deputy came to me at the beginning of the austerity piece and said that he was going to take retirement because he could not see himself dismantling what he had built up — he said he did not have the energy or appetite to do it. So tackling organisational change is the biggest challenge. The second challenge is that there is very little succession planning in the service. I have seen people leave and when we look around to see where our next leaders are coming from there is no one there. A third challenge is the potential merging of the blue light services. There is not enough visioning taking place about what that could look like. There is a lot of protectionism and defensiveness going on with this issue which is, in itself, a challenge. A further challenge is implementing a leadership approach. If you see how an incident is managed when life and death is an issue, it is a very task-focused activity and everyone knows their place in that task. You then have fire officers who also do a functional job, such as HR or Risk, but when they are at an incident the way that the incident is managed is very structured and formulaic. It is about instructions going down the line and you follow the instruction to the letter, because if you do not something could go wrong. So in that situation the leadership style is 'do as I say'. What happens is that leaders come out of that scenario and bring that style back to their functional role. So we are having to address how they adapt their leadership style.

As stated previously, one of the biggest challenges for leaders is leading organisational change. When you are delivering change and there is tension and fear from people, you are not going to get buy-in by giving them instructions. One of the things I have talked about with my staff is situational−transactional−transformational leadership and looked at the different leadership styles which work in different situations and why. We have looked at different styles, what they look like, and how individuals can transition from one style to another. The impact of this has been that the leaders who have got it are still here and the ones who have not have left.

In summary, I would suggest: trust your gut and your instincts; soak up knowledge; learn quickly; develop your resilience strategy; and seek out support early and use it.

3.5.6. *Local Authority*

Carlton Brand

My experience is unusual in local government in that it spans the private sector. I spent 20 years in the automotive engineering sector as a design engineering manager working across a number of countries, cultures and operations, and at all three levels of local government: District (providing local services), County (providing strategic services) and Unitary councils providing all services. I have held leadership positions spanning small teams to my current position as Corporate Director, Wiltshire Council, one of the largest authorities in the country.

For me, management and leadership are inextricably linked. I believe that good managers are good leaders and that you can't lead without being able to manage. For me, there is a credibility gap with leaders who can't manage. Why would you follow a leader without credibility? This is probably controversial as the literature tends to separate the two. Leadership and followership are linked for me.

Good management is about performing a role covering three distinct but related domains: task, team and individual. They include: definition and achievement of the task in hand; developing the team as a collective; and developing individuals and one's self to learn and improve. I like to think about these three domains existing in a model of management and leadership comprising four levels: vision, strategy, operations and tactics. The leader has to operate at all four levels and in the three domains to be successful. Leadership then goes beyond this into the realm of change. Change related to improved performance, better customer satisfaction, reduced costs, and enhanced staff well-being and learning. Change is the important differentiator between management and leadership; change is a psychological journey to be led rather than a task to be managed.

The skills required to manage and lead are closely related. They include: a passion for and a skill to communicate; displaying the appropriate behaviours; and being competent technically but also across the whole system, not just the immediate part of the organisation. Leaders need to be conversant in systems thinking competencies. Above all, they have to deliver change and deliver the performance demanded by customers, citizens and politicians.

It is a multi-faceted role but the bottom line is that it is my job. I am employed to lead. Everything else is secondary. It is about all of the following:

- Attracting, growing and developing the best people and setting them free to deliver
- It's something to be measured and worked at continuously to improve — forming the major part of my annual CPD
- It's lonely, complex, difficult, challenging, frustrating and hugely exciting and thrilling

- It's about caring: for staff, customers, the organisation and yourself
- It's about challenging the *status quo* with a dogged desire to improve things
- It's about detail as well as big picture and also simplifying complexity for others
- Taking risks and being comfortable with prolonged exposure to those personal and organisational risks

Above all, it's about having a vision for the future that you know will be better than today.

The world of management and leadership is changing because the world is changing. The global debt and government deficit crisis means that spending is massively constrained in the public sector and will be for another 10 years. Customers and citizens expect better service, customised to their personal preferences all at a cost that represents better value to them, as buyers, or as tax payers. This requirement is driven by an increasingly sophisticated and developed consumer mind-set and market where the customer or client is in full control. In this world, local authorities are having to move from a model of 'we'll tell you what you can have' to a model of 'what do you need and how can we help to provide this?' This is a difficult cultural and behavioural shift for staff, managers and leaders to make if they have only ever experienced the former.

Key challenges in this new world include: doing more with less; doing different things with less; innovation and creativity and funding and exploiting it; better data and information and how to use it; exploiting new technology and ways of working; personal resilience to continual change and pressure; communication and influence with customers, clients, stakeholders, partners and co-production; and how to work with communities and individuals to enable service provision. Leaders who do not understand this, and merely propose service cuts, are failing.

Local authorities are undergoing the biggest change that they have ever experienced. Funding reductions of 30% plus, and the same again, is to be announced over the next few years which makes the job of leadership very difficult. Most managers in local government have never experienced challenge of this magnitude and it is becoming the discriminating factor between personal success and failure.

In this respect, key challenges for leaders include: finding a common purpose to galvanise effort and spirit in organisations which deliver over 350 largely unrelated services; managing complexity between the interrelated parts of the organisation and the wider community systems within which the organisation operates; developing communities to co-deliver services to reduce unsustainable demand; innovation, including cross sector innovation, and how to leverage this to the benefit of communities and the organisation to improve performance and reduce costs; and better management and leadership competence to inspire staff and communities to make the journey of change that society is demanding.

The major challenge is for leaders to move on from their professional background and to embrace the profession of management and leadership. In a world where whole-system thinking will differentiate between those that succeed and those that fail, the following, I believe, will be the new leadership competencies: the ability to think in terms of systems and knowing how to lead systems; the ability to understand the variability of work in planning and problem solving; understanding how we learn, develop and improve; leading true learning and improvement; understanding people and why they behave as they do; understanding the interaction and interdependence between systems, variability, learning and human behaviour; knowing how each affects the others; and giving vision, meaning, direction and focus to the organisation.

It will also be important to be aware of the experts, particularly those selling simple ideas as the panacea to address and meet the problems of today and tomorrow. In addition, new delivery models such as outsourcing, commissioning and staff mutuals have a role to play but they are not the solution or even a major part of the solution to the problems facing the public sector over the next 10 years.

Finally, leadership is lonely. I try and be prepared for the mental and physical effects of this and seek out sources of support from friends, a coach or a mentor. I have learnt from sport where the best have great support systems in place. Lastly, I consider that local government officers who do not listen to and understand their politicians always get themselves into trouble.

Sue Bruce

My understanding and experience of leadership, and all that it means, has developed incrementally over a lifetime, informed and challenged by a diversity of experience and circumstance. I firmly believe that my appetite for change and risk was embedded at an early age as my parents pursued employment and forged a future for my siblings and I. During my childhood, I attended nine different schools in four or five local authority areas across the United Kingdom, adapting as necessary as I was presented with a different curricular experience, varying regional accents and of course, always with the wrong school tie. On reflection in later years, I consider that the sense of being on the outside and surviving, and making the most of repeated new and challenging environments, as a youngster, have all become attributes in my world of work that has followed. Through an ability to adapt to new environments and to deal with people from many different backgrounds, and without realising it, I was becoming a change manager. I learned at times how to harness the power of one. The values of trust, humility, respect and integrity drawn from my parents have underpinned the journey and have been relied upon ever since.

Commencing employment in adult life in social and economic regeneration, initially through youth and community work and in a variety of roles since, including three as a CEO (City of Edinburgh Council, Aberdeen City Council and East Dunbartonshire Council), have further honed my experiences, understanding and thinking of leadership in all of its facets and guises.

My perception in the United Kingdom today is that we have, unsurprisingly, a wide variation of leadership examples, in a somewhat mixed bag from a spectrum of very strong leadership through to weak, less effective leadership. To take a positive view, examples of strong leadership come to mind with ease, such as the outstanding leadership behind the delivery of the London Olympics in 2012 and the delivery of the annual festivals in Edinburgh, with the International Festival, the Fringe and the Tattoo. I am struck by the personal resilience demonstrated in individuals and there are many examples here too. The leadership role that manager Ally McCoist played to support his team, colleagues and fan base during the 6-month period leading up to the liquidation of Scottish football club Rangers, then one of European football's biggest clubs, exemplifies an individual providing leadership, primarily to his team in a complex scenario where others were controlling the outcomes — a context that provides interesting dynamics between responsibility and accountability. For it is in these times of crisis that the metal of a leader is truly tested.

I advocate inclusive and distributed leadership which, when working effectively, can produce substantial leverage in terms organisational capability, capacity, ownership and productivity. A successful model of distributed leadership must have absolute clarity about roles, responsibilities, and accountabilities and clear parameters to provide a supportive environment to release leadership potential. Indeed one of the key attributes of a good leader is to remove ambiguity for those that follow.

In terms of what leadership means to me, I believe that people look for direction, guidance, challenge and care, in other words, supported empowerment. Effective leadership, in my view is not, however, about heroic leadership where an organisation has all of its leadership capacity vested in an individual or 'star chamber' who does not engage with others. We can all achieve greater benefit from leadership that develops and importantly, unleashes the capacity and capability in people, organisations and communities to engage and contribute constructively.

Within the public sector, we all face substantial new areas of complexity at present. Even as we cautiously welcome signs of growth in the economy there are huge challenges facing both individuals and organisations. And here we face a conundrum. On the one hand our constrained budgets, and on the other, the need to stimulate inclusive economic development. To illustrate, I can draw on two cases which demonstrate the delivery of successful outcomes in and around my own working environment.

3.5.6.1. Case 1 — UK Green Investment Bank

The decision by the UK Government to site the HQ of the UK Green Investment Bank in Edinburgh was a case in point. Once the opportunity had been identified, team Scotland got behind the effort to secure this asset and investment in Scotland, and then agreed that Edinburgh, as the main centre for financial services, would be the preferred place. Many stakeholders were involved including the Scottish Government, Scottish Enterprise, The City of Edinburgh Council, Scottish Financial Enterprise, The Chamber of Commerce, Edinburgh Business Forum and not least, the support of all of Scotland's local authorities. This is an excellent example of leadership both political and non-political where securing the outcome for Scotland transcended individual interest. The collective and distributed effect of the leadership was powerful and secured the outcome.[26]

3.5.6.2. Case 2 — The Edinburgh Guarantee

Working in partnership with the public, private and voluntary sectors, the City of Edinburgh Council seeks to increase the number of jobs, education or training opportunities being made available to young people in the 16−19 age group. With a baseline of December 2010 showing proportionately the poorest performance in Scotland in this area, an effort has been made to harness the collective power of leadership to make a substantial and sustained impact on youth unemployment. Having identified the challenge and analysed it in granular detail, employers in the public, voluntary and the further education sectors were asked to consider what we each could do and what that would look like if we developed an approach collectively. Two years on, The Edinburgh Guarantee has 150 business partners and has created 1000 opportunities for young people. Edinburgh has been identified in a recent independent survey as the best place in the United Kingdom for young people seeking employment (Legal & General, 4/10/13). The Edinburgh Guarantee is a partnership[27] — a coalition of the willing — whose constituent partners have all sought to contribute to the common cause of supporting young people into opportunities. The aim is to help them look forward to their futures rather than to just suspect their fates. The environment of mutual understanding and respect along with effective collective and individual leadership has led to the best outcomes for 15 years for these young people. And if I was fortunate enough through my early experiences to develop insights for my career, they will need this and more in such a fast changing world.

In conclusion, we can all bring the range of tools we have in our personal leadership toolbox and deploy them as the situation demands, underpinned by the values that drive us. The delivery of effective leadership, which includes being directive, and also the courage to stick our heads above the parapet, will support our capacity to deliver effective outcomes. An effective *distributed* leadership model will support our capacity to deliver exceptional outcomes because it makes everyone a leader.

Sophia Looney

My experiences of leadership within local government have often, although not always, come from unexpected places. Peers and colleagues have

---

26. http://www.greeninvestmentbank.com
27. http://www.edinburghguarantee.org

inadvertently (or perhaps consciously?) led me by the power of their personalities and the attractiveness of their thinking, ideas and ways of operating. Members of the community have provided that extra motivation, and given me the push I have needed to get the right things done. People from outside the workplace have shown me that there are different ways of thinking about how I approach the challenges in the workplace. This transferability is striking and connects to a big future challenge as the boundary between personal and professional becomes increasingly fuzzy.

My experience of formal leadership is marked by its inconsistency. When it is poor, it appears to be because it fails to recognise the changes that have happened within the context in which we operate; or it is so inflexible and rigid that it stifles and restricts. But it is also where I have seen, and more importantly felt, the most significant transformational leadership that I have experienced.

Political leadership has had a significant impression on the nature of relationship between managers and politicians feeding the atmosphere, driving expectations and behaviour, shaping what I do, and what those I lead are encouraged to think about. My experiences of this have been generally very positive; both individuals demonstrating leadership through their behaviour and collectively through the decisions they make and the way in which they interact with managers, the wider workforce, and most importantly for me, the communities which they serve. Where this has not been evident, the vacuum is palpable. The political leadership, perhaps because of the democratic mandate they acquire through the ballot box, has always been more significant for me; providing legitimacy and a clearer link to my own values relating to public service which drives me to work hard and consistently seek improvement.

My experience of leadership has more variety and contrasts. The poor practice — where leadership is missing completely and I have been left to my own devises — has been liberating at times and preferable to that where those leading have monotone styles and a lack of creativity. Weak leadership, which has been marked by an emphasis on control and exerting managerial power, has stifled flexibility and constrained innovation through the reinforcement of bureaucratic and permission-seeking hierarchies. Where it has been positive, leadership has been inspirational — it has enabled me to work differently to find solutions, deliver work effectively, and provided the space to take risks. These leaders have been calm, breeding confidence and assurance. But alongside this, these leaders have also created tension, to good effect, enabling and encouraging change and quickening pace and movement. Some of the most creative leaders in local government have been able to truly exploit tensions in the organisational machinery in support of their overall direction of travel and those following rarely notice what it is that is happening.

Leadership is a strange, nebulous force that motivates, drives and cajoles me. It emanates from a variety of sources from managers, from peers, within the organisation, or within the community that is being served. At its best, when I am not conscious of being led, I feel empowered, supported and convinced, confident and certain. The best leaders have worked with me, persuading and influencing, encouraging and without me realising, carefully directing.

My experiences of being led have shown me that leadership is enormously powerful. It has had a significant impact on my personal attitudes to work; to my motivation and confidence in what I am doing and in some respects, to my own self esteem. It has shown me that used creatively and positively, leadership can make a massive difference to my own willingness to push the boundaries and really extend my own efforts. While the best has shown me that carefully used, tactics enable and support the delivery of a leader's strategy and vision. More than anything, my experiences have shown me that leadership can come from many places, and when it is most effective in its impact, for me, it is when those multiple leaders coalesce.

The opportunity that is presented is to broaden the concept of leadership to a more diverse, fluid concept that acknowledges and understands that leadership can and should come from anywhere; the risk is that the homogeneity of formal leadership is maintained. Meeting the challenges that the public sector is facing will require leadership which is flexible and liberating, that draws out the other leaders in the system and supports and enables them to apply creativity to solving the big problems. This will be extraordinarily hard, when the narrative will be for strong leaders and the temptation to hunker down will be ever present.

The leadership challenges in local government are substantial. The pace of change and transition is quicker than ever before and the context of the work more uncertain and in many respects more complex. Expectations about what local government is for, what public servants do, and how councils should be run are changing. The reduction in resources available and the reduced size of organisations is already having a direct impact in the way in which local government can and should be led. Communication and dialogue with local communities are changing and technological developments are reinforcing difference. This changing environment requires leaders to hold and understand what is happening now and to be better able to predict what may happen next in a way they have never had to do before. They need to be able to translate and interpret what they see on the horizon and to make sense of the implications. It requires new emphasis on the ability of those leaders to build sustainable relationships, to build a sense of value, and enable people to understand why things are being done, even when they do not agree with them. This presents a big challenge for leaders — politically and managerially as it is genuinely unchartered territory.

Leaders need to be opportunistic, to enable risk taking, to embrace the changing perceptions of public services and to seek out new ways to build relationships with the communities they serve. They need to be in a position to lead this transition. This requires acknowledgement that a more collective and distributed leadership approach which recognises the strength that lies in leadership beyond the hierarchy and understands that everyone, including communities and the workforce, has a leadership role to play. The need to be flexible, agile and innovative in order to build these new relationships and support the tactics that are needed to deliver organisational ambitions and vision is greater than ever.

Given the current context of local government, it is unlikely that the organisations we are familiar with now will remain. Leadership will need to be highly distributed to enable local government to embrace fluidity and encouraged and enabled by those with formal leadership roles. Individuals will need to be able to move across and between organisational forms focusing on task, rather than role; stripping away the bureaucratic hierarchies and power bases that they are familiar with. Leaders, wherever they are, will be challenged by the complexity that this creates. They will need visibility, openness and highly developed relationship skills, being inclusive whilst retaining the ability to be visionary and to bring it to life.

3.5.7.   *Government: Education*

Roger Mullin

Where there is no vision, the people perish

Proverbs 29: 18 (King James Version)

For the last 20 years, I have been involved in providing various types of support to leaders of major public sector bodies, both within the United Kingdom and elsewhere. The elsewhere has included Canada, Ireland, Namibia, Oman, South Africa, The Marshall Islands and Yemen. At times, I have been specifically contracted to provide leadership on major projects, but most often contracted to assist leaders. For most of my professional career, I have been unaware of the fact that I am, apparently, a 'third space' professional.

Most of my work has been within the education sector, but I have also been involved in the vocational training, science and fisheries sectors. Regardless of the sector, however, I have found leadership challenges and responses surprisingly similar.

What do I mean by leadership? This is a question that has helped make many an academic career. Most people, I would guess, have a very clear intuitive sense of what is meant by leadership, but once something more formal and precise is required, it becomes a much more elusive concept. Part of the problem, in my view, is that it is often considered to be an inherent quality of people inhabiting senior positions, whether a chief executive, a university principal, a senior partner or some other post. It is also unlikely to be immediately associated with those lower down the organisation, whether these be lecturers, laboratory technicians, fishermen or indeed anyone not at the top of some hierarchy. My experience, however, suggests that leadership is not so neatly distributed.

It is easy to find the university principal who lacks leadership capability, and yet refuses to learn about management or leadership from his own academic community, or the chief executive, who, faced with a major business crisis, refuses to mobilise the talents in his employ to address the challenge. Yet such people often believe they deserve the epithet leader while they refuse to confer the term on those who could actually help them become leaders.

Reflecting on personal experience, I would argue that leadership has got very little to do, indeed anything to do, with position in a hierarchy. Furthermore, I would argue it has little to do with charismatic features either. In my experience, the more charismatic the leader, the more prone he or she is to hubris.

In our modern fast changing world, where the rate of change of an organisation's external environment is on an exponential path, I would argue hierarchical authority is no basis for effective leadership. In such fast changing environments, where new forms of knowledge, new technologies and ever changing social norms have become the norm, leadership requires intelligence and foresight.

Where can we find intelligent leadership? Intelligent leadership is, in my judgement, most often found in collectives, often unofficial, unplanned collectives at the start, which come together to fill the gaps left by hierarchical authority. Sometimes those gaps can be huge. Such collectives usually mobilise a range of skills, including both analytical and creative skills, to help understand situations and predicaments, and also to create a sense of what is possible. In my experience too, intelligent leadership avoids basing judgement on purely intuitive approaches, whereas hierarchical authority is often steeped in it. As a result, there are different orientations evident when we compare intelligent collective leadership, and traditional forms of hierarchical leadership. Indeed, the future of leadership is probably going to see the fall of traditional forms of hierarchical leadership, in addition to the rise of new, collective and intelligent forms. Only through such new forms of leadership can we expect to effectively shape our future.

In dealing with the huge uncertainties regarding the economy and society, whether we talk of the United Kingdom, Europe or the world more generally, we find traditional forms of hierarchical leadership, whether in the fields of business or politics, failing to effectively understand the fast changing nature of the modern world, and failing to provide any compelling sense of the possible. At a time, therefore, when leadership is required as never before, we can often find a lack of intelligent leadership. In such circumstances, too often hubris comes to the rescue.

Take the debate in Europe about the economic challenges that are faced. Most leaders failed not only to predict the banking crisis, but have presided over a collective economic policy failure ever since. They may have been willing to spend billions on shoring up past banking failures, but when faced with the fact, according to Eurostat, that only 34% of Europeans aged between 15 and 29 were employed in 2011, there has been a collective failure to respond. Even in terms of creating an education response to this crisis, the very modest proposal made by the Scottish Government in 2011 to provide a guaranteed place in education or training for all 16–19 year olds, was met with criticism from college leaders who saw this disruption to their complacent leadership as compromising 'lifelong learning'. Oh the irony of it all.

Working within the education sector, there are intelligent voices in both our universities and colleges that recognise the world is changing, and that the education sector needs to change and develop. However, those arguing for change are often drowned out by the complacent and vested interest of hierarchical leaderships.

Working in both the college and university sectors, hierarchical leaders often spend more time in turf wars, in establishing their place in league tables, or simply defending traditional practice, than in providing a leadership that is in tune with a changing society.

My experience is that hierarchical leadership, in long established educational institutions, is least likely to have a vision of the future. Such vision as exists is often predicated on seeing their existing institutions as 'centres of excellence', 'world class' or some other complacency inducing description. The complacency of educational leadership is, in many respects, not unlike the complacency found in the banking sector before the crash of 2008: arrogant, ill-informed, unreflective and resistant to organisational change, seeking complete freedom to do as they will.

Michael Russell

All members of a Cabinet also have a collective leadership responsibility, working under the leadership of the First Minister. So after six years as a Minister, as well as many other senior roles within the Scottish National Party, and before that much time leading local organisations, my own and others' companies and a variety of different bodies, I have had several decades of leadership experience in a wide range of settings.

In all those circumstances I have also seen leadership as a collective as well as an individual responsibility. Certainly the buck stops with the leader but the process of keeping the buck moving and ensuring action is, for me, one which requires the building of *relationships* that underpin leadership by consent, example and agreement.

One of the best human development consultants I ever worked with, an American Professor from the Mid-West, used to use a range of cartoons to drive home his point. One has stayed with me for the past thirty years — a rather petulant looking figure with a crown askew on his head, shouting 'A king does not have to give reasons'. The consultant used to use this to illustrate the weakness of solitary and dictatorial leadership for in failing to give reasons, a king would quickly lose the support of his subjects and descend into force, brutality and probably irrelevance.

It is almost a truism to say that in education, everyone has a leadership role. But given the nature of today's schools, colleges and universities it is true that leadership in learning is no longer simply left to teachers or even head teachers or principals. Students are, and should be, encouraged to lead their own learning activity and to share leadership with others with whom they work. All teachers help to lead their students and the collective process of learning whilst educational managers lead both continuing activity and the shared responsibility for change. Where then does that leave an Education Minister particularly in a country where decisions about the delivery of learning in schools as well as in universities and colleges is the *de jure* as well as the *de facto* responsibility of others?

Leadership in education is a matter of persuasion, inspiration and example. An Education Minister has to set the tone, support others who are taking ideas forward and hold a space open for positive growth and development, within the context of his or her strategic vision. The interactions with all parts of the educational spectrum need to take place in a constructive but clear fashion, with collaboration the key note.

Successful educational leadership from Ministers and all other educational players is about giving reasons and showing cause, ensuring that there is a process of collective consideration that leads to movement forward. Of course, sometimes the pressure of circumstance makes this ideal difficult to achieve, and the intervention of the human misunderstanding, mischief and even malevolence can play havoc with it. But it must always remain the ideal and as much the norm as possible.

For a nationalist politician in Scotland over the past few decades, leadership has also meant ploughing — which has appeared to be (at times) — a lonely furrow. The present progress towards the referendum was by no means a foregone conclusion even a generation ago and for those of us who remained in the party after the rise and fall of the SNP in the 1970s, political leadership was as much the sound of voices in the wilderness as anything else. Scotland was led at that time by those who had, to misquote Parnell, said 'thus far and no further' and the challenge of keeping the leadership of a cause and a vision alive was a difficult one. It is even harder to make it grow and flourish from such arid ground, something that the present First Minister has been almost single handedly and quite brilliantly able to do.

The wider question of Scotland being led to independence within the context of the difficult financial situation across Europe needs those skills like never before but they can only be fully exercised if all the levers of power are available here in Scotland. That is not yet the case, as the final decision on completing the powers of the Parliament still needs to be made by the Scottish people.

Contrasting what Scotland can achieve by leading these islands in human concern and compassion with the wholesale callous destruction of potential which is taking place south of the border would be one good way to do it. Another will be to point to the success of small countries across Europe and the leadership their people provide to the continent.

Scots will also want to be reassured that those things they regard as central to their sense of themselves will not only be preserved if they choose independence but will also flourish. Education, one of the few areas of distinctively Scottish policy actively protected after the Act of Union of 1707, is undoubtedly amongst those issues and, therefore, a clear direction, a confident leadership — *primus inter pares* — and a firm advocacy of what makes our system good, becoming great will be crucial in the weeks and months ahead.

3.5.8.   Government: Non-Departmental Public Body

Neil Hunter

I have experienced both good and indifferent management and leadership over my 20 years in providing health and social care services in the public and voluntary sectors. The most inspiring leaders I have worked with have vision, create direction, can motivate others and demonstrate passion and enthusiasm.

People respond to positive leadership and leaders that can demonstrate understanding and empathy, clarity and certainty, promote stability and diminish ambiguity, are much more likely to be positive leaders. Having the confidence to help people surface issues individually or as part of the team, knowing that the solution is almost certainly within the orbit of the people concerned is an important feature. The alternative is to not allow issues to surface, for them to remain hidden, unresolved and distorted.

People, no matter what their role, do not thrive in circumstances of anxiety and uncertainty, lack of clarity and understanding, and a climate of fear or duress. Quite often muscular, aggressive leaders have a sense that they are doing what is needed to get the job done in the short term, but they are at risk of eroding the very resource, using everyone's skills to best effect, they will rely upon in the longer term to get the job done, not just once but from here on in. Leaders need to be able to create the conditions in which people can develop, thrive, be productive and feel professionally and personally satisfied.

Good leadership feels like you have got someone at your back keeping you moving forward, encouraging you to do even better, to find creative solutions, giving you a sense of permission to move things on, to engage with others, and to make things happen. Good leaders relish and value teamwork and work to the collective whole.

Leadership for me is a way of optimising human potential amongst people who work for the team/group/organisation you have been given responsibility for or work within. Leadership may not always be hierarchical, but it is always, in my view, about the quality of relationships, about the creation of a direction and vision, and a sense of security and solidarity amongst and with each other. Good leadership builds confidence, does not destroy it, and seeks to eliminate anxiety and not promote it, brings people together, and does not divide them.

Creating more devolution within organisations, distributing leadership responsibilities across organisations and investing and bolstering leadership at the level of operational front line delivery to individuals and communities are consistent with socially progressive movements that seek to empower people to promote engagement, dialogue and understanding. Leadership seeks to — if not dismantle, then certainly to — limit the influence of remote, technocratic, inert structures divorced from the reality of the lives of many of our communities. It believes that people, working in organisations and providing services, have skills and talents that need to be given a platform to flourish and develop. The challenge for leadership in the United Kingdom and Europe at this moment in our history, then, is to: ensure that these ideas and principles are used progressively; to value the ethos of public service; to ensure they are tasked to promote social justice; to challenge inequality and discrimination; and to value human solidarity and the place of community, in the face of economic and political forces that value accumulation, concentration, centralisation of power and decision-making in the hands of a narrow elite.

The challenges in public sector organisations, particularly those working and engaging with vulnerable communities and 'at risk' populations, will undoubtedly be to avoid decision-making becoming increasingly centralised and removed from the day-to-day concerns of our communities, the people who live in them, and the staffs who service them. That is not to say that doing things once, and doing them efficiently and well is not important — it is. The leadership challenge for us all is about ensuring we can deliver improved quality and efficiency at the same time as devolving as much control and power to front-line managers and services. This is to ensure decision-making is as close to our communities as possible and not concentrated in an ever diminishing cohort of managers, planners, technical experts and policy makers.

Devolving responsibility and power in organisations is difficult. It can be seen as a weak response by those leaders who seek to centralise and create omnipotence in command and control structures. But yet it is crucial, I believe, to building sustainable, sensitive public organisations, in touch with their communities, and making decisions with people, informed by real world known needs, concerns and priorities.

Organisations which embrace devolved and empowering practices can improve the management, innovation, communication and problem solving of its (previously constrained) team leadership arrangements. Similarly, empowered organisations, with high levels of devolution to unit/team level, have stronger team performance, increased employee satisfaction and better employee relations.

Key to the challenges faced by organisations going through this kind of journey is the extent to which the organisation, its leadership and its teams can create a genuine empowerment climate, with open channels of communication, trusting relationships, understanding of organisational purpose and direction, and a commitment to high standards of principled ethics and shared values amongst and between its leaders and staff.[28]

Responding positively to this challenge for culture change will, in the future, enable us to respond much more sensitively to local needs to make decisions that will take account of local and community issues in a much more robust and systematic way. This is a much more sustainable model for the future, with operational and resource deployment decisions being made at a much closer point to the needs of people in need, as opposed to being made at the centre of organisations, allowing co-production and co-design of services to be much more realistically attainable.

Engagement within organisations at all levels is absolutely key to the creation of an empowering organisational culture, improved performance, motivation, morale and job satisfaction. It is the job of leaders to create this dynamic, to generate the vision and energy to move it forward, to keep it on track and to coach others in its virtue and efficacy.

3.5.9.   The Forestry Commission

Douglas Howieson

My experience of leadership stems from early discussions with my father in the 1980s. My father — who by that time was nearing retirement — used to offer such maxims as: *You should never ask a man to do something that you can't do yourself.* To be fair to dad, I have taken the time to reflect upon whether this maxim stands the test of time in the modern environment.

Whilst no longer at the coalface, I do have in my team, machine operators who are highly trained, skilled and talented in the way that they operate state-of-the-art timber harvesting monster machines — I could never do what they do without their level of training and consolidation and I could not get anywhere near their output or professional competence given our rigorous trainability testing and our machine operator selection criteria. So, in order to show good leadership, should I aim to make a fool of myself by trying to compete or impress them? I think not, but my father's maxim may have stood up in a previous generation where manual output was possibly less complex.

As a young forester with a front-line squad of workers, I certainly had to push them on a daily basis through piecework payment methodology but now in a strategic planning and larger team leadership role, I look to pull the team

---

28. For example, see Hartog and De Hoogh (2009).

around me in to a cohesive force where everyone buys in to, and understands, the intellectual and physical challenges that we face in modern forest ecosystem management.

I guess my perception of leadership could be gauged to be a cousin of my father's maxim to the extent that leadership should understand, value and reward everything that contributes to good team performance and output whilst not necessarily taking direct charge of every task or intervening in every aspect of daily delivery when effective controls are in place. I do, however, put great store and trust in the traditional management hierarchy as experience has shown me that a flat structure can more often simply result in the delegation of inappropriate levels of authority without credible or reasonable remuneration. This can also cause ineffective and confused decision-making.

For me, leadership means that I am respected but not necessarily liked by everyone. The latter aspect is seldom always possible given that — although in my organisation we have succeeded in our desire to achieve unified terms and conditions for the whole organisation, where previously there was a management team and an industrial workforce — there will always be a need to take up the less pleasant challenges of management which, on occasion, includes dealing with, for example, poor performance. Paradoxically, to fail to do so is, in itself, poor performance but to manage people properly, giving no quarter to those who would seek to undermine the team or the organisation for personal gain or because there is a resentment harboured, is simply right and fair to others.

The great task for me in leadership is to bring a team member back in to the fold or to achieve improved morale through effective leadership of our greatest asset — the team. Moreover, spotting and developing potential that exists in the team and watching as that talent flourishes, as a result of our organisational encouragement and facilitation, is without doubt, one of the greatest pleasures in management and a sure signal of effective leadership, both as an individual leader, and within an organisational culture.

I foresee that for the United Kingdom and Europe, in these times of change and recession, the biggest challenge in leadership will be to develop our skills, confidence and willingness in delegation and to ensure that those being delegated to are properly trained, empowered and remunerated for the extra responsibility that is surely coming their way. Behind this is that every public sector organisation seems to be working on or implementing plans to respond to austerity measures. My observation of these plans seems to have a reduction in workforce (and hence salary and overhead costs) as a central plank. I then find myself wondering what other organisations are doing to respond to the need to work more smartly with the resources that remain at their disposal in terms of the workforce. My organisation has been incredibly skilled and successful in creating a staff reduction strategy, which gives management the ability to reduce the head count while ensuring that all of the skill and talent does not walk out the door at the same time with experience and dedication being lost to early retirement and redundancy.

It is only with forethought and the ability to look ahead that good leaders maintain the resource necessary to grow the business during times of forced or chosen austerity. Unfortunately, there is tension between making redundant the longest serving staff that generally cost the most, and at the same time, losing vital experience and operational knowledge.

We are going to need to develop new maxims to take over from some of those used by my father and his generation. Our new maxims should address how to do more with fewer staff in the public sector. I feel a maxim coming on now … . *Never gold plate the job when you haven't the resources to do so.* What does this mean? Should we work smarter and find new ways of doing things and continue to investigate and innovate so that we don't drop our standards in the public sector — you're dead right, and it's going to need good leaders.

3.6.   Analysis and Conclusions

The analysis of the reflections in this section follows a structured approach. First, the reflections essays are summarised in tabular form with the themes Experience, Perception, Means, Challenges and Sector. This summary is shown in Table 3.1. Second, thematic interpretational content analysis is used to analyse the summaries, allowing knowledge to be generated via the emergence and interpretation of themes. Content analysis was used rather than a software package such as NVivo to ensure that we were not distanced from the data gestalt (Davis & Meyer, 2009). Third, the themes are grouped into a 'totality'. This approach allowed the themes to become (and form) a comprehensive picture of the contributors' collective thoughts on leadership in the public sector. This, then, offered and would offer:

- Comparison with extant academic leadership thinking within this sector
- Comparison with the third sector

3.6.1.   *Content Analysis*

3.6.1.1. Experience

> My understanding and experience of leadership, and all that it means, has developed incrementally over a lifetime, informed and challenged by a diversity of experience and circumstance. I firmly believe that my appetite for change and risk was embedded at an early age
>
> Sue Bruce

Table 3.1: Essay summaries — Experience, perception, means, challenges and sector.

Name	Experience	Perception	Means	Challenges	Sector
Bhogal	• Provision of leadership to staff • Operationalising strategy	• A 'way of working' • Not just from top of organisation • Product of behaviour, situation, contexts • Need to see behaviours at all levels	• Allows organisation to consider its purpose • How it will fulfil this purpose • Allows engagement and empowerment	• Must innovate despite restrictions in finance • Must continue to empower and engage	• Organisation to embrace business changes associated with technology
Clare	• Leadership (esp. project planning and negotiation) skills developed from private sector previous roles	• Communication (transmission and listening) • Focus • Involvement • Setting example/role model and explaining outcomes/benefits	• Listening, learning from all • Apply arguments to suggestions • Persuasion to encourage buy-in of command and control	• Overcoming resistance and having to change workforce shape and size	• Widen recruitment pool (esp. from private) and strategy • Performance management needs to be better • Flatter organisation • Reduce clinicians' power • Change structure — too managerial/bureaucratic
McKenzie	• From university and work • Very practical • Requires a broad perspective • Not command and control	• Reality of what is really going on is always found at the coalface • Speak to one's 'troops' • Work with good people and build your team to complement strengths • Collective benefit	• Leadership is not well understood • About us as people • Authentic • Developing the right culture in an organisation is key	• Economic environment • Ability to adjust to working in a different way	• March of technology and science • Increasing population of elderly people

Table 3.1: (*Continued*)

Name	Experience	Perception	Means	Challenges	Sector
Ireland	• Variety of roles in the NHS/medicine since graduating from medical school	• Galvanise the development of teams, organisations and strategy • Style: empowered, enabled and supported • Develop values and a culture that enables trust and respect, leading to a sustainable distributive model of leadership	• Self-awareness, personal development, strategic 'nous' professional focus • Influence/place one's head 'above the parapet' if required	• Media, demographic, technological advances • Our inability to understand and articulate the opportunities of above	• Demographic changes, financial challenges, the need to invest in community proactive services, the need to disinvest in Acute Care environments, and understanding the impact that possible Scottish independence could have
Sunderland	• From poor performance	• Visibility	• Communicate	• Lack of command and control/structure • Designated leadership roles for doctors • Reward and discipline • Leading disparate groups • Need to agree a medical agenda	• Meeting spaces allowing for sharing of values and aspirations • Information management skills • Few identifiable medical leaders • Confusion between leadership and management
Grice	• From sport • First boss	• Made not born but certain natural attributes are	• Do something with purpose and value • Soft power	• Declining resources • Rising demand • Identify resources	• Independence referendum

	• Practice in leading more demanding teams • Work in progress	important (intellect, extroversion, optimism)	• Authenticity	• Make difficult decisions	• More with less • Use of reserve forces • Loss of interest in the military • Soldiers need to valued, supported and resourced
Cooper	• From 36 years as soldier • Same as platoon to 3*, general star but many shades • Key words: cohesion, unify, resourced, empowered	• Selection and maintenance of the aim • Do not be swayed by this	• Requires study and self-analysis • Structure does help leadership: it gives moral and intellectual framework • Needs of mission and team may take priority • Truth-based leadership culture • Need ARAR • Need to give direction and be empowered with ARAR to get effect	• Finance	
Giles	• From 33 years in Royal Air Force	• Multi-layered series of relationships • About people — it is messy • An art form • Be self-aware, know what is to be achieved, how it will be done and why it needs to be done • EQ, IQ, SQ and combination raises	• Individual or collective service to community • Serve to lead • To act as a catalyst to enable and empower the contribution and growth of others to achieve a shared, meaningful aim	• Need to work collaboratively • Build respect, rapport and trust • Nurture, establish and maintain cooperative and mutually supportive relationships	• To ensure that its people are fully empowered to operate independently and as members of a team, both within their own service and with wider parties • To achieve more than has been asked of them than before is directly related to the

Table 3.1: (*Continued*)

Name	Experience	Perception	Means	Challenges	Sector
		management to art of leadership			quality of the leader–follower relationship and the support provided by third parties
Gray	• Difference between strategic, operational and tactical level • Different requirements at each level	• In defence, leadership is luxury because, at the end of the day, leaders at all levels just give orders • The alternative viewpoint is that those in defence have raised the art (and possibly the science) of leadership to new levels	• To embrace development and education	• To maintain the standards and levels of leadership education • Technological challenges and innovation • Organisations are led by an older generation who are invariably more conservative than the younger and more technologically adept. Admitting one's shortcomings in this field for the greater benefit of the organisation is not easy	
Jupp	• Examples of leadership around	• Everyone's view of leadership is coloured by their experience of	• Every leader at all levels needs to know the context within	• Low or no growth • Leaders need to shape the expectations of	• How do we do more with less?

- me — both good and bad
- The old expression that if you want to learn about something, teach it, is also true!

- it wherever that be from

- which they are working and the purpose their team is there for
- Leadership then becomes the relationship between the leader and his or her followers where the leader persuades the followers to do (or not to do) things
- Philosophy of Mission Command
- Attributes don't make leaders; they help the leadership in an organisation

- everyone to fit these circumstances as public sector spending inevitably shrinks
- We need to understand the new context within which we work and think differently about what we do

- How to lead without authority, how to lead different types of groups
- Flexibility and agility
- Leaders will need to know all the different types of people who make up their team and to lead the necessary changes in behaviour and attitude

Gargan

- From police career
- Leadership is a great privilege and pleasure
- False paradox that was presented between leadership and management

- Quality of strategy and quality of the relationship between the leader and the led at all levels in the organisation

- Indispensable ingredients:
  - ➤ Integrity
  - ➤ Knowledge
  - ➤ Strategy
  - ➤ Ambassadorship
  - ➤ An understanding of, and a commitment to, effective organisational performance

- Modernising, connecting and shrinking simultaneously
- Learn a new skill set from a leadership cadre who, in most cases, learned how to lead in times of relative plenty
- Wide-spread re-thinking of the role of Government

- The emerging cyber threat
- Incentives to collaborate are sometimes difficult to find given its challenges
- Governments demand economies of scale

Table 3.1: (*Continued*)

Name	Experience	Perception	Means	Challenges	Sector
				• The ability for the United Kingdom and Europe to defend themselves effectively from external threats and from threats that cannot be authenticated • Developing the skills to deal with this changing world will be a key challenge	
Thornton	• From career	• Leadership and management are both necessary • No self-interest	• Relationship with followers and outside world to get an outside-in perspective • Set example • Creating supportive and trusting culture	• Austerity	• Relationships with professionals changing: more wary and critical, require more openness and trust • Lead transformational change
Johnson	• From work/career	• Develop those who come after me • Resilience • Call on support • Taking time to invest in yourself is time well spent	• What one would see in the organisation as being different • To consider how one's staffs see you, as the leader • Strategic planning — to paint a picture:	• Driving and delivering change is the biggest challenge • Succession planning in the service • Potential merging of the blue light services	• Leading organisational change

Brand	• From private sector and public sector in a variety of roles	• L & M are required: 3 domains and 4 levels • Change leads on from this	• Change is a psychological journey to be led rather than a task to be managed	• You need time out — you need thinking time about the future, the opportunities, the behaviours expected and how we should interact with each other • Senior teams are shrinking and the time they have to discuss and think ahead is very limited	• Reducing budgets • Customers and citizens want more • Customer and client are in full control • 'What do you need and how can we help to provide this?' • Many key challenges: leaders who don't understand this and merely propose service cuts are failing	• Finding a common purpose • Managing complexity between the interrelated parts of the organisation and the wider community systems within which the organisation operates; developing communities to co-deliver services to reduce unsustainable demand; innovation • Better management and leadership competence
Bruce	• Grown and developed (incrementally) over a lifetime via a range of experiences including childhood • I provide managerial and professional	• Strong and weak leadership in the United Kingdom today	• People look for support, direction, guidance and defence • Effective leadership is not about heroic leadership • Distributed leadership model		• Referendum in Scotland • Financial position of the United Kingdom and the importance of sustaining and developing further our economy	• Focusing on the delivery of effective outcomes, providing public leadership and supporting the development of leadership in all our communities

Table 3.1: (*Continued*)

Name	Experience	Perception	Means	Challenges	Sector
	leadership and the political leadership is provided by elected councillors and officials				• We must provide 21st century services and meet 21st century expectations in a construct that is, arguably, 100 years old • Very little headspace to have these conversations
Looney	• Peers and colleagues • Members of the community • Political leadership • Managerial leadership • Leadership is enormously powerful	• At its best when I'm not conscious of being led; I feel empowered, supported and convinced, confident and certain • The best leaders have worked with me, persuading and influencing, encouraging and without me realising, carefully directing	• Strange, nebulous force that motivates, drives and cajoles me • Emanates from are variety of sources	• Expectations about what local government is for, what public servants do, and how councils should be run are changing • The reduction in resources available and the reduced size of organisations • Communication and dialogue with local communities	• Pace of change and transition is quicker than ever before • Context of work uncertain and in many respects more complex • Expectations are changing • Reduction in resources • Reduced size of organisations • Technological developments
Mullin	• From support to leaders of major public sector bodies, both within	• Most people have a very clear intuitive sense of what is meant by leadership, but	• Leadership has got very little to do with position in a hierarchy	• At a time therefore when leadership is required as never before, we can often	• Those arguing for change are often drowned out by the complacent and vested

the United Kingdom and elsewhere
- Regardless of the sector however, I have found leadership challenges and responses surprisingly similar

once something more formal and precise is required it becomes a much more elusive concept. Part of the problem is that it is often considered to be an inherent quality of people inhabiting senior positions
- Also, it is unlikely to be immediately associated with those lower down organisations
- Leadership is not so neatly distributed

- Leadership requires intelligence and foresight
- Intelligent leadership is most often found in collectives
- The future of leadership is probably going to see the fall of traditional forms of hierarchical leadership, in addition to the rise of new, collective and intelligent forms

find a lack of intelligent leadership

interest of hierarchical leaderships

Russell
- Note: all from work

- In education, everyone has a leadership role
- Leadership in Scottish education is a matter of persuasion, inspiration and example
- The interactions with all parts of the educational spectrum need to take place in a constructive but clear fashion, with

- Leadership as a collective as well as an individual responsibility
- Leadership is about giving reasons and showing cause, ensuring that there is a process of collective consideration that leads to movement forward

- The wider question of Scotland being led to independence within the context of the difficult financial situation across Europe (exacerbated by the UK coalition's dangerous deflationary austerity agenda) needs those skills like never before but they can only be fully exercised if all the levers of power

- Clear direction, a confident leadership — primus inter pares — and a firm advocacy of what makes our system good, becoming great will be crucial in the weeks and months ahead

Table 3.1: (*Continued*)

Name	Experience	Perception	Means	Challenges	Sector
		collaboration the key note		are available here in Scotland • Persuading Scots to take on that leadership role will be a vital task	
Hunter	• From local government and from a variety of sources	• You've got someone at your back keeping you moving forward, encouraging you to do even better, to find creative solutions, giving you a sense of permission to move things on, to engage with others and to make things happen • Good leaders relish and value teamwork and work to the collective whole	• Optimising human potential • Not always be hierarchical, but it is always about the quality of relationships, about the creation of a direction and vision, and a sense of security and solidarity amongst and with each other • Builds confidence, doesn't destroy it and seeks to eliminate anxiety and not promote it, brings people together and doesn't divide them	• Avoid decision-making becoming increasingly centralised • Deliver improved quality and efficiency at the same time as devolving as much control and power to front-line managers and services	• Extent to which the organisation, its leadership and its teams can create a genuine 'empowerment climate', with open channels of communication, trusting relationships, understanding of organisational purpose and direction, and a commitment to high standards of principled ethics and shared values amongst and between its leaders and staff

| Howieson | • Maxims
• Tactical level: 'push'
• Strategic level: 'align' | • Plurality and team performance
• Empower/do not 'micro-manage'
• Hierarchies are relevant/appropriate | • Importance of earning respect
• Coaching and development of individuals
• Improving morale | • Delegation
• Empowerment
• Correct remuneration
• Workforce, talent and resource planning and management | • Work smarter
• Criticality
• Innovation |

In considering these reflections, it was judged as important to understand where one's experience of leadership comes from in addition to how it is actually 'experienced'.

In looking at the reflections, it would seem that the authors' experience of leadership seems to come from work itself. Few authors (bar Bruce and Grice) have mentioned leadership development from school and sport — we consider this to be very interesting. Is this because we only assume that leadership is an 'adult thing'? This is in contrast to the literature where there is an emerging and significant body of knowledge around pre-adult leadership development including coaching/mentoring at school (Murphy & Johnson, 2011) and indeed, as far back as infancy including the relationship between attachment theory and predicted leadership outcomes (Howieson, Kahn, & Thiagarajah, 2003; Keller, 2003; Popper & Amit, 2009).

In terms of how leadership is experienced, Gray and Howieson comment on leadership being different (with different competencies being required) by level; for example, at the strategic, operational and tactical levels. In this respect, Howieson offers that his leadership style (philosophy) changed from 'push' to 'align' as his seniority increased in his organisation.

All authors do comment on leadership development as their careers and lives have advanced (e.g. see material by Ireland and Cooper). In parallel, McKenzie and Bhogal note that their experience has actually come from 'doing leadership'. Of note, few, if any, authors attribute education (higher and executive) to their leadership experience. Johnson does mention the fact that she did an MBA as part of her overall development.

Various authors (Sunderland and Jupp) note that learning from others (both good and bad) has been a leadership experience and Looney makes the point that it [leadership] has surprised by its source: *My experiences of leadership within local government have surprised by their source; often although not always, the best leadership has come from unexpected places.* She goes on to state that sources have included peers and colleagues, members of the community, and people from outside the workplace. Of note, she further comments: ... *there are different ways of thinking about how I approach the challenges in the workplace. This transferability is striking and connects to a big future challenge as the boundary between personal and professional becomes increasingly fuzzy.*

Leadership as a 'powerful experience' is stated by several of the contributors. In addition, some suggest that it is broadly similar across the sector and in and between sub-sectors. For example, Mullin comments: *Most of my work has been within the education sector, but I have also been involved in the vocational training, science, and fisheries sectors. Regardless of the sector, however, I have found leadership challenges and responses surprisingly similar.*

Several contributors (Brand, Gargan, and Thornton) comment about the experience of leadership being different to the managerial experience. Gargan notes: *As I developed through the Police Service I was very conscious of a false paradox that was presented between leadership and management.* Gray does, however, introduce another variable to this duality (leadership and management) — that of command authority:[29] *But actually having to tell someone to do something or more usually not to do it, is a much rarer occurrence outside of actual combat. In any event, in most circumstances the military-speak term is command rather than leadership — an equally complex subject which involves the right to legal sanction to back up those orders.*

3.6.1.2. Perceptions

I perceive leadership to be a multi-layered series of relationships. It is a relationship between a leader and one or more followers and we are all both leaders and followers depending on the situations we inhabit. Leadership is also a relationship between conflicting desires, limitations and opportunities which must be balanced in order to achieve an aim. A leader needs to know: who he is — be self-aware; what is to be achieved; how he intends to achieve it; and, fundamentally, why it is worth his efforts and those of her/his followers

Amanda Giles

According to the Concise Oxford Dictionary (1995), perception is defined as: *An interpretation or impression based on one's understanding of something.*

In setting this question, we were interested in understanding how the authors perceived leadership. In addition, it was considered to be important to determine if this perception was different to their leadership experiences.

The answers to this question were grouped, for ease of analysis, into four subthemes: ideal state; what it looks like; good and bad; and confusing.

Ideal state. In this respect, we understand 'ideal state' to be what leadership should be. Several authors describe this state:

Bhogal: *My perception is that leadership is 'a way of working' and it requires behaviours to be demonstrated rather than just personality.*

Gargan: *But the two biggest determinants of successful leadership in my perception are the quality of strategy — the leaders' thinking, the plan, the mission and second the quality of the relationship between the leader and the led at all levels in the organisation.*

Ireland: *My perception of leadership is that leaders should create opportunities to galvanise the development of teams, organisations, and strategy that address key issues in a way that enables all that are involved to feel empowered, enabled, and supported.*

---

29. See again Howieson and Kahn (2002) and Grint (2005).

What it looks like.   In this respect, we regard this as how the authors see leadership at present or how they think others see leadership. For example:

> Giles: *Leadership founded on trust and mutual respect between leaders and followers; shared goals and a sense of achievement when those goals are met or exceeded; and honest empowerment and acceptance of responsibility are universally important, no matter the context.*

> Gray: *All too often, the perception of leadership in defence is that it is a bit of a luxury because, at the end of the day, leaders at all levels just give orders.*

> Looney: *Leadership is enormously powerful. It has had a significant impact on my personal attitudes to work; to my motivation and confidence in what I am doing — in some respects to my own self esteem. It has shown me that used creatively and positively, leadership can make a massive difference to my own willingness to push the boundaries and really extend my own efforts; while the best has shown me that carefully used tactics enable and support the delivery of that leader's strategy and vision. More than anything, my experiences have shown me that leadership can come from many places, and when it is most effective in its impact, for me, it is when those multiple leaders coalesce.*

> Thornton: *Leadership is essentially about having a relationship with followers and so the need to engage, to listen, and to build trust is paramount.*

Good and bad.   Several authors note and comment on this area. For example:

> Bruce: *My perception in the UK today is that we have, unsurprisingly a wide variation in leadership examples — from a spectrum of very strong leadership through to weak, less effective leadership — a somewhat mixed bag.*

> Sunderland: *Poor leadership leads to poor team performance — this is recognised in many walks of life and in organisations, big and small.*

Can be confusing.   Several authors allude to the confusing nature of leadership. For example:

> Giles: *Leadership is messy. It is about people. It is not a science but an art.*

> Gray: *Leadership in defence is a complex and emotive issue.*

> Looney: *Leadership is a strange, nebulous force that motivates, drives and cajoles me.*

Mackenzie: *I don't think leadership is that well understood. I always think it's very hard to define but you do know it when you see it. I perceive it as fascinating and it has drawn me to it.*

Overall, the answers were different to leadership experience. Experience, we consider, is how leadership is developed and actually enacted. Perception on the other hand is how the authors 'view' or understand it.

3.6.1.3. Means

Leadership may not always be hierarchical, but it is always, in my view, about the quality of relationships, about the creation of a direction and vision, and a sense of security and solidarity amongst and with each other

Neil Hunter

There are literally thousands of books and articles on this subject. Reminding ourselves why this book was written, we were very keen to understand what leadership means to these people who undertake a variety of demanding jobs at the 'coalface'.

Unsurprisingly, a variety of responses are offered. This is commensurate with the many ways of interpreting leadership which is introduced in Chapter 2. For ease of analysis, however, the answers are grouped again around five sub-themes: levels of analysis; personal qualities; philosophies; self-awareness, insight and soft skills; and its difference to management and command and control.

Levels of analysis. Mullin is very clear that leadership is not a function of hierarchy. He notes: *Reflecting on personal experience, I would argue that leadership has got very little to do, indeed anything to do, with position in a hierarchy.* Although not a function of status or position, Giles, Gray and Jupp (all Royal Air Force officers) comment on the importance of understanding leadership by level of responsibility; for example Gray points out: *Issues of leadership are further complicated by the levels at which it is exercised.* This thinking, and comment, is consistent with the literature. For example, levels of conceptualisation for leadership are shown at Figure 2.1 and discussed in Chapter 2.

Johnson's reflections and self-analysis, for example, is clearly set at the strategic level of her organisation, which is commensurate with her role as Chief Executive Officer.

Personal qualities. Many authors offer personal qualities associated with leadership. Representative examples include:

Claire: *Specialising in business change leadership is about listening to ideas ... involving people, leaving no one out of the loop, and communicating clearly to everyone.*

> Gargan: *Leadership has a handful of Indispensable ingredients: integrity, knowledge, strategy, and ambassadorship.*

Philosophies. This sub-theme elicited most responses. We consider that the authors were keen to comment on their own leadership philosophy. We also suggest that these answers align with the 'philosophy approach' that was introduced in Chapter 2. Several key words appear in the analysis including: 'servant' leadership (Giles); the importance of engagement (Bhogal, Ireland, Grice, Gray and Hunter); empowering (Bhogal, Giles, Bruce and Hunter); and a creative and supportive culture (Ireland, Mackenzie, Cooper, Thornton, Johnson, Brand and Hunter).

Self-awareness, insight and soft skills. Many authors also comment on the importance of self-awareness and analysis and developing greater insights of themselves (i.e. Johnson). Giles introduces emotional and spiritual intelligence in addition to the accepted intellectual intelligence accepted as a necessary attributes for a leader. In addition, Ireland comments on the importance of personal understanding and an acceptance of personal limitations and Grice discusses conscious self-development and the importance of authenticity.

Not command and control and management. Several authors also comment on the difference between leadership and management including Brand, Gargan, Gray and Thornton.

3.6.1.4. Challenges

> They need to be able to translate and interpret what they see on the horizon and to make sense of the implications. It requires new emphasis on the ability of those leaders to build sustainable relationships, to build a sense of value, and enable people to understand why things are being done, even when they do not agree with them. This presents a big challenge for leaders – politically and managerially as it is genuinely unchartered territory.
>
> Sophia Looney

The leadership challenges were generally described at the macro-(environmental) level. These challenges are grouped around the sub-themes of: political, economic, socio-cultural and technical.[30]

Political. Russell — perhaps unsurprisingly — makes political comment in his essay. Mackenzie is perhaps more forthright and critical in the challenges of dealing

---

30. A full PESTLE analysis would normally include legal and environmental considerations. It is interesting to note that none of the authors commented on these (legal and environmental) challenges.

with politicians. For example she states: *Politicians need to work differently to achieve this, it's a totally changing set of circumstances ... Politicians are still operating under the old rules and have been very slow to grasp this nettle.* Perhaps, this is also alluded to by Bruce when she offers: *We must provide 21st century services and meet 21st century expectations in a construct that is, arguably, 100 years old.*

Economic. This sub-theme is analysed further via:

- Demography: Ireland comments on an ageing demographic becoming a significant challenge. Of note, Gray actually comments on the challenge of being led by older people. He states: *The highly structured bureaucracy of defence, and the costs of shedding senior personnel, means that the organisations are led by an older generation who are invariably more conservative than the younger and more technologically adept. Admitting ones shortcomings in this field for the greater benefit of the organisation is not easy.*
- Many authors make reference to money/austerity (Bhogal, Cooper, Thornton, Brand and Bruce). Perhaps this is not surprising considering that the authors operate in a sector that has undergone a significant financial 'squeeze' since 2010. Grice writes more generally commenting on declining resources and Jupp makes note of the problems of little or no economic growth.

Socio-cultural. Several authors (e.g. Giles and Jupp) recognise that socio-cultural changes will affect leadership thinking and practice.

Technological. Many authors discuss the on-going challenges of technology: innovation (Bhogal, Gray); IT/IS/www — where is this taking us? (McKenzie, Gray); and associated threats (Ireland, Gray, Gargan).

More generally, some authors look at these challenges from a meta-level of analysis. For example, McKenzie states: *The leadership challenge has to paint a picture of a new future balancing some of the downsides with possible upsides, like our food may actually be what we thought it was!.* In addition: Ireland is concerned about our inability to understand and articulate the opportunities of these challenges; Jupp who talks about a new context; and Gargan who offers modernising, connecting, shrinking simultaneously and the leadership implications thereof.

Certainly, these challenges do suggest:

- New forms of leadership and not management will be required (which echoes the thoughts of Brookes & Grint, 2010)
- Some people may have trouble accepting this/keeping up (see Looney, Hunter and Clare)
- Changing leadership philosophies including distributed approaches (Bruce and Looney)
- The importance of alignment towards common goals
- The management of multiple expectations by many stakeholders
- Succession planning

- Implementing, urgently, a new leadership approach
- Critically, our actual inability to understand and articulate the opportunities of above

3.6.1.5. Sector

> What does this mean? Should we work smarter and find new ways of doing things and continue to investigate and innovate so that we don't drop our standards in the public sector — you're dead right, and it's going to need good leaders
>
> Douglas Howieson

The reflections offer many sector-specific challenges, which include:

- Meeting spaces allowing for sharing of values and aspirations
- To deliberate, be allowed not to understand, and to try and make sense of this change and what it means (Bruce discusses the importance of 'headspace')
- Helping people develop, learn, and skills uptake
- The importance of valuing, supporting and resourcing
- Empowering and team membership
- Importance of leader−follower relationships
- Leading without authority and leading diversity
- Flexibility and agility
- Managing and understanding complexity
- Common purpose
- Galvanise effort and spirit
- Leadership and management as a profession — what competencies are required?
- Is there a difference between public, political and managerial leadership?
- Enabling
- Problems with hierarchical leadership
- Critical thinking
- Role of leadership and innovation

On reflection, we do wonder if it is these that are important or is it what kind of leadership will be required to meet these challenges.

3.6.2.   Totality

A significant insight into leadership is offered by studying the authors' reflections on what leadership means to them.

Focusing specifically on leadership philosophies, we are struck by the importance of putting the *follower* at the centre of leadership (i.e. servant leadership, the focus on empowerment and creating a supportive culture). In terms of self-awareness, insight and soft skills, we also note the honesty and acceptance by the authors of their limitations and an understanding thereof of their desire to learn and develop. In addition, and in all the authors' reflections, we see a rich flavour of the philosophies that were introduced in Chapter 2; for example, adaption, authenticity, distribution, ethics, servant and sharing.

Moving on to the challenges (general) and challenges (sector specific), it is interesting to note that, from the Concise Oxford Dictionary (1995), that the words *leader* and *leadership* are actually nouns, which we judge has focus on the individual.[31] In juxtaposition, leading (enactment) is a verb and its absence is noticeable in the general discourse on leadership. The commentary, by the authors, suggests that the act of doing is very important, particularly drawing on soft skills. For example, 'doing' words and phrases include: *implementing an approach; helping people develop, learn, and skills uptake; valuing, supporting and resourcing; empowering and team membership; leading without authority and leading diversity; managing and understanding complexity; and enabling.* Perhaps, then — and on our reflection — it is time to put the verb back into leadership.

In addition, the intellectual demands of this leadership commentary are noteworthy. Gargan, for example, comments on this when he says: *But the two biggest determinants of successful leadership in my perception are the quality of strategy — the leaders' thinking, the plan, the mission and secondly the quality of the relationship between the leader and the led at all levels in the organisation.* Mullin offers: *Indeed, the future of leadership is probably going to see the fall of traditional forms of hierarchical leadership, in addition to the rise of new, collective, and intelligent forms. Only through such new forms of leadership can we expect to effectively shape our future.*

In this respect, several comments are also worth noting: *our inability to understand and articulate the opportunities of above*; *to deliberate, be allowed not to understand, and to try and make sense of this change and what it means*; *managing and understanding complexity*; *critical thinking*; and *the role of leadership and innovation.*

At this stage, it is not clear how this will be advanced. We do, however, comment about this in future research in Chapter 5.

Turning to leadership thinking within the public sector, we are reminded of some of the theory which is included earlier in this chapter:

---

31. Howieson and Summers (2014) argue that we need to reconceptualise leadership as a public good. That is, as something not embodied in a few individuals but possessed and drawn on by all in an organisational community. They state that leadership, as is currently and widely conceptualised, taught and understood, is focussed on the exemplary individual, their special ability to produce enhanced organisational performance, and yet this is divorced from the society in which organisations are situated. This approach dominates the management (academic and practitioner) literature and suggests that leaders are seen as 'something different' or special. But, this concept of leadership is deeply flawed and has, arguably, led to a divorce of business from social usefulness (the failures in the banking industry for example) and from the communities within which they are located and upon whom their actions and decisions impact. The result has been, arguably, instability in organisations and in society.

- The criticism of individuality in leadership
- Collective endeavour, where individuals can contribute to the establishment and development of a common purpose (a common vision)
- From individuals as leaders — to the relationship between leaders and followers (or constituents, colleagues, collaborators)
- Leadership as perceived as one of the cornerstones of innovation, because it plays an important role in changing the *status quo*
- The potential for leadership is broader than has been thought hitherto. Leadership, then, seems to be about making it possible for everyone in the institution or within a network of institutions to contribute
- A shift away from traditional technical or operational roles on the one hand and from advisory roles on the other to more collaborative, networked leadership roles.
- Developing the insights necessary for successful change within complex systems
- Building the cognitive skills to manage effectively in demanding environments
- Demonstrating the emotional intelligence to motivate their people
- Building leadership at all levels of the organisation, by developing capability and ensuring that overly complex structures do not impede the ability of individuals across the organisation to exercise leadership
- A form of collective leadership
- Collaborative advantage
- Reflecting trust

We suggest that the material offered by the authors complements and supports further this theory/thinking particularly around the areas of collaboration, collective endeavour, relationships between leaders and followers, the importance of networks, insight, cognitive skills, EQ, and capability.

In addition, we judge that the authors' reflections will help scholars and theorists develop and advance further the theory in this sector, particularly the leadership philosophies that will be required to meet the many sector-specific challenges.

References

Antonacopoulou, E. P. (2010). Making the business school more 'critical': Reflexive critique based on phronesis as a foundation for impact. *British Journal of Management, 21*, s6–s25. doi:doi: 10.1111/j.1467-8551.2009.00679.x

Bekkers, V., Edelenbos, J., & Steijn, B. (2011). *Innovation in the public sector: Linking capacity and leadership*. Basingstoke: Palgrave Macmillan.

Brookes, S., & Grint, K. (2010). *The new public leadership challenge*. Basingstoke: Palgrave Macmillan.

Concise Oxford Dictionary. (1995). *English*. New York, NY: Oxford University Press.

Crosby, B. C., & Kiedrowski, J. (2006, 31 March). Theoretical foundations of integrative leadership. Presented at the Humphrey Institute Research Symposium, Minneapolis.

Davis, N. W., & Meyer, B. B. (2009). Qualitative data analysis: A procedural comparison. *Journal of Applied Sport Psychology, 21*(1), 116–124.

Dunning, J. (2008). Location and the multinational enterprise: A neglected factor? *Journal of International Business Studies, 40,* 5–19.

Ferlie, E., Ashburner, L., Fitzgerald, L., & Pettigrew, A. (1996). *New public management in action.* Oxford: Oxford University Press.

Flynn, N. (2012). *Public sector management* (6th ed.). London: Sage.

Forth Sector Development Limited. (2012). *Leadership in the new order.* A Discussion paper. Forth Sector Development Ltd. Retrieved fom www.forthsector.org.uk

Gill, R. (2012). *Theory and practice of leadership* (2nd ed.). London: Sage.

Goleman, D. (1996). *Emotional intelligence: Why it can matter more than IQ.* London: Bloomsbury Publishing.

Grint, K. (2005). Problems, problems, problems: The social construction of leadership. *Human Relations, 58*(11), 1467–1494.

Gudelis, D., & Guogis, A. (2011). Integrating public and business management: A model of interaction between public and private sectors. *International Review on Public and Non-Profit Marketing, 8*(1), 1–9.

Hallikas, J., Karkkainen, H., & Lampela, H. (2009). Learning in networks: An exploration from innovation perspective. *International Journal of Technology Management, 45*(3–4), 229–243.

Harris, A. (2009). Distributed leadership: What we know. *Studies in Educational Leadership, 7*(1), 11–21.

Hartog, D. N., & De Hoogh, A. H. B. (2009). Empowering behaviour and leader fairness and integrity: Studying perceptions of ethical leader behaviour from a levels-of-analysis perspective. *European Journal of Work and Organisational Behaviour, 18*(2), 199–230.

HMSO. (1999). *Modernising government.* London: HMSO.

Holzer, M. (2008). Culture and leadership. In R. S. Morse & T. F. Busset (Eds.), *Administrative leadership in the public sector.* Armonk: M. E. Sharpe.

Howieson, B., & Kahn, H. (2002). Leadership, management and command: The officer's trinity. In P. W. Gray & S. Cox (Eds.), *Air power leadership: Theory and practice* (pp. 15–40). Norwich: HMSO.

Howieson, W. B., Kahn, H., & Thiagarajah, T. (2003, November). Attachment theory and its implications to leadership. Presented at The British Psychological Society Annual Conference, Perth.

Howieson, W. B., & Summers, J. C. (2014). *Leadership as a public good.* Unpublished synopsis for RSA Journal.

Jessop, R. (2002). *The future of the capitalist state.* Cambridge: Polity Press.

Keller, T. (2003). Parental images as a guide to leader sensemaking: An attachment perspective in implicit leadership theories. *Leadership Quarterly, 14,* 141–160.

Kellerman, B. (2008). *Followership: How followers are creating change and changing leaders.* Cambridge, MA: Harvard Business School Press.

King, P. (2009). *Understanding housing finance* (2nd ed.). London: Rutledge.

Lawler, J. (2008). Individualization and public sector leadership. *Public Administration, 86,* 21–34.

Leavy, B., & McKiernan, P. (2009). *Strategic leadership.* Basingstoke: Palgrave Macmillan.

Leifer, R., & Delbecq, A. (1978). Organisational/environmental interchange: A model of boundary spanning activity. *The Academy of Management Review, 3*(1), 40–50.

Leslie, K., & Canwell, A. (2010). Leadership at all levels: Leading public sector organisations in an age of austerity. *European Management Journal, 28*(4), 297–305.

Lindkvist, L. (2004). Knowledge communities and knowledge collectivises: A typology of knowledge work in groups. *Journal of Management Studies, 42,* 1189–1210.

Lord Turnbull. (2012). What do we expect of public leaders. In S. Brookes & K. Grint (Eds.), *The new public leadership challenge.* Basingstoke: Palgrave Macmillan.

Lüscher, L., & Lewis, M. W. (2008). Organisational change and managerial sense making: Working through paradox. *Academy of Management Journal, 51,* 221–240.

Moran, M. (2003). *The British regulatory state.* Oxford: Oxford University Press.

Morse, R. S., Busset, T. F., & Kinghorn (Eds.). (2007). *Administrative leadership in the public sector.* Armonk: M. E. Sharpe.

Murphy, S. E., & Johnson, S. K. (2011). The benefits of a long-lens approach to leader development: Understanding the seeds of leadership. *The Leadership Quarterly, 22*(3), 459–470.

Ojasalo, J. (2008). Management of innovation networks: A case study of different approaches. *European Journal of Innovation Management, 11,* 51–86.

Performance and Innovation Unit. (2001). Strengthening leadership in the public sector. A research study by the PIU, Cabinet Office, UK.

Popper, M., & Amit, K. (2009). Attachment and leader's development via experiences. *The Leadership Quarterly, 20,* 749–763.

Raffell, J. A., Leisink, P., & Middlebrookes, A. E. (2009). *Public sector leadership: International challenges and perspectives.* Cheltenham: Edward Elgar.

Starling, G. (2010). *Managing the public sector* (9th ed.). Boston, MA: Wadsworth.

Stevenson, A. (2013). *The public sector: Managing the unmanageable.* London: Kogan Page.

Thorne, J. I. (1992). Oregon plan approach. In M. A. Strosberg, J. M. Wiener, R. Baker, & A. I. Fein (Eds.), *Rationing America's medical care: The Oregon plan and beyond* (p. 31). Washington, DC: Brookings Institution.

Thorpe, R., Gold, J., & Lawler, J. (2011). Locating distributed leadership. *International Journal of Management Reviews, 13,* 239–250.

Trevor, J., & Kilduff, M. (2012). Leadership fit for the information age. *Strategic HR Review, 11*(93), 150–155.

Van Wart, M. (2003). Public-sector leadership theory: An assessment. *Public Administration Review, 63*(2), 214–228.

Van Wart, M., & Dicke, L. (Eds.). (2008). *Administrative leadership in the public sector.* Armonk: M. E. Sharpe.

Vermak, H., & Weggeman, M. (1999). Conspiring fruitfully with professionals: New management roles for professional organisations. *Management Decision, 37,* 29–44.

Worrall, R. (2009, November). Co-Creating public service leadership development in a new era of collaboration. *Proceedings of the 5th European conference on Management, Leadership & Governance,* Greece.

Zohar, D., & Marshall, I. (2000). *SQ: Connecting with our spiritual intelligence* (pp. 3–4). New York, NY: Bloomsbury Publishing.

Chapter 4

The Third Sector

A leader sees greatness in other people. You can't be much of a leader if all you see is yourself

Maya Angelou (2013)

4.1.　Introduction

In this section we aim to address the relative paucity of reflection about leadership in the third sector. First, we define what is meant by the third sector and outline the challenges it faces. Second, we provide a brief overview of the existing research on leadership in the sector, which aims to identify any common perceptions or themes. Third, we go beyond academic discussion and draw on the reflections of leaders in the sector, written in their own words. These reflections help to promote open and honest discussions of what leadership is and the challenges faced. The reflections illustrate that the organisations in the third sector are led by people who identify strongly with the work that they do and are passionate about meeting the needs of the communities that they serve. They also highlight the challenges posed by a decline in funding, coupled with a rise in demand for services. A picture is painted of how the landscape of the sector is being reshaped and how the individuals within it are being forced to reassess their approach to leadership.

4.2.　Defining the Sector

The third sector is a hugely contested terrain (Macmillan, 2010). From within the sector, lively debates eschew over what 'it' does and with what effect, whether and how it should be publicly supported or promoted, and the consequences of a closer relationship with government. Externally, there are debates about whether there is, in fact, a coherent sector (Alcock, 2010) and, if so, what it should be called (Billis, 2010).

There is, however, general agreement that delivering services of various kinds, such as welfare, is one of the many things that organisations in the sector do, with a long history going back several centuries. This has been charted by historians who have shown how the sector has operated in the development of welfare services and in relation to the emergence of the welfare state (Harris, 2010). Whether in the relief of poverty, the provision of education or rudimentary attempts at healthcare, there is a long history of people in the United Kingdom and elsewhere voluntarily coming together to serve others who are less fortunate than themselves. Many of the great social changes and innovations have been brought to fruition through the creation of voluntary, charitable and non-profit organisations. Hospital services, education, services for people with disabilities, research into disease, environmental protection and human rights campaigns have all emanated from such organisations (Hudson, 2011). The sector's role in delivering such services has been at the centre of an animated set of debates around its role, structure and reform over much of the last 25 years as well as how the sector should be defined.

In recent years, the term 'civil society' has gained in popularity as a way of defining the activities and organisations that inhabit this third sector space. Although the term 'civil society' is a relatively recent one, and been subject to a variety of different interpretations, the idea originates in the writings of the 18th century Scottish Enlightenment philosophers who, essentially, saw civil society as a bulwark against the state (Edwards, 2009). Whether today the emphasis is on civil society as the embodiment of associational life, as a promoter of the 'good' society, or as the guarantor of the public sphere, it has increasingly been seen as a banner around which different elements of the third sector can coalesce.

Civil society is, however, a concept, which encompasses more than just the third sector. First, it is wider than a group of organisations, although the role of voluntary groups and organisations is central to it. It is associational life that brings people together and allows civic values and skills to develop. Second, civil society is defined by values associated with the 'good society', which aims for social, economic and political progress. Third, civil society is defined as a space — a public sphere where debate and deliberation allow the negotiation of the common interest. Civil society is, we consider, far more extensive than the third sector, and, therefore, not an appropriate term for the sector we are examining in this chapter.

In an attempt to agree a definition, Halfpenny and Reid (2002) pose the question *what organisations comprise the sector?* They have reviewed a number of different definitions and perspectives, concluding that the sector is very diverse and that the temptation to impose homogeneity may be questionable and lead to the exclusion of some potentially important dimensions. Halfpenny and Reid (2002) found no definitive definition in the literature and this, according to Alcock and Kendall (2011), has remained an underlying feature of the practice debate and policy development across the sector.

This lack of consensus extends not just to the definition. Leading commentators on the sector have challenged the very notion that a 'sector' can even be found. The Wolfenden Committee (1978, p. 15) report on *The Future of Voluntary Organisations* opens with the claim that: *It is not helpful to imply that there is anything like a unified voluntary movement with a common philosophy guiding its work.*

Similarly, Deakin (1996) pointed out that there was no single authentic voluntary sector for which a simple master plan could be drawn up.

Such a general and, in some cases, dismissive approach has in practice been a feature of the way in which the sector has been defined, and even described. For example, to distinguish third sector organisations from the public sector they are sometimes referred to as *non-government* or *non-statutory* organisations; and to distinguish them from commercial market activity they are often referred to as *non-profit* organisations. These negative definitions have wide currency and, to some extent, are linked to the broader political and cultural contexts within which the sector is discussed. For instance, the term *non-government organisation* (NGO) is often used to refer to international agencies engaging in overseas development work, where it is important they are separate from the national government agencies. The *non-profit* sector is the concept commonly used within the US literature on the sector, where the primary concern is to distinguish organisations from the profit orientation of the market. This can be contrasted with the European literature where relations with the public sector are more developed and the notion of a non-statutory sector is more common (Evers & Laville, 2004).

The problem with such negative definitions is that whilst they might tell us what the sector is not, they are not of much help in trying to understand what it is. The concept of 'civil society' is too wide; while using either 'charitable' and/or 'voluntary' terms to describe the sector as a whole are too narrow and tend to be used to define sub-sectors; and using 'non-profit' has negative connotations about not making a financial surplus, which many organisations in the sector do. Definitions from government organisations provide us with a little more clarity. The Office for the Third Sector (OTS) defines organisations in the sector as non-governmental organisations that are value driven and which principally invest their surpluses to further social, environmental and cultural objective.[1] While the National Audit Office describes the sector as a range of institutions which occupy the space between the State and the private sector. These include small community and voluntary groups, registered charities (both large and small), foundations, trusts and the growing number of social enterprises and cooperatives.[2]

As the definition from the National Audit Office illustrates, the term 'third sector' provides us with a useful umbrella for referring to numerous spheres of activity that respond to terms such as social enterprise, cooperatives, charities, mutuals, voluntary and community organisations. Within the sector there are a number of sub-divisions and groups. Some of these have specific legal definitions while others have blurred boundaries. Nonetheless, these terms can be useful in providing a conceptual map of the sector and provide an indication of the diversity of organisations that exists within the sector. Table 4.1 offers a summary, with definitions, of third sector organisations.

---

1. http://www.cabinetoffice.gov.uk/third_%20sector.aspx
2. http://www.nao.org.uk/our_work_by_sector/third_sector.aspx

Table 4.1: Third sector organisations.

Charitable foundation and trust. General charities whose primary purpose is awarding grants to other voluntary organisations, other institutions or individuals.

Community organisation. A broad term with no legal definition usually referring to organisations that work with a confined local or regional focus. Community organisations may have a legal status or a constitution but there are numerous groups, which have neither.

Cooperative. An autonomous association of people united voluntarily to meet their common economic, social, and cultural needs and aspirations through a jointly owned and democratically controlled enterprise.

Charity. General charities are defined as private, non-profit-making bodies serving individuals.

Social enterprise. Trades for a social purpose. A wide range of organisations fit the definition of social enterprise. These include cooperatives, community businesses, trading arms of charities and a variety of other businesses that use their trading activity to meet social goals.

Mutual. An organisation based on the principle of mutuality. A mutual exists with the purpose of raising funds from its membership or customers, which can then be used to provide common services to all members of the organisation. A mutual is therefore owned by, and run for the benefit of, its members. It has no external shareholders to pay in the form of dividends, and as such does not usually seek to maximise and make large profits or capital gains.

The legal definition of the various organisations that are outlined in Table 4.1 may vary according to the country that the organisation operates in. In addition, the regulation, tax treatment and the way in which local laws affect the organisations may also vary.

The primary objectives of the organisations outlined in Table 4.1 are social rather than economic. They include charities (regulated by the Charities Commission), community organisations, arts organisations, campaigning organisations and other organisations carrying out voluntary actions, often on too small a scale to be registered as charities and too numerous to count. Cooperatives and mutual societies have also increasingly come to be seen as part of a more widely defined third sector, as well as social enterprises, including well-known names such as the Eden Project, Cafédirect and the Big Issue.[3] The ethos, that all those organisations share, is that they are driven by a cause. They tend to share two common characteristics: (i) they do not distribute profits to their owners; and (ii) they are not subject to direct

---

3. www.edenproject.com; www.cafedirect.co.uk; www.bigissue.com

political control. They have a common heritage and the same motivation and desire to improve the world in which they live. They are established and led by people who believe that changes are needed in society and the environment, and who want to do something about it themselves.

In this book we use the term 'third sector' to include all organisations that:

- exist for a social purpose rather than having a profit making objective
- are independent of the state because they are governed by an independent group of people and are not part of a government department or local authority
- reinvest their financial surpluses in the services they offer or in the organisation itself

4.3. Context

Since the expansion of social action during the Victorian age, the third sector has grown to employ well over half a million people and contribute billions to the UK economy (Hopkins, 2010). The voluntary sector workforce has grown by 24% since 1997 compared to 9% in the private sector and 16% in the public sector. Organisations in the sector collectively generated a record income of £36.7 billion in 2009–2010, but their expenditure also hit a new high of £36.3 billion, leaving many struggling to cover their costs (UK Civil Society Almanac, 2012). The National Council for Voluntary Organisations (NCVO, 2012) puts the rising costs down to two main factors: (i) organisations continue to invest in services to meet the additional need for their support caused by the recession; and (ii) rising inflation is forcing up the prices of the goods and services that they have to purchase.

Despite rising costs, the third sector continues to attract attention as an integral driver of social, economic and ethical progress. The organisations in the sector are the primary voices of social and environmental justice, as well as deliverers and sources of services to vulnerable people. The sector is characterised not only by distinct legal formations, but also by an ethos that puts social and environmental interests above economic imperatives. This ethos is not, however, mutually exclusive with professionalism, innovation and value for money. Indeed, the blossoming of social enterprise, and the many organisations who implement multi-faceted fundraising strategies to deliver on their ambitious visions, have demonstrated that the so-called 'not-for-profit' sector is also, in many cases 'not-for-loss'.

The organisational profile of the third sector is different from that of the public and private sectors. Almost one-third of voluntary organisations have fewer than 10 employees compared to 8% of public sector organisations. Only 4% of organisations in the sector have over 500 employees compared to 13% in the private sector and 31% in the public sector. Overall, the sector has grown in size due to an increase in demand for its services, as well as through contracting for service delivery. Although income from statutory sources continues to stimulate growth in the sector, the majority of this money comes through contracts, which often allow less independence than grant funding relationships. There is a split occurring in the sector between the three-quarters of charities who do not receive money from statutory sources and those organisations with an income of over £1 million which receive three-quarters of statutory funding. As a result, the sector is having to ensure that the increased contract funding does not erode the critical independence of the sector or create funding disparities where large organisations entrench their relationship with the state leaving smaller and, perhaps, more nimble and innovative third sector organisations out of the loop (Hudson, 2011).

4.4. Changes

In recent years there has been a radical shift in the social, political and economic environment in which the third sector operates. Organisations need to be robust and contextually aware to navigate through this environment and the changes it brings. Since 2008, as a result of the economic crisis, the sector has been operating under the shadow of austerity, with an increased demand for services against reduced resources (Wilding, 2010). As a result of this, much of the sector's activity has shifted towards an emphasis on survival and resilience, along with an intensified focus on collaboration and to demonstrate impact and value for money. The financial crisis which began in 2007−2008 hit many third sector organisations with a fall in public donations and the availability of far fewer Government grants. According to Finance Hub (2008, p. 4), this has led to:

> ... a creeping sense of crisis regarding voluntary sector funding and a widespread perception in the sector that funding has not only changed markedly in character in recent years but has also significantly reduced. In particular, it is felt that grant funding for the third sector available from local authorities has faced the greatest decline, gradually being replaced with more restricted types of funding, such as contracts and funding for the purchase of commissioned services.

In response to financial cutbacks there has been significant growth in the establishment of strategic partnerships across organisational boundaries and in mergers between organisations of all sizes.

At the same time there have been major changes in the expectations placed on organisations in the third sector. Accountability requirements have increased with the adoption of more rigorous accounting standards (Statement of Recommended Practice, 2005), and organisations are expected to be more transparent in reporting what they do, how they spend their money and what they achieve. There have also been changes in how performance is managed, as organisations have striven to get a better grip on measuring and understanding the differences they make to people's lives. The governance of many organisations has also been reviewed and restructured to achieve greater value and to meet the new demands for greater accountability. There have been even more changes with the government recognition that third sector organisations are best placed to address some of the intractable social problems which society faces, such as poverty.

The growing diversity of the sector, in terms of size, purpose, legal form and scale of reach, is a significant change. Although there may be commonalities of approach and of origin between all third sector organisations, it can be challenging to find a common experience between a multi-million pound social enterprise such as Cafédirect and a small community organisation relying entirely on the help of volunteers. Moreover, a small local charity may struggle to identify with larger national charities typified by an organisation such as Barnardo's, with an annual income approaching £200 million and over 6000 paid staff.

A further change for the sector is a drive for creativity and innovation. For despite the proclivity to see the sector as a leader in innovation, research has shown that there are issues which need to be addressed in order for the sector to create and maintain an innovative approach. Osborne, Chew, and McLaughlin (2008, p. 66) found that innovation in the third sector has reduced dramatically. On the basis of a mixed-method comparison of third sector organisations in 1994 and 2006, they found that innovative capacity is not a constant or inherent organisational characteristic, but varies according to the cues and incentives of the public policy context:

> Far from being a constant in terms of their role in delivering public services, innovation has been revealed as a variable. It has argued that the prime driver for this shifting pattern of organisational activity has been a significant change in the public policy context ... In 1994 this context privileged innovative activity above other types of activity. This led organisations both to focus more of their activity on innovative work and to portray their other work as innovative, irrespective of its true nature, in order to gain governmental funding. In 2006, this context has shifted to favour the development and provision of specialist services that enable local authorities to meet their own performance targets from central government.

This supports the findings in a report by the Young Foundation on social innovation, which concluded that most of the literature on social innovation in the sector points to a sector that is 'better at believing they are innovative than being innovative' (Mulgan, 2007). Leaders in the sector may disagree, but it would appear from such findings that there is a need to drive distinctiveness and innovation across the sector.

There is underway a long-term re-balancing of the roles and responsibilities of individuals, the state and society. This has led to a blurring of the boundaries between the public and third sectors. There are third sector organisations, which share similar values and also have characteristics in common with the public sector. This is most evident in the development of social enterprise and in the charitisation and mutualisation of public bodies. These are set to become increasingly significant parts of the third sector landscape. One implication of this is that it will become more difficult to clearly set out the dimensions of the third sector. This would be an unfortunate backward step since until comparatively recently, the third sector was not recognised as a sector at all. Instead, it was perceived as a group of disparate and unconnected organisations that championed good causes but were often viewed as inefficient and badly managed. Today, it is seen as an essential part of the fabric of society and the organisations within it are acknowledged as one group that has a common cause: to take independent action to make the world a better place without excessive personal gain.

Such changes, as outlined above, open up questions about the role of leadership in the sector, which until now has been largely unchartered territory. There has been little previous discussion about 'what leadership is' or 'what role leadership should play' through and beyond 'the age of austerity' in the third sector. Although leaders, in the sector, give interviews, make individual speeches and write occasional blogs, there appears to be no sector-wide conversation about leadership and the impact on it of the shift in the social, political and economic environment. Yet the question of leadership in the sector is a significant one, due (not only) to its neglect in the academic literature but also because of the transformation taking place as a result of the external drivers for change. Such issues are highlighted in this chapter through the voices of those who are, or have been, in leadership positions in the sector. It is through these individual voices that we can start to gain a deeper understanding of what leadership is and is becoming in the third sector, as well as the challenges that are present and lie ahead.

4.5.   Leadership in the Third Sector

The nature of leadership has been extensively researched, and while there is still some debate over the impact of leaders on important organisational outcomes, the general conclusion is that top executives matter (Finkelstein, Hambrick, & Cannella, 2009). Senior executives, however, have also come under increasing scrutiny because they can get it wrong (Hodges, 2011). Following a decade or more of corporate scandals where the behaviour of leaders has been severely questioned, and the inadequacy of previously feted leaders during the global financial crisis, there has been a 'falling out of love' with the charismatic/heroic/leader-centric models of leadership that dominated the literature and business press from the 1980s onwards (Hamel, 2009). In their place, models of shared or distributed leadership have become popular (Pearce & Conger, 2003), which are aimed at dispersing leadership throughout organisations (Hodges & Martin, 2012). More recently, ethical leadership has gained currency (see Chapter 2).

With the growing interest and importance of ethical leadership, in parallel with rapid and continuous organisational change, questions around how leaders lead ethically are of paramount importance in the third sector, as well as elsewhere. As Trevino and Brown (2004, p. 77) argue: *The environment has become quite complex and is rapidly changing, providing all sorts of ethical challenges and opportunities to express greed.* In order to address such challenges, leaders in the third sector need to understand the ethical boundaries within which they are called to operate. The ethical and moral dimensions of leadership are crucial, according to Diefenbach (2013, p. 166) for the *success or failure of management, leadership and organisational change.* Mendonca (2001, p. 266) goes onto say that, *it is the leader's moral principles and integrity that give legitimacy and credibility to the vision and sustain it.* In this sense, researchers like Spangenberg and Theron (2005) demand 'ethical leadership'. It is important that leaders in the third sector focus on how they behave, how they treat others and how they conduct their office. Third sector organisations are altruistically driven and focus on morally responsible action (for example, working for human rights, animal welfare or environmental protection). In contrast, profit organisations are driven to influence the behaviour and emotions of their stakeholders and the need to outperform competitors. Although some profit organisations engage in forms of morally responsible action, it is not usually the dominant focus or core business, as it tends to be in third sector organisations. The ethic morality within the third sector will only prevail if all organisational stakeholders are able and prepared to ensure that ethical rather than unethical behaviour is pursued by leaders in a democratic way.

The democratic approach of third sector organisations emphasises the decentralisation of power, whereas senior leadership positions in profit organisations concentrate on legitimate power over collective resources (Knoke & Prensky, 1984). Leaders who are high on using their power for motivation and have a high concern for responsibility seem to fit the third sector context well. Engaging in morally responsible action, emphasising values and behaving in ways that reinforce the values inherent in the mission seem to be especially important to leaders in the sector. In contrast, using power for purely personal gains runs counter to the altruistic values inherent in the mission of third sector organisations (De Hoogh et al., 2005). It also goes against the high value these organisations tend to place on employee involvement and control (Wilderom & Miner, 1991). There are, therefore, distinct values, behaviours and use of power by leaders in third sector organisations which impact on how they address the complexities of stakeholder management.

The leadership within the sector is facing multiple and diverse demands from a wider range of stakeholders. This is creating a new level of complexity with major implications for the nature of the leadership which must be exercised. Leaders need to understand the demands of stakeholders, who reflect the demands of the wider range of external elements that the modern leader faces — in particular the three triple bottom-line elements of economic, social and environmental values (Dunphy & Benn, 2013). An IBM Global CEO survey, *Capitalizing on Complexity* (IBM, 2010), emphasises that the world's public and private sector leaders believe that a rapidly escalating complexity is their biggest challenge and one that will only increase rapidly in the near future. Part of the increasing complexity faced by leaders in the third sector is, and will continue to be, the broader task of meeting the demands of a wider range of stakeholders than has traditionally been taken into account. This involves identifying and collaborating with an increasing set of external stakeholders across the public and private sector. So, not only is the leadership in the sector being driven to be more ethical, there is also a growing need for this to be done in a collaborative manner.

4.6. Leadership Theory

There is a dearth of research into leadership within the third sector (Boal & Hooijberg, 2000). The leadership literature tends to assume that leadership occurs in the private and public sectors. This leaves third sector leaders to either interpret the empirical findings regarding leadership in other sectors to fit their own sector, or to reject the findings as non-applicable. Common sense would suggest that leadership in the third sector might be different (Thach & Thompson, 2007). Indeed, there are unique challenges in the sector which are intimated by Warren Buffett (2003, p. 3). Buffett says that the nature of the problems that the sector faces is exactly the opposite of business:

> In business, you look for easy things; very good businesses that don't have very many problems and that almost run themselves ... In the philanthropic world, you're looking at the toughest problems that exist. The reason why they're important problems is that they've resisted the intellect and money being thrown at them over the years and they haven't been solved. You have to expect a lower batting average in tackling the problems of philanthropy than in tackling the problems of business.

Research to address such problems is embryonic in the third sector. Despite some attempt to consider leadership as a broader set of processes, the focus of much writing appears to remain on individuals in leadership roles or positions of formal authority. The sparse research that does exist tends to emphasise the role of Chief Executives of relatively large voluntary organisations. For example, Kirchner (2007) has developed a leadership model in which the Chief Executive is seen as leading upwards (managing governance), downwards (harnessing resources and running an organisation effectively) and outwards (representing the organisation). Other studies have also tried to identify and describe the typical attributes and characteristics of Chief Executives. Paton and Brewster (2008) note the relatively high visibility and scrutiny faced by Chief Executives and draw attention to the 'soft leadership' roles they need for handling relationships with a diverse but committed range of people in and around their organisations. Drawing on work from organisational psychology, Paton and Brewster (2008) have developed a conceptual framework for 'what is it like being a Chief Executive'. The framework includes: system and field awareness, or the 'helicopter view' of seeing the bigger picture; emotional awareness; detachment from dilemmas, that is, beyond binary either/or thinking; and intuition. A much longer list of characteristics is provided by

Cormack and Stanton (2003) which includes: emotional attachment, passion, enthusiasm and affinity with the cause: a strategic perspective and a customer service orientation: networking and influencing; personal humility; motivating a team; resilience; self-confidence and being a visionary and inspirational communicator involving others; the ability to paint a picture of the future that appeals strongly to others; showing passion and emotion in visioning and representing the work of the organisation to others; a powerful communicator in all forums from one-to-one to public speaking; visibility; and being seen to speak out and represent the organisation. A common characteristic from such lists appears to be the importance of sense-making. In a study into the type of leadership required by voluntary organisations Kay (1996, p. 131) explores and extends this characteristic by conceptualising leadership as a process of creating and sustaining meanings in negotiation with and influencing others, and depicts the concept of leadership as a 'sense-making' process involving: *A multi-dimensional process of social interaction, creating and sustaining acceptable meanings of issues, events and actions. Leaders are conceptualized as those who have involvement and influence in this leadership process.* Kay (1996) focuses on the process of 'sense-making' between people around shared understandings and meanings which involves vision setting, interpretation and take-up, influence, and credibility. Four dimensions to sense-making are identified: (i) social and cognitive (creating meanings acceptable to others); (ii) socio-political (influencing commitment to particular meanings); (iii) cultural (setting meanings within an organisation's culture); and (iv) enactment (ensuring that meanings are reflected in actions). Similar sense-making characteristics are highlighted by Schwabenland (2012) in her discussion of the role of leadership in the foundation and development of organisations to achieve social change.

Although there has been several studies carried out into the role and characteristics of Chief Executives, little attention has been given to leadership in the third sector as a whole, or in its sub-sectors, such as 'the charity sector' or new and growing movements within the sector, such as 'social enterprise'. This is one of the reasons why, in this book, we have included the views of leaders from a cross-section of organisations in the third sector.

4.7. Leadership Development

The most important issue confronting the sector today and in the near future relates to leadership, wrote Thomas J. Tierney (2006), former Chief Executive of Bain and Company, and co-founder and chairman of the Bridgespan Group, Incorporated, a non-profit strategy consulting firm in the United States. Until recently, leadership was not a word that many people used when talking about third sector organisations. Leadership was seen to be part of the culture of the corporate world and was not thought to be appropriate in the third sector. This perspective has thankfully begun to change due to the dramatic growth and the increasingly professional approach of organisations in the sector. Today, the concept of leadership has been colonised for organisations in the sector and its language and jargon are becoming increasingly common. Arguably, this reflects the need for leadership as a potentially creative and transformative reaction to third sector 'managerialism' (Paton & Brewster, 2008). More specifically, it can be viewed as accompanying the growing realisation that there is a 'leadership deficit' in the sector (Kirchner, 2006). While the sector navigates intense periods of change and continues to expand year-on-year, studies show that there is a deficit of leadership capabilities:

- Schmeuker and Johnson (2009) found that the third sector needed to improve its skills in key leadership competencies such as strategic thinking, influencing, negotiating and communication
- Hailey and James (2004) found an increasing deficit in leadership abilities because of rapid turnover of managers in the sector
- Research by the Clore Duffield Foundation (2007) concluded that there was a scattergun approach to leadership that lacked coherency

Such studies show that that leadership within the sector is in need of special attention. Venter and Sung (2009) point out that many in the sector are worried that there are not enough prospective leaders in the labour market. Key questions which need to be addressed are: how does the sector develop their future leaders; how does it utilise individuals who have gained skills in other sectors; and how does the sector demonstrate the many ways those skills that make a good leader can be developed? (Clark, 2007).

Leadership cannot, however, be imported from the corporate world and imposed on third sector organisations, without changes so that it is relevant within the context of the sector. It requires subtle and critical adjustments to be made in order to reflect the different ethos and culture. Leadership theories and frameworks, which abound in private and public organisations, may bring great benefits; however, they are of limited value unless they are tailored to address the different context of third sector organisations. These organisations attract extraordinarily diverse people, as illustrated in the individual reflections later in this chapter. Many of these individuals believe in the creation of a fairer, more caring, better educated and healthier world. How they lead is influenced by the mission and values which pervade all aspects of the organisations in which they work. According to Frances Hesselbein (2002) such leaders need to understand 'how to be'. Hesselbein describes this as having quality, character, values, principles and courage. Leaders, who appreciate how to be, build dispersed and diverse leadership and hold forth the vision of the organisation's future in compelling ways that ignite the spark needed to build an inclusive enterprise. This raises the issue of development for leaders.

The range of third sector leadership development initiatives can be seen simultaneously as impressive but also as somewhat limited (Reid & Pearson, 2011). Key initiatives include the establishment of the Governance and Workforce National Hubs of Expertise, and the subsequent Governance and Leadership National Support Service, the establishment of the Skills-Third Sector, the expansion of the School for Social Entrepreneurs, a range of local and regional leadership initiatives plus the Clore Social Leadership Programme, NCVO's Leadership 20:20 Commission (O'Boyle, 2010) and NAVCA's (National Association for Voluntary and Community Action) work on 'Inspiring Local Leadership' (NAVCA, 2011).

A great deal of valuable work has been carried out through these initiatives, and continues for some of them. From a distance, however, it looks like a whole lot of organisations, networks and partnerships falling over each other to stake a claim around third sector leadership, and to proclaim their particular leadership 'takes' for their particular interests or constituencies — wanting to be leaders in leadership (Hudson, 2011). The unfortunate demise of the Third Sector Leadership Centre is perhaps a case in point. Established in late 2006, as a partnership between the NCVO and the Association of Chief Executives of Voluntary Organisations (ACEVO), it aimed to raise the profile of leadership and leadership development across the third sector (Plummer, 2009). Its demise has created a gap which needs to be addressed, in order to improve leadership capability.

This gap was highlighted in a recent review which investigated skills and leadership across the sector. The review was led by Dame Mary Marsh, founding director of the Clore Social Leadership Programme and a former Chief Executive at NSPCC — the Children's Charity. Marsh says that it is a critical time for organisations and that they need to develop their skills and leadership to enable them to deal with the challenges they are facing as well as respond to opportunities. The review identified three overarching themes: (i) the importance of personal responsibility in personal development; (ii) the sector's responsibility for developing people and making the most of existing potential; and (iii) the existence of specific skills gaps in the sector. The conclusion is that there is a critical need to attract and develop leaders in the sector.[4]

The findings of the review have ignited the spark for the sector to invest in leadership development to create a talent pool of people with the right skills and attitudes to boost the sector. The Institute of Fundraising (IoF) has recently designed a programme to help the profession build a leadership 'pipeline'. While the Resource Alliance — the international charity devoted to supporting voluntary organisations to be financially sustainable — has launched a Future Leaders Programme. The programme offers potential leaders 360-degree feedback, a one-week residential course about the key skills for leadership, and mentoring and professional support to complete a personal action plan.[5]

These are all praiseworthy initiatives, yet spending on leadership development in the third sector still lags significantly behind that in other sectors (Hudson, 2011). Without investment in leadership skills there will continue to be a small pool of appropriately skilled leaders, a continued drain of talent to the public and private sector, and a restricted pipeline of future leaders.

---

4. www.thirdsector.co.uk/management/article/1182570/Leadership-skills-review, accessed 26 May 2013.
5. http://www.theguardian.com/voluntary-sector-network/2013/jun/25/leadership-development-fundraising

4.8.   The Reflections

In the following section are the personal reflections from individuals in the third sector in the United Kingdom. Like those in Chapter 3 on the public sector, the individuals do not speak for the sector but provide their own views on leadership within the sector, based on their experience. These personal reflections provide us with an insight into what it really is like to be a leader in the third sector. Our thanks go out to all who have taken the time to write their reflections and for making this book possible. We are especially grateful to the contributors for being so open and honest about their experience and providing us with a small glimpse into their working lives.

As the sector is broad in context, it is outside the scope of this book to include all the different types of organisations within it. We do, however, have contributions from individuals who work in the following sub-sectors: Charity; Mutual; Cooperative; Community, Voluntary and Social Enterprise. As mentioned in the introduction to this book, contributors were asked to provide, in their own words, commentary on: their experience and perceptions of leadership; what leadership means to them; the leadership challenges for the United Kingdom and Europe, particularly in times of change/recession; and the leadership challenges for the sector in light of the challenges identified.

4.8.1. Voluntary

Gary Bishop

I was in my late twenties when for the first time I began to consider leadership as a unique discipline and skill. It was only then, out of necessity that I really began to study leadership and seek to grow my own capacity in that area. I was appointed as the leader of a team of 20 young adults who relocated to a very troubled estate in Manchester. Based in a church, which was virtually derelict, our task was to initiate a youth and community project, which would make a positive impact on the neighbourhood. I lived and worked in what sometimes felt like a very alien and hostile environment with many pressure points and which was incredibly daunting. It seemed that overnight I had some pretty big expectations to fulfil and I started devouring books by John Maxwell, Zig Ziglar and Ken Blanchard. Maxwell, in particular, writes in very memorable sound bites, many of which I can still recall but none more influential than this: *Everything rises and falls on leadership.* Maxwell taught me that in leadership there is nowhere to hide, as a leader if there is a problem it is your problem, if there is a mistake it is your mistake, if there is failure it is your failure, and the only thing you don't own is the success — that belongs to the team.

Seven years of leading that project taught me that our people were our greatest asset and the better I looked after the people and maintained the complex web of relationships, which our team represented, the stronger our project became. Today, as the Managing Director of the Justlife Foundation I maintain this principle and believe that the most important contribution I make to the organisation is in recruiting the right staff and developing the people that we have. John Adair's Action Centred Leadership model suggests that leaders should spend equal time on tasks, team and individuals. Of course, most of us find it incredibly easy to get sucked into achieving the tasks, which each day throws up and it takes real discipline to shut the laptop lid and get focused on the team and the individuals who really power the organisation and determine its future. It is a constant process of balancing and re-balancing but I tend to think of myself as a team leader rather than an organisation leader, knowing that if the team is motivated, resourced, focused and supported then the rest of my job is pretty straightforward.

Ninety-five percent of the time leadership feels like an enormous privilege, a wonderful opportunity and a lot of fun. For the other 5%, it is desperately lonely, emotionally draining and wholly undesirable. I say this because I think there are some myths about what leaders are like, and how their lives should look: stressed up to the eyeballs; working 75 hours a week, high blood pressure; and constantly under enormous pressure to make the big decisions and get them right every time. That is not my experience, nor is it my aspiration.

Now, I am not denying that occasionally work leaks into the weekend, that I struggle to put my Blackberry down or that sometimes I wake in the night worrying about budgets or personnel but I know that I am not cut out for a leadership life which lurches from one major crisis to another, constantly fire-fighting and chasing the next big thing. Naturally those things land on the desk of every leader from time to time but I need 95% of my leadership to be actively engaged in innovation, creativity, team building, business development and working with outstanding individuals. It is those life-giving aspects of my role, which make the occasional pressure points bearable and fuel my desire to get the big and sometimes difficult calls right.

More than that though, I regularly say to our staff team at Justlife that I so believe in the charitable work that we do that given the chance, I will gladly continue to lead the organisation for the rest of my working life. I think that claim comes with more credibility and authenticity when I am working at a sustainable pace and my leadership performance at work is genuinely enhanced by regular rest, exercise and relaxation and knowing that I make good time for my family who remain my priority at all times.

For me leadership is the opportunity to create, to innovate, to develop and ultimately to change something, be that addressing a social problem with community innovation, equipping a Doctor's surgery to become more community orientated or coaching leaders through challenges and seeing them thrive and grow in the process. There is great joy for me in seeing things work better. At a personal level, for me leadership is all about the great people I get to work with and I am very fussy about who those people are. I love to work with people who are clever and have skills that will stretch me — I need those people to be passionate, loyal, open and motivated. The more senior you become in your leadership the harder it is to find people who will honestly critique your performance or tell you when you are screwing up. When I find people who will encourage me but also 'lock horns' with me in a constructive and peaceful manner I want to hang onto them. Personality profiling identifies me as a slight introvert and I am aware that I thrive with familiarity, so having a solid, trusted and diverse team around me enables me to press onto new opportunities with strength and confidence, fully aware of my own weaknesses, but secure in the collaborative expertise of our people. If the Justlife team were to report that I care about them as people and I inspire them to lead well then I would be very happy.

The United Kingdom and Europe have been in economic meltdown for over 5 years — at the time of writing, the growth forecast remains gloomy, even the 'good' news in the financial press is not that good. Much of the leadership chatter focuses on rejuvenating failing economies and returning to the way things were a decade ago with strong UK markets and large scale infrastructure investments, but I am not sure a return to the so-called glory days is really what is required. We are in a situation where our old systems have failed, the shutter-clad shop fronts on many of our high streets are a graphic illustration that consumerism is perhaps not the cultural deity that it once was and even if wealth and growth return, we should expect it to look very different because people's values, ideals and principles are shifting all the time.

The challenge for leaders is the drag towards returning to the old ways when what is needed is totally fresh thinking, which builds on the success and failures of the past but creates a new future. Much of today's most creative, innovative and opinion forming leadership is coming from unexpected places. For example, we could look at the Occupy movements around the world, which have sought to challenge the dominance of capitalist culture in western society. How can a movement with no obvious hierarchy and no constitution mobilise tens of thousands of individuals to raise their voices around huge cultural issues and expect to challenge the dominant cultural symbols of a generation? Most of the leadership literature from the last half century would have us believe that such a movement is not possible and yet we see a wide range of senior societal figures from politics, the financial sector and faith communities associating with the Occupy cause recognising its value and embracing its message. This is just one example, but culture is moving fast and leaders will have to learn quickly to listen to alternative voices, adopt a new set of strategies and adapt to a new set of demands from very well informed and demanding communities.

I recently took part in a launch event for a large scale funding programme being offered to regions around the United Kingdom. I made a short presentation about the work of our charity Justlife. A Whitehall policy maker followed me onto the podium. He kindly endorsed our work but insisted that unless the projects are scalable they are of little significance or interest. Now I am not averse to growth — in fact, I would go as far as to say that I like it and actively seek out opportunities to do more of something that I passionately believe in. However, bigger is not always better, especially in our sector. Some of the unique competencies the third sector has are our rich local knowledge around key themes and/or geographical areas and the potential to make a significant impact in these fields. These competencies come from being embedded in local communities and gaining a depth of understanding which cannot easily be grasped by a large corporation or global provider.

The idea of scaling up successful models has a certain allure to a social entrepreneur but we need to ensure that the drive for size does not replace a drive for quality, authenticity and social impact. Equally, in an era when local authorities look to become commissioners of service rather than providers of services, the voluntary sector should approach large contracts with a degree of caution especially where public sector partnerships risk compromising the independence of the community or voluntary sector organisation by overbearing governance or local authority intrusion.

Perhaps then the challenges for leadership in this decade will not be so different to those gone before. Knowing when, how and where to grow and critically who to grow with are all central challenges for today's leaders. Those who manage these challenges well will continue to thrive and grow their work and its impact in the world.

Alison Elliot

It is easier to describe what leadership is not in the third sector than what it is. The third sector consists of fiercely independent organisations that resist being spoken for. At the same time, representing the third sector, its strengths and its concerns to Government and to the public is an important job, with which the Scottish Council for Voluntary Organisations (SCVO) is tasked. It takes fine judgement to do this. The challenge is to stay close enough to the third sector member organisations to ensure that the predominant messages are identified, while stretching that consensus to focus on a forward direction.

It is worth making a distinction between leadership behind the scenes, in dialogue with government and other agencies, and leadership in the public sphere. For the former, expressing the lived experience of third sector organisations and the people they work with, as a reality check on policy, is an important part of the task. Secondly, calling national and local government representatives to remember the contribution of the third sector and identifying its importance for the effective implementation of policy is often necessary. Finally, it is important to promote in the discussion values that are thought of as 'third sector values'. This often entails emphasising the need to put the service user at the heart of the policy, although that principle is more widely adopted now than it used to be.

Third sector leadership in public debates hinges on the importance of articulating a civil society perspective on issues that are not aligned with the views of a political party. Sometimes that involves the same reality checking as above but it can also involve arguing for values and principles that promote democracy, rather than party political views. Protecting that space in the debate is often a contested activity, particularly when the parties line up on either side of a clear dividing line, as is the case in the present referendum debate.

For SCVO, there is a potential tension between supporting the interests of our members and adopting a normative civil society role, which concerns itself with what is in the best interests of society as a whole and, in particular, with the concerns of the most marginalised people within it. Many of our members work daily with people 'on the edge' and so ensuring that their voices are heard in public, debate can be argued to be a core part of our purpose. On the other hand, many of our members are dependent on public funding to such an extent that they are anxious if we are thought to be taking a political line that could offend present or future governments.

I see leadership as supporting those who have appointed me as a leader, giving them the confidence and the opportunities to speak for themselves and using my position sparingly, so that any intervention I do make is given full value. I have a good collegial relationship with SCVO's CEO and I see my role as that of giving him constructive support.

At a time of change and recession, people need to find ways of connecting with the non-financial resources that are present in their sector or in their environment. In recent years, this has led to an emphasis on the insights and capacities that people and communities have within themselves to address problems that might otherwise be dealt with by the attempts of outsiders. Focusing on the assets people have, rather than the deficits that are often the object of policy, is not only an attractive approach when money is tight but is also likely to lead to more sustainable solutions. This is the natural habitat for the voluntary sector, which tends to be close to local communities. The sector often has a more immediate relationship with the people it works with and encourages innovation and person-based approaches to service provision or problem solving. Therefore, involving the voluntary sector in the development of policy as well as its implementation is a canny approach at times of recession.

The leadership challenge for the sector is to make the case that this is a way of ensuring better policies and more secure implementation and is not just a way of saving money and doing things on the cheap. Another challenge is to mobilise a sector, which is disparate and predominantly small-scale to rise to this challenge effectively.

John Lauder

My experience of leadership comes partly from being led by others in my earlier career, observing both good and bad practice and considering how best to apply the former and avoid the latter when I got a chance to lead an organisation. In addition, like many leaders I have reflected and learned the theoretical approach to leadership by attending training and leadership courses. What you cannot be taught and what you might not understand as you watch others at work is the ability to be confident about taking decisions, making sure you communicate well with your teams so that they understand you and vice versa and having the skill to make sure you have a good team around you who understand what you are trying to achieve and support into your vision and approach. Finally, not everyone will be happy with your leadership and if not expressed well they can hurt you and themselves, my experience is to do all you can to plan ahead, consider the unexpected consequences of your decisions, listen to people, ensure they understand they are being listened to and understand how best to express themselves when they do not feel a decision is the one they would have taken.

My view of leadership has evolved over the 7 years that I have been leading a team. When I took over, my approach was to build consensus and trust that a commonly held vision was enough to make sure people would move forward in the way I wanted them to. I have learned since then, and continue to learn every day, and my perception now is that leadership is about establishing clarity of purpose and agreeing a common mission and approach to the tasks at hand then making sure that you are driving that mission and approach forward. If it is your idea, why not make sure it's working? Taking time to be really clear, listening but not being dragged in different directions and following a course of action once it has been agreed is now how I perceive my role as a leader to be. Not to say that I get everything correct or that we cannot change direction, but that people like clarity in their work. Finally, when I started as a leader I did not have any perception of how much time and energy is required and how lonely things can be when all is not going well, particularly the case in the third sector when funding can be hard to find and jobs are on the line. But the rewards far outweigh the distractions and disappointments.

For my part, leadership is about listening and being seen to listen, being confident that structures are in place and are working and, as stated above, making sure that the direction we are taking is understood, being followed and being seen to be followed, and that work is being reviewed to spot inconsistencies, iron out errors and celebrate successes. Perhaps the last part is one of the most important and easiest to overlook, particularly in charities where the mission is all important and if you are not careful, a very puritanical outlook can prevail that says that we have nothing to celebrate until the final mission of the charity has been achieved. That is a laudable sentiment, but not a way to inspire and motivate staff. This all sounds easier than it is and it takes more time than I had ever imagined. Leadership is also about being prepared to front the organisation but not take the credit, take the hard decisions and be prepared to face up to mistakes when they occur, as they must surely do.

It seems to me that ignoring climate change by focusing on the need to survive in the orthodox economic model is the biggest challenge to leadership across the United Kingdom and Europe. We seem to be adrift in a miasma that focuses only on economic survival at the expense of everything else when at the same time the climate of the world is changing rapidly. There is no shortage of advisers highlighting the need to adapt to a changing environment and reduce carbon emissions that both offer economic advantages and opportunities for growth. In addition, as people in Europe live even more sedentary lifestyles the need to take more exercise in our daily lives and so help to lead more healthy, and less costly lifestyles should be challenging our leaders to act to allow people to choose to travel in ways that benefit their health, well-being and the environment.

The big challenge to leadership as I see it is to keep a clear focus on the vision, mission, aims and objectives you hold, make sure you are monitoring your progress towards achieving all four, and being prepared to take hard decisions as funding, political changes and other factors come to affect your work. Perhaps the easiest thing to do in recession is nothing, but I don't see hunkering down and hoping that the storm will blow over is either a good plan or much of a position for a leader to take. Another major challenge is to look at the organisation itself, its aims and objectives, mission and vision and consider whether we can achieve everything on our own. Too much time in the third sector is spent bidding for funding against sister charities and not enough time is spent finding a common purpose. If we are struggling to generate enough income are we alone or are others in a similar position?

Perhaps this is the right time to review the fundamental foundations of the charity and move on to agree new alliances and partnerships.

Steven Paterson

Throughout my life I have been exposed to a range of effective leaders including teachers, mentors, coaches, consultants, mentors, managers and friends. This has shaped me as a person, my career path and my leadership approach. For the last two decades I have been steeped in leadership roles in national organisations which are concerned with improving the experiences and outcomes of looked after children.

I have learnt a lot during this phase of my career. The organisations, in which I had a significant leadership role, have undergone significant change programmes. For example, in one organisation the change took place in a time of growth, while in another organisation the change reflected a reduction in funding, despite an expanding remit and scope. Critical to the success of both these change programmes was an effective leadership approach and a commitment to the process of change, highlighting the importance of understanding and applying effective leadership skills in practice.

Extensive research and theory has been undertaken to define or categorise leadership using a variety of traits, values, measurements and constructs, which all have their merits. From a personal perspective, effective leadership is: for the organisation; within the organisation; and beyond the organisation.

Perhaps the most obvious role of a leader relates to their ability to create and implement a strategic plan *for the organisation* and this should be informed by the expertise within the organisation. This aspect is critical to engendering confidence, while providing direction and aspirations. Leadership for the organisation requires the development of a vision, values and principles and a strategic plan. This aspect of leadership requires an ability to conduct environmental scanning which can inform the direction of the service with due consideration of external and internal capacity and need. With this insight, leaders are able to act with courage and conviction to provide a road map and directions which will enable the organisation to reach its destination.

Contemporary leadership *within organisations* requires a more 'transformational' than 'transactional' approach. The former reflecting the importance of motivation and morale in benefitting the individual and the organisation. Although not all leaders are necessarily charismatic or comfortable with the engagement of staff, good leaders will recognise their value, contribution, expertise, potential and limitations. This can be reflected through their collaborative approach and/or commitment to appropriate leadership at all levels. This links directly to what Daniel Goleman defines as Emotional Intelligence (EI), which has the capacity to make a measurable impact on people and organisations. EI skills are self-awareness, self-regulation, motivation, empathy and social awareness. These skills enable leaders to capitalise on the performance of themselves and those with whom they work.

In the contemporary landscape, *leadership beyond the organisation* is equally critical. A combination of the emphasis on stakeholder engagement and partnership requires an ability to provide leadership in contexts where there is no locus of power. This requires a leader skilled in negotiation and collaborative approaches to retain the position of their own organisation while respecting the place of others.

The aspects of leadership outlined above benefit from consideration of *personal leadership*. The consideration of values, self-awareness and self-regulation will make a significant contribution to how leaders are perceived. A leader needs to have clarity about their principles and work in a way that is true to their principles. Leading with courage, conviction and transparency will instil confidence and provide motivation for staff.

A significant challenge for leaders in the United Kingdom and Europe in the current climate of recession is the issue of poverty. There is evidence of concerns about how to deal with welfare issues and reduced levels of funding, while continuing to deliver high-quality services with positive outcomes. Dealing with these so-called 'wicked problems' requires a considered leadership response that differs from what might be described as traditional leadership approaches. These problems are compounded as a result of the decreasing resources available to address inherent and complex issues which are resistant to homogenous solutions. This has led to increasing demand for the delivery of bespoke solutions and products rather than depending on 'off-the-shelf' packages which have a better chance of delivering tangible outcomes and value for money. Within this bleak financial environment the combination of reduced resources and increasing promotion of partnership working presents a conundrum. The competition for a reducing pot of money can lead to organisations moving beyond their area of expertise in order to diversify and secure other sources of funding. This can create a culture where there is concern about sharing knowledge and information which can help sustain a competitive edge. This can be compounded if partnerships become fractious at a time when collaborative solutions have the potential to provide additional benefits through their synergistic effect.

The additional challenge of an increasing, yet appropriate, focus on outcomes and measurements of impact can be a source of consternation. While this is critical to the future of the organisation, it is also important to allocate the correct level of resources to provide this evidence. In addressing this challenge, it is equally important not to be overly influenced by outcome bias. It is essential that there is clarity about the cause and effect of outcomes and not an ill-conceived response which applies an overly positive or negative halo effect.

Leadership in times of recession and change presents additional challenges that can affect the relationship dynamic within organisations. Making difficult decisions in difficult times means leadership can be viewed as a necessary evil, and become the focal point of culpability. This is a reality of leadership, although conversely this can be easier than making difficult decisions in prosperous times. It is vital in such a context that there is an emphasis on individuals in the organisation, maintaining a balance between support, development and performance management.

The principal challenge for organisations in the looked after children's sector is to deliver services which improve experiences and outcomes. This is particularly relevant as these children and their families are affected by poverty and welfare issues which will contribute to their complex needs. In order to tackle this challenge, it is vital that organisations are flexible and adaptive as well as being reflective and open to learning.

Collaborative and partnership working can present an enigma which is a challenge but one which also offers potential solutions. As previously indicated, organisations have to find a balance of preserving their own place in the sector while being confident enough to share knowledge and information for wider benefit. By establishing some low risk transactions, it should be possible to benefit from collaborative working as long as the time is taken to develop high levels of trust. Looked after children and young people go through their lives dealing with and adapting to change; therefore, the irony for leaders is the need for them to prepare, cope and respond to change in a timely and effective way.

Richard Taylor

My experience of leadership began in 1978 as a Shop Manager for Boots the Chemist. Running a business as if it were my own, worrying about staff wages, bookkeeping, purchasing, customers and profit. I learned to thrive in an unrelentingly competitive world and came to realise that any lack of confidence or fear of being found out was no more than a commonly held self-doubt. A professional vulnerability that can affect most of us, at some point, in our career. I joined a fledgling Early Learning Centre in 1984 as an Area Manager and adapted to its fast paced, dynamic and innovative environment. I embraced the responsibility of remote management and the accountability for performance and development for 500 people. I enjoyed numerous promotions which culminated in me becoming their Operations Director in 1994, which meant assuming operational and strategic responsibility for all shops in the United Kingdom and Europe, generating £150 million of revenue a year.

Following 20 years in commercial retail, I moved into the third sector where I discovered well-intended people who lacked in my narrow view, commerciality. However, real and dynamic leadership more than compensated for the perceived deficiency that I interpreted as unprofessional — qualities I had not witnessed in such abundance before. These were people who had foresight, influence and talents to challenge the norms at that time. Comparisons with the commercial world today are more favourable and thankfully the visionaries are still here.

I currently lead a team of 2000 paid staff and 50,000 volunteers across a portfolio of 10 business disciplines generating close to half a billion pounds of revenue a year for world class science. Since my first role, I have progressed from being a manager who got things done, to someone who endeavours to inspire others to do the very same. It is no longer fashionable to universally foster control and command practices; it is now about the individual's role in visioning, decision-making, creativity and organisational winning.

My perception of leaders today is divided as I still come across those increasingly redundant types who cynically exercise control over others through high-handed interventions. And when they do not delegate, I imagine it is because they are too fragile or do not trust themselves to believe in others. Their power games derive from that same old fear of failure and of being found out. They are rarely liked or admired but they do have the confidence to make big and bold decisions. They do keep the rudder firm. They navigate financial difficulty, and are invariably passionate, so they are not all bad. The others are those who not only think deeply about what they do, but care as much about how they do it. These are the encouragers and enablers who demand courageous thinking from others, who dream and innovate, nurture creativity, take risks and adopt perspective beyond immediacy. They understand their own limitations and that of others. And their investiture comes from ordinary people who look for greatness in others and who want to be a part of something new, different and successful.

Leadership for me means the engagement of people through intellect, imagination and heart. It requires excitement, vision and passion from people who think and care deeply. They shoulder risk, create space, unlock creativity and demand rigorous planning. They work at many levels including the task in hand. Great leaders zoom in and hover out, seamlessly balancing day-to-day detail with dreams, visions and hopes of future possibilities. They not only exercise imagination of a world where anything is possible but also have the nerve to plan for it. They diligently learn from others, watch trends, worry about reinvention and bravely destroy their own business before the competitor does it for them. They encourage an insatiable appetite for change and a relentlessness that sniffs out the slightest hint of complacency. But that can be unhelpful if driven from ego. My expectation of good leadership acknowledges that true success rarely relies on a single individual. It comes from the notion of team, the celebration of others, and often at the expense of self-promotion. And even though you are good, it is likely that the people who work for you are even better and having the courage to acknowledge that creates a higher likelihood of success. A leader like that intrigues me, seduces me and gives me a sense of my own worth and that can be powerful when witnessed across an entire workforce.

The leadership challenge for the UK pivots on the adaption to its environment that is spinning out of control whilst retaining focus on the mission in hand. Maintaining clarity on the goal with a watchful eye on the competition as the pace of change quickens and opportunities emerge through new channels in narrowing time frames. Leaders must intuit, plan, invest, calculate and manage risk, within finely honed parameters. The challenge of adapting to emerging markets and technologies from the East, within the bankruptcy of Europe, will require a balancing act which may well separate one philosophical business model from another. Those who respond to the new rules with agility and fewer home grown embedded doctrines will survive.

The main leadership challenge for my sector involves the adoption of a consumer-centric mindset. It must understand and meet its customers preferences, beliefs and behaviours by predicting next actions from increasingly complex data points. The growing removal of Government funding for charity services will lead to more calls on the public purse. Charities will need to reach out to a discerning public that understands where value resides and what is worth backing. The third sector can still challenge the world's conscience but its leaders must be noticed and speak out to both the benefactor and beneficiary alike, and those who do so with compulsion and clarity will most likely address the pressing needs of society.

4.8.2. Community

Jane Ashcroft

Like most people, my experience of leadership started as a follower. Early in my career, I held a role where I was responsible for arranging and supporting senior meetings in a large utility company. While the majority of my time was spent on administrative tasks, including endless photocopying, part of the role involved taking the minutes of senior level meetings which gave me an opportunity to observe leaders in action, in a formal environment. I moved through a series of managerial roles in personnel and then Company Secretary's functions, during a period of change as the utility company, I worked for, was being privatised.

Leaving this sector, I moved into a regional Housing Association as the first occupant of a full time HR Manager role, from which my role increased to include other corporate service activities such as the Company Secretary role, office facilities, insurance, car fleet etc. In this role I worked with a CEO who became my mentor throughout my career, and who continued in that CEO role for many years, growing the organisation, developing his people and constantly refreshing his skills and reinventing his approach during his tenure.

Moving into the care home sector as a Personnel Director I joined a listed plc, operating 135 care homes with a workforce of 15,000. The nature of care services means that the workforce is absolutely central to business success, not least as people make up over 50% of the costs of delivery, and this was at a time when the employment market was very competitive. In addition, as a listed plc, the pressures of city expectations featured in decision-making at every level.

My move to Anchor, in 1999, was driven by an interest in the combination of housing and care services, and brought me back to the third sector. Recruited as Head of HR in an organisation working across England, I moved into my first general management role outside of my functional specialisms. Initially, I took on broader roles within support functions, and then became Director of Community Services. In 2007, I became Managing Director for all of Anchors care services and in 2010 I was appointed CEO of the whole organisation. Anchor provides housing and care services for older people across England, working from around 1000 sites, with almost 40,000 customers, and around 9000 colleagues.

Leadership has many definitions. One of the important issues for me when identifying effective leadership is that it fits the needs of the organisation. Understanding and responding to external challenges and opportunities for the organisation, as well as reflecting internal issues, culture and personalities are all critical in identifying what will work — right leader, right style, right time.

Although there are attributes which provide a solid foundation for leaders, I do not hold with the 'leaders are born' approach. Virtually anyone can lead, with the intention to do so, the support of others, and an objective to aim for. A clear goal or aim is a common theme of effective leadership and while this can change over time, a focus or driver is something, which a leader must describe, in a compelling fashion in order to fulfil their role. While a 'burning platform' is sometimes provided by circumstances, where this is not the case, my experience is that something must be identified which a team can coalesce around. Making that aim meaningful for individuals in the team is an important part of the leader's role.

The leadership challenge for the United Kingdom and Europe in times of recession is complicated by the other changes, which are affecting society. The economic pressures created by recession require leaders to focus on efficiency and cost management, and can result in short-term decision-making. While these pressures can produce positive change through necessity, there is also less capacity for innovation and for trying new methods and approaches, which may require investment of money or time, which cannot be made available.

Working in older people's services for over 17 years, I am very interested in generational change and inter-generational issues — demographic change, and particularly the increases in longevity and the consequences for society, our economy, and local communities across Europe and more widely. For leaders, this will also mean leading an ever more diverse team — the changing expectations of Generation Y and the new millennials. Indeed, as careers lengthen we should anticipate that leaders will work across many sectors, be able to transfer their skills and experience.

The third sector leadership challenges in this decade are a reflection of the macro picture. The constraints on public funding are already having a profound effect, and the duration of this economic environment affects all customers' confidence and concerns, regardless of how they are funded. The need to attract new funding adds complexity to the task of leaders, and extends the skill set as not all leaders are finance people, but our knowledge of financial issues must be current.

Following the decline in trust of traditional institutions in the United Kingdom (such as banks, the NHS, the BBC, the political establishment), there is a growing interest in governance and probity. One result of this will be increasing regulation, something that leaders will need to embrace in a way, which enhances services, whilst also reflecting the drive for reduced costs. In a less structured way, increased transparency through social media, as customers, colleagues and others share information and views about our services and our organisations will require a breadth of view and a speed of response, which will change the role of leaders.

Despite all of these demands, the expectations of the people using our services will only increase. Being totally in touch with the changing needs of our customers will continue to be a key element of being a great leader in the third sector.

Rory MacLeod

I have enjoyed an inspirational career, paid and unpaid, in the community-based sector amongst many inspiring people. I have found myself in lead roles in the voluntary and public sectors, in small teams, divisions and council departments, in local and national agencies and organisations.

All such enterprises have benefitted from a mix of paid and voluntary contributors to the tasks in hand. All involved putting new ideas into action —

the actions were always original in their context and often inspired by others. All were about community, about change and challenging the *status quo*, always engaging with groups of people. All took longer than anyone wanted or understood, all required patience, understanding, and clarity of task and clarity about my role. Part of it was being a modeller, an equaliser and having faith in the task, tinged with risk and confidence, with and for all involved. Most positions involved letting go of the role at the right time. Most of the learning, initially at least, was transformative for me.

In work settings, there were leaders everywhere, above, beside and below me. The effective ones, in the minority, quietly but significantly stood out. Others simply quoted rules and systems. It was often managers managing messes. One learns from this, from immersing and being hands on with tasks, learning to be reflective, visionary and honest — to see yourself and your behaviours, and your actions, as others see you. Almost all effective actions involved sharing, distributing and giving away, tactically, tranches of the leadership position. Tinge any boldness and confidence with humility because these characteristics follow initial learning, for better and for the worse.

Effective and meaningful engagement with people is an art, a collection of capabilities and knowledge. If you hit the wrong note, pitch in at the less than best time, the tune does not sound right. Empirically placed leaders are too often poor at this. The hoped for outcome gets in the way of the delivery and the process. As leaders we need to learn to handle the silence that prevails before the next sound, the next piece of the tune, beat of the drum. If you do get the tune wrong, people will tell you or let you know. This is not a personal thing. Don't take it so. Too many leaders can't handle the challenge with their mix of office, status and ego overwhelming their stifled humility. They are, of course, too often whistling their own tune, alone. The tune is a lament to the mantra 'Everyone is a leader' — without knowing how to play it at all.

I learned to be wary of these leadership clichés. Ironically, they can lower the standard of debate and the potential to lead. They feed off insecurities, affirm a mutual inability to stand back from the lead role and give others in the complex network space the opportunity to lead forward, walk on an edge, take risks and persevere.

In my experience, leaders in the public sector often wanted to but rarely took risks. There was a great deal of fear and nervousness. Too often a meaningful change in the public sector was achieved despite the cloud of corporate guidance. Such leaders are now learning to have conversations with key players about meaning in tasks. There seems to be endless rules and reasons about not doing original things. In reality there aren't, so a great deal is possible. Where it works effectively, is where people free themselves of the imagined limitations and are prepared to deconstruct hierarchies and build support networks, complex networks at times, working with people in the community. Local leaders with bottle and who persevere achieve much. Let them.

The third sector benefits from an identified focus, purpose, and a belief as well as a fluctuating, but critical mix of passion and science in structure and approach, which results in the emergence of creative leaders. Many effective leaders adopt a cultural leadership approach in, and amongst, a set of networks. The leader, when at the centre of the action, has a heightened sense of the dynamics of his/her colleagues and an awareness of the potential of their colleagues to work in cohesion to a common purpose. I have found in this sector that leaders will intuitively know when to own tasks and when to let them go. They will maintain purpose and meaning, on track, with decisiveness and clarity and the evidence is when actions follow on soon after conversations take place. The action is about change, growth and evolution. It is not about the individual making a mark.

Leaders will persevere with patience without stubbornness but also in their own way, being fearless of the new territories and handling the concerns and anxieties that others bring to these moments. Leaders will be settled in their own, sometimes isolated, company, but will recognise the benefits of and value the company of others. They will learn from others with humility but recognise that they carry the conch when it matters. They will not feel the need to be a hero but wear some of these garments when required and, at times, be a bit mischievous — almost a guerrilla action, comfortable with creative chaos. It is a bigger toolbox than we know.

Our leaders, given the opportunity, must return to leading people and not systems that are often driven by single ideas. Recession itself has become a reason for not doing meaningful things and appearing to be lost, so we search for the good old days. Instead, we should be considering new beginnings, an opportunity for change. Tinkering with old models must cease, redesigning is not only the way ahead, it is critical.

We must pay attention to our language. It is increasingly aggressive, accusatory and divisive. Sound bite culture lives and dies in a moment. Leaders learn from conversations, decide when to have them, when not to and make sure that listening and hearing are in the leadership mix — the leadership DNA. The strategists need to have these conversations more frequently with people who action the work. It is time to let go of the past and push forward.

Our systems are gridlocked with the clashing of boundaries. Leaders need to lead beyond these limitations and explain in straightforward terms why they are doing this. This involves us all as both explainers and listeners. Leaders must turn the talk of values into distinctive action. Too often it is a task in itself carried out and modelled by managers alongside annual communications plans and team building business lines. Selfless leaders who will challenge dated paradigms must lead the change in culture that is required for the community sector to be recognised as the key player it is.

Chris Mould

I began working in the voluntary sector at the beginning of 2004 after twenty-two years primarily in the public sector. For sixteen of those years, I held chief officer level roles in the National Health Service and in the Police. I also had a foray into Education as Chairman of Governors at a primary school, a non-executive position held alongside the other paid employment. Throughout my career, because of the type of work I have done and some of the one-off projects I have been involved in, I have additionally had insight into politicians as leaders when they have held government roles. Finally, in the NHS, the Police and currently in the voluntary sector, I have held leadership roles in, or involving other European nations, which have helped me note in particular that not everyone does it the same way.

The principles I want to reflect on are not especially specific to the voluntary sector, so I would encourage anyone anywhere in leadership to consider them. But the voluntary sector is a distinct territory, as the context is significantly different. In the sector, organisational vulnerability is often amplified, uncertainty and unpredictability about the future are constant companions, financial circumstances are frequently edgy, and the stakeholder mix is as complex if not more so than in any other sector you could work in. It is cross-over territory, borderlands in all sorts of senses, which make the need for sure-footed leadership and good judgement all the more pressing.

I am going to write about values, faith, humility, personal morality, emergence, teamwork, persistence and having your feet on the ground. I start with personal morality as whenever I reflect on leadership I find myself circling back there frequently. This is because I have had the privilege of working with a host of very fine leaders over the years whose worlds have in the end unravelled as a result of profound misjudgements in the area of personal morality spilling over into their work. At the extreme, a few have taken their own lives in consequence. Several had no choice but to leave their jobs and have never again had a platform, where others could draw on their talents and creative leadership. Stopped short, in other words.

In my mind good leaders embody what they are about. They live it and whatever angle you probe them from you should find the same strengths at the fore. There can be no dissonance between what you say and how you live it. Good leaders have strong values and they have thought about those values deeply. They know how their values apply in all sorts of contexts such as making decisions about money, assessing strategic business opportunities, deciding whom their organisation should partner with and dealing with challenging people problems.

Truth is, though, it is not as easy as it may sound to hold to your values. I lead the Trussell Trust, a Christian, faith-based organisation, which launches and develops community-based sustainable projects that tackle poverty. Because of who we are and what we aim to do, how we go about our work is especially important. Integrity is at a real premium. I look outside my organisation and beyond myself for help to stay true to those values. My personal faith means for me prayer, as reaching out to a God who can chide me as well as guide me is my route. But religious faith or not, good leaders should ensure they have someone to mentor them, perhaps a coach, or at the very least, someone who does not work with them, who knows them well enough and is secure enough to tell them when they are not doing it right. Good leaders will listen to those voices.

In January 2004 the Trussell Trust trustees held their annual vision day. We decided then that if our food bank project in Salisbury was needed in Salisbury — as evaluation feedback clearly told us it was — every town and community in the United Kingdom should have one. Where we had just one food bank, we saw a need for at least 700. Where we were operating in just one provincial city, we saw a need to be operating UK-wide. To make the challenge more attainable we set ourselves the interim target of establishing 50 food banks in five years, a target that still looked huge. By the summer of 2013, the Trussell Trust had launched over 350 food banks. It had also stimulated a market too, which means that beyond the food banks in the Trussell Trust's own network, there is now a host of independent projects seeking to tackle the issues we tackle, using similar approaches. In relation to hunger in Britain, the landscape of awareness and organisational response has entirely changed in less than 10 years.

Knowing clearly where you want to get to and getting up every morning with that goal in mind are qualities in leaders who persist, who demonstrate resilience, and are qualities worth consciously nurturing. I like to partner this idea of persistence with something that might seem contradictory: a taste for emergence — spotting an opportunity when it comes along and being flexible enough to take it before it is too late. In any business on the edge, where finance is uncertain and political context can so easily move the goal posts, comfort with emergence is immensely useful. It is particularly so when your commitment to the long-term goal drives everything, because then you are able to use emergent opportunity to serve that goal and able to spot when an opportunity is actually nothing more than a distraction in disguise.

The Trussell Trust decided in 2005 to diversify its income streams because we wanted to avoid the vulnerability that comes when an organisation is over dependent on one source of funding. Today we receive no government funding, have seven different categories of income and 40% of our turnover comes from 18 social enterprise projects. Individuals with drive are vital to success. But the reality of enduring success is always rooted in teamwork. More so than a leader would deep down like to acknowledge, it is the team that gets an organisation where it needs to get to. Consciously stating to themselves, and to the world at large, the importance of each individual's contribution helps a leader get the balance right.

Leaders with staying power, stay in touch. However frenetic the pace and however rapid the growth, listening to clients, going to where the job's being done and listening to the people doing it, has to be given priority. Intentionality makes the difference. Good leaders block that time out in their diaries. Good leaders know they have to give themselves the chance to be brought down to earth, and they know they have to do it regularly. The Trussell Trust has grown 13-fold in 6 years. Growth does not provide an excuse. It makes time spent listening and observing all the more important.

Three certainties strike me. First, with leadership comes power. Second, with power comes the temptation to believe the rules are different for you. And third, abuse of the power leadership conveys is so common. There is no doubt I too could abuse any power I have. However much I might like to think otherwise, I am not immune.

Four hundred years ago the eminent poet John Donne, who after a lifetime of personal struggle and deeply disappointing career setbacks, had eventually become Dean of St Paul's Cathedral in London, found himself reflecting on his own vulnerability. Chewing it over in 'A Hymn to God the Father', and musing on forgiveness, he concludes: *When thou hast done, thou hast not done, for I have more.* It may be self-awareness. It may be humility. Enduring in leadership long term will require that you consciously develop both qualities. They are the ground on which the other ingredients flourish. Times are tough in the United Kingdom and in Europe. Recession and austerity continue to take their toll. These realities have sharpened the challenge for leaders but for me they do not change the priorities. Honing the personal qualities of leadership is where the difference between success and failure will always reside.

Verene Nicolas

I came to play a leadership role in the community after being involved for many years in community empowerment and transformative learning. I am originally from France and moved to live in Scotland in 1997 where I got involved in the Centre for Human Ecology, an educational charity whose mission is to bridge academic education with community-based learning. In 2004, my husband and I moved to Govan in Glasgow. We wanted to be closer to the Galgael Trust whose work with people struggling with unemployment and addiction inspired us. In 2010, myself and others created the Govan Folk University, an initiative to join up areas of our work on learning in the community. Under this banner, several local organisations launched a project into how Govan could become a more resourceful and resilient community, particularly in the light of the economic crisis and climate change issues.

My present voluntary role in the community includes working with other local people and agencies on specific projects, facilitating learning events, and supporting the community to organise events around practical issues, such as offering a weekly communal meal in Govan's main community centre, campaigning for local representation in one of the Govan's key organisations, and enquiring into how we could more effectively work across differences in the community and voluntary sectors.

My perception of leadership in a place like Govan is that it is a role played by highly committed, creative and hard-working individuals, whether they are originally from here or not. Leaders act on behalf of the community, with deep concerns for the dignity and well-being of the people and are anchored in a long-term vision of inclusion, self-reliance and cultural vibrancy. However, in their role as leaders, they are often confronted with challenges that few are fully equipped for, either organisationally or individually. They also often operate from a conception of leadership that has become outdated and needs deep rethinking.

Unlike more diverse and wealthy areas of Scotland, communities like Govan have multiple layers of deprivation and are highly socially stratified. It means that local people are confronted with high levels of mental illness, low individual resilience and a narrow range of skills to tap into in order to initiate, run and sustain local projects. As a result, it is not unusual for the boards of local organisations to be made up primarily of professional people living outside the local area.

In terms of leadership, it means that the fabric of the community makes it difficult to gather solid, skilled and reliable individuals to share the load. Trying to bring about change in a community like Govan requires the ability to work consciously on developing resourcefulness and leadership capacity amongst people who do not identify themselves as leaders. This, in turn, requires a particular need to identify where the leadership potential might lie, as well as perseverance in creating the right conditions by which people feel safe and motivated to engage. By way of comparison, in wealthier communities, people are thirsty to get involved in meaningful, community projects to counteract the stress of high performing jobs and the isolating effect of individualistic lifestyles. They often bring with them professional skills, networks of contacts, and the kind of work ethic that organisations and communities thrive on.

By contrast, many organisations in hard-pressed areas have a particular challenge in balancing effectiveness (the daily tasks of running and sustaining an organisation) with inclusion. Whilst local people benefit from a rich, vibrant community and voluntary sector, their chaotic personal circumstances make it difficult to trust their ability to come together around a common vision and seize the opportunities for self-transformation that this represents. It also means that human dynamics within organisations can be particularly time and energy consuming. How to balance people's immediate needs and create enough space for long-term visioning at an organisational and community level is hugely challenging, especially at a time of shrinking resources for local services.

My sense is that it is time for a radical rethinking of the notion and role of leadership. In the eyes of many, a leader is still someone who puts himself or herself forward to represent and take initiative on behalf of the community. This person is seen to have particular qualities and influence. And they are given legitimacy to use a particular type of power.[6] However, we all bear the scars of living in an increasingly de-humanising society where economic and political structures are based on an authority-based model of decision-making

---

6. For more on this topic, check http://baynvc.blogspot.co.uk/2013/05/leadership-101.html#more

and where worldviews such as competition, consumerism and scarcity create cultures of fear and disempowerment. In this context, the kind of leadership we are familiar with is not working anymore. In particular, I hear people I am working with[7] questioning the usefulness of representative democracy in a political and economic context where it has become critical for people to organise and take control of their lives. How to rethink leadership then? First of all, we want to witness a shift from 'hero' to 'host':[8] the leader's role is to create space (or social containers) for the community to articulate its concerns and set its own agenda. Then, at the heart of this is the challenge to transform cultures of fear into cultures of trust, in ourselves as leaders, our teams and our organisations, so that the community can in turn regain the trust that everyone matters, that their voice counts, and that they can mobilise the resources to tackle their own problems. This is particularly important in the context of building self-reliant communities as only when people feel they matter can they start rebuilding their self-belief and a sense of the preciousness of their own health and destiny. This has two implications with regard to leadership: one is in relation to conflict; the other one is commitment to self-transformation.

There is a need to seriously engage in transforming conflict dynamics within and across organisations. How can we expect a wide range of people to be inspired and resourced to take their future in their hands if we cannot model collaborative leadership within the community and voluntary sectors? This, to me, requires particular skills such as dialogue, speaking truth with care, giving, and receiving feedback and facilitating collaborative decision-making processes. Crucially, this involves transforming destructive patterns of power, such as power over others (where we prioritise meeting our own needs over those of others) or abdication of power (where we prioritise meeting other people's needs to the detriment of our own) and privilege power and moving to collaborative power. At this point, and because we all carry these destructive power dynamics in ourselves, we are confronted with a very personal challenge. The kind of leadership that I am envisioning requires of us what might be called a spiritual practice of self-reflection, surrender and ultimate trust to develop: an openness to change and being changed; to embody qualities of authenticity; courage and care; and to nurture a quality of connection with self and others that can lead to genuine organisational and community renewal.

To conclude, I would say that whilst anchoring our leadership role in an intention to serve the community and care for the whole is important, it is often not enough. Because the task at hand is to transform deeply engrained and destructive power dynamics, it is critical that we learn the skills of

---

7. I am particularly indebted to Gehan Macleod and Kate Driscoll Erickson for their contribution to this article.
8. See Wheatley and Frieze (2011) for the notion of leaders shifting from 'Heroes to Hosts'.

collaborative leadership and nurture cultures of trust wherever we are. This, I believe, is a critical path to reconnect people with themselves, neighbours, nature and the rest of society.

Pam Schwarz

I came across housing, as a career, by accident. In the early 1970s, after 2 years voluntary teaching in southern Africa, I returned to the United Kingdom with the intention of looking for a fill-in career until I was 40, and then mature enough to teach. It was during this time that I came across housing management, described as administration plus working with people. Jobs were scarce but I sent a letter of enquiry which landed on the desk of a charismatic community leader who also worked in a community development way. This gave me a link back to my Africa experience. I had come across community in rural Africa and now I found an organisation founded on community development principles, in urban UK. I became the first employee of this thriving Housing Association which was seeking to interpret and meet the housing needs of its own community — pure community development.

Thirty-seven years later, I retired from that same Housing Association as its second Chief Executive. For the years between joining in 1973, as a Trainee Housing Manager, becoming Chief Executive in 1997 and retiring in 2010, I was part of the growth of the organisation which increased from 40 units of accommodation in ownership to over 4000 and from 1 to 110 staff. The housing association had begun as a group of people in Moss Side, Manchester, England. Its aim was to deal positively with the aftermath of a well-meaning housing policy. This policy of slum clearance and demolition had resulted in the mass movement of people around and outside the City of Manchester. Communities, families and individuals were being torn apart. The delicate ties which bind people together were not recognised and not taken into account. Waste swathes of land were made free of buildings for the first time in four generations. The bold premise of the housing association's founders was that housing can be organised in such a way as to respond to individual needs and to communities' needs. The founders held that high-quality housing and a high-quality housing service could be delivered in a way which works with the grain of peoples' needs and wants and which takes into account the community perspective.

Leadership within this housing association had a particular dilemma to address. The whole reason for its being was a response to identified community needs. Those needs were to be addressed in a community development way, in particular to take into account individuals and communities. In this way, it was hoped that the unintended consequences of the grand solution approach to housing policy and practice could be avoided. To run a staff team with a similar community development approach would be a logical and fitting approach. This would mean encouraging and empowering front-line staff. But the pressure to run a staff team as a conventional hierarchy with bosses who tell you what to do, bosses who take the blame, and bosses who treat you badly was compelling. So, my leadership experience, within the housing association, was an attempt to balance these two approaches in a staff team — community development versus hierarchical — while working with communities and individuals and responding to the demands of local government, central government, lenders and suppliers.

As well as my experience of leadership within the housing association, I have also served as a School Governor in Moss Side and as a Council of Management member of a heritage building in Manchester which has been saved from demolition by the determination of local residents. Looking back at my working life, leadership, within a social business, means to me:

- Living the values, vision and mission
- Employing the best available people — avoiding only employing people not as clever as the boss
- Giving people as much control as possible over their working lives
- Trusting, encouraging, and supporting people
- Keeping calm when those around you are in panic mode — dealing with your own panic elsewhere
- Saying the hard thing when appropriate and hearing the hard thing when it is said to you
- Balancing the needs of the individual with the needs of many whether they are residents, staff or members of the governing body
- Hearing and recognising the lone voice, as they may be right. But also recognising when they are wrong

Both method and approach are important. A comparison can be made between the community development approach to relating to individuals and communities and the importance placed on customers in modern business management approaches to service and product delivery. Perhaps the community development approach and modern business methods are not as different as they seem at first sight. Both are 'person centred' (to borrow a concept from counselling theory). Both are consistent with participatory democracy, which is considered important by western democracy and capitalism.

Leadership challenges within Europe and the United Kingdom seem to me to be:

- How to get more value for less cost? Only £££s, budgets and deficits seem to matter. We need to take into account people and communities as they are often forgotten. Are we about to repeat the mistakes of the last generation? This time with a different reason and when we have already learned better
- Is the only way to lead and manage to create a burning platform? If so, which of the values or elements of leadership which I have described above must be sacrificed? And how is that to be decided?

The challenges for leaders in the community-based sector of the housing association movement would seem to be:

- Can the values, vision and mission be stuck to? Of course not, they are always changing with new perceptions or changed circumstances. But what should the new approach be? Can the people-based and community-based approach be retained? Or should that fall off the burning platform? If so, what comes in its place?
- Taking Government's money (or The Queen's Shilling as the Press Gangs called it) means doing the Government's job and presenting the Government's view. This has been the case for over 30 years and has resulted in subtle or less subtle changes in emphasis. Can this sector still speak a special truth to government? Or is it to become just another government agency?

If the last becomes true, the community-based housing association sector could become part of the problem for individuals and communities rather than an agent of communities, which takes them into account and stands alongside them.

Over the years of its existence, the housing association I worked for has adapted and changed. It has been pragmatic in its responses to change. It has ducked and it has woven. But it has kept its values at the centre of what it does. Looking now at how it is responding, and, particularly, at the current leadership, it is continuing to do that. It continues to ask questions, to seek for and recognise solutions which are sensitive to communities and individuals.

4.8.3.   Charity

Bernard Collier

I first started leading organisations in 1990, when I joined PIP, a small charity teaching independent living skills to adults who have learning difficulties. In 2000, I moved to Voluntary Action Westminster, which helps to build local community organisations and enable community voice with public authorities. I have been a Trustee of many organisations including London Voluntary Service Council and the National Association of Voluntary and Community Action. The latter afforded me many opportunities to play a role in civic space on a national level. My experience is of leading small- and medium-sized charities with between 3 and 40 staff.

Charities are an idea or purpose of the original trustees, captured in the founding document, which sets out a vision of the world they would like to create. Leadership in the charity sector takes place in the context that every activity leads towards the longer term purpose. Leadership is, therefore, the process of gathering all stakeholders, including internal staff, volunteers, trustees, beneficiaries and outside interested bodies, around a collective understanding of the endeavour. Then creating a compelling story that will motivate stakeholders to give their energies and resources towards the big vision. Uniquely, if the charity has fulfilled its purpose, the role of the leader can be, with the board, to close the organisation down.

As a leader, my objective is to try and gain commitment to the purpose of the organisation internally and externally. I do this externally by trying to align goals by building partnerships and internally by getting all staff, trustees and volunteers to feel that they equally own the end purpose of the organisation. For me leadership is about communication, coalition building and motivating people. But whilst overseeing and evaluating delivery in the present, leaders also need to be evaluating: are we doing the right thing now and how do we adapt to what will be needed for the future? All this can never be done in isolation so the role of the leader is to nurture a thinking culture where people throughout the organisation are posing questions about efficacy and debating the way forward.

As part of strengthening the organisation, leaders need to encourage others to take responsibility. Leaders need to back their judgment, as if it were their own supporting success, but also learning when things don't go to plan. Leaders need to be visible and take personal responsibility when organisations are having a difficult time, but to push others to the fore when there are successes to celebrate.

A prolonged period of slow or no growth will suppress wages and create under-employment and long-term unemployment. Such a period of stagnation will lead to societal tensions as individuals' living standards are undermined and their dreams thwarted and they feel the need to find someone to blame for their misfortune. The conditions are ripe for divisions to grow: inside and between countries in Europe: between old and new members; North and South; rich and poor; East and West; and developing and developed. And within the United Kingdom between: North and South; rich and poor; employed and unemployed; a United Kingdom or divided; in versus out of Europe; and bankers versus everyone else.

Leaders will need to create consensus on a number of areas including the following: their approach to sharing the proceeds of wealth; climate change; energy policy; the aging population; and the growing competitive challenge from BRICs (Brazil, India, Russia, China) the CIVETs (Colombia, Indonesia, Vietnam, Egypt, Turkey, South Africa), instead of diverting their attention to unproductive divisions, such as those described above. Leaders will need to find a balance between supporting those disadvantaged by the depression, while investing in the infrastructure for innovation to flourish.

The single most important challenge leaders will need to face is to keep people believing in the special nature of voluntary association. Leaders will need to show what the purpose of the sector is, why it is needed and what its special contribution is. The key leadership challenges will be:

- *Legitimacy.* As the economic slowdown continues and the social consequences of government policy become more apparent, the space in which the sector operates will become more contested. Politicians and commentators have already started questioning the legitimacy of charities campaigning on social issues, especially if they are in receipt of government funding. This questioning of the legitimacy of the sector will intensify, and its voice will come under greater scrutiny
- *Authenticity.* At the same time the sector's role will be held up to scrutiny by the wider community, but particularly by the people that it serves. As government policy impacts on people's lives the sector will be expected to stand up for the less well off. It will lose credibility if found wanting. The leadership challenge will be to stay relevant whilst not overstepping the legitimacy question raised by politicians
- *Civic leadership.* At a time when so much in the public space is contested and politicised, and views are becoming polarised the risk of social breakdown becomes greater. Although sector leaders may have profound concerns about policy they have a duty to beneficiaries to add to the debate in a positive way
- *Sectoral cultural dissonance.* The sector will be faced by a number of dilemmas especially if it is to continue to deliver services. Involvement in contracting will be riskier, involve consortia and because of the size of contracts they will increasingly involve the private sector. The dilemma goes further than this for many in the sector, given that the way to fund services will be through donations, socially enterprising activity, corporate giving or philanthropy. To maintain services organisations will not be able to rely on donations and for many the size of social enterprise activity needed to fund services would dwarf them. This leaves corporate giving or philanthropy and both will expect something in return for their resources. The inevitable coalition will disturb many in the sector and finding the blended value and reciprocity in these relationships will be a challenge. Sector leaders will need to find a way of harnessing these opportunities in a way that empowers beneficiaries
- *Innovation.* Given that for the vast majority of the sector there will not be enough resources to fund services, leaders will need to find new ways of providing services. They will need to find new organisational models, which use technology and utilise volunteers more in a way that enables them to support beneficiaries

All these elements are vital for leadership in the third sector now and in the future.

Edel Harris

Like many people, I did not learn my leadership skills from going on training courses or from reading books but rather from working for, and alongside, both great leaders and very poor managers over the period of my career. The qualities I admire in people whom I perceive to be exceptional leaders are not their qualifications or their accolades but rather their human behaviours. By this I mean those people I have worked with who are kind, take time to know you, and appreciate that you have a life, hobbies and interests and a family outside work that are important to you too. Individuals who are honest and always act with integrity and who will always put the needs of the organisation before their own.

I am often asked what the difference between management and leadership is and for me it boils down to one important factor — *vision*. Good managers are able to get the best out of people, systems and other resources in order to achieve a goal or a target, which has often been set by someone else. There is a place for good management in every business and we should not see good management skills as inferior in any way to good leadership skills. Good managers will thrive alongside good leaders. However, a leader has a very clear vision, often they can see a journey's end before others have even thought about packing a case. But seeing the vision is not enough. A good leader needs to be able to articulate the vision, clarify the steps required to get there and be able to inspire others to join them on the journey.

As the leader of one of the largest third sector social care organisations in Scotland which employs over 1800 people, I adopt a relatively straightforward approach to leadership which I can describe best as my top 10 tips. I do not profess to be a management guru nor do I have an MBA or other academic qualification to back up my theory but these are the tips I would pass on to anyone aspiring to undertake a role such as mine. Some of the tips, which you might recognise, have been 'borrowed' from others, in particular Jim Collins the author of 'Good to Great':

- *Clear vision.* Avoid putting everyone on the bus and driving it yourself. You need others to want to get on the bus and help you to work out how best to reach your destination. Once the vision is articulated and endorsed someone else with the right skills can drive the bus — you are the navigator. Lots of activity does not equal realising the vision. There may be several strategic priorities and action plans sitting on the shelf because everyone is too busy to deal with them
- *Employ the right people with the right attitude.* Find roles for great people to fill rather than always seeking the right person to fill a post. People with the right attitude and values can make all the difference. At all times eradicate negativity and surround yourself with people who want to work, who believe in the organisation and who try to find solutions not problems. There is no place for 'mood hoovers' in our company

- *Apply the spirit not the letter of the law.* In large organisations subject to regulatory influence you will often find policies and procedures written with the very best intentions but are often so inflexible. In our desire to treat everyone fairly we often create a beast that leaves little room for human response and the ability to treat certain situations on their merit. I am not always popular with my HR colleagues, with such views, but as long as I can justify why I take a particular course of action that is what is important. As a leader you need to have the confidence to make decisions and not hide behind policies and procedures, rules and regulations. Be human in all your endeavours
- *Greater empowerment of colleagues.* Central or tight management control stifles creativity and innovation. Greater empowerment is likely to increase the risk of error but I believe the benefits outweigh the risks
- *Ambitious for the company first and foremost.* Great leaders attribute much of their success to good luck rather than personal greatness. Great leaders, in my opinion are often the ones we have never heard of
- *Understand the company's risk profile and the risk profiles of the key decision-makers.* We will all have a particular view of risk and this may differ from that of our colleagues. When working together as a team it is important that you all understand each other's risk profile so when important decisions have to be taken they are taken in the context of the organisation's appetite for risk and not based on the group's personal view
- *Don't focus solely on the potential financial impact of any decisions.* Balance the financial risk with the potential risks associated with maintaining quality, staff retention, undermining previous decisions/activity/strategy and being true to your values. Our values are: Caring, Customer focused, Professional and Pioneering. Ensure you and the senior decision-makers understand the business values[9] and ensure they are always considered when making important decisions
- *Be outward facing.* Recognise the relevance of good relationships and never let an opportunity go cold. It takes strong leadership to 'look up' during difficult times
- *Understand the competition.* Sometimes it takes a crisis or challenge for us to see ourselves compared to our main competitors. We don't tend to look when all is going well. It is easy to become complacent. But challenged organisations can and do emerge stronger, leaner, more focused and better able to compete

---

9. Our business values:

- *Performance*: we expect the highest standards from the organisation ourselves and each other
- *People*: we promote a positive work culture; we respect each other, take accountability for our actions and work as a team to deliver great results
- *Integrity*: we are always professional, authentic and honest

- *Always feel passionate about what you do.* Whatever business or industry you are working in ideally you should wake up every morning feeling positive about the working day ahead. If you lose that passion and purpose you are in the wrong job

The recession and the rapid change, particularly in public service delivery, expose weak leadership where we see many examples of responsive management. A strong leader has to stand by the vision and even when times are tough make sure that the business values are not compromised. The consequences of this approach can sometimes be devastating in the short term, but if you are certain that your principles are sound and that a compromise or a purely financial decision may result in a poorer service being delivered, you will emerge with your company reputation intact when others fail to survive.

In the context of social care, I worry that the UK government has not woken up to the fact that the numbers of vulnerable, disabled and older people are increasing while at the same time there is a race to the bottom, in terms of what public commissioners will pay for care services. We need to see strong political leadership and ask ourselves what sort of society we want to live in. Nick Clegg famously said in 1990 *you can judge a society on the help it provides to those who need it most*, and yet we don't see that value underpinning many of the decisions currently being made by our politicians.

Managing our operations through these financially challenging times without compromising on quality is probably the biggest challenge we face as an organisation. The current external environment is threatening the basis on which we have built our business. We have experienced so much change and many of the challenges we are facing today could not have been predicted.

We have some insight into the complex and evolving social care market which will undoubtedly have a major impact on our organisation and the way we currently work. Although we continue to recognise the local authorities as significant stakeholders, it is unrealistic and impractical for us to continue to work with them as our primary customers. This allows us to focus our attention on doing what is always in the best interests of the people we support and in managing the complex and challenging relationships we have with our key funders without always meeting their expectations.

Our relationships with our local authority colleagues are being tested in some areas as they retreat behind the commissioner/provider contractual relationship rather than the partnership approach we would prefer. There are both threats and opportunities presented with the advent of self-directed support and the integration of health and social care. We need to ensure that we are not left behind in the technology revolution and we need to face some cultural issues associated with our historical paternal approach to the care of vulnerable people. In our attempts to be leaner and to respond to the cuts required by local councils, we are stretching some of our managers to the limit and if we do not address this issue immediately it may begin to impact on the quality of the care we provide. However, despite these challenges I continue to take pride in all we have achieved particularly the difference we are making to the lives of over 2000 children, adults and families who require our support. We remain focused on our aim 'to enable the people we support to enjoy a valued life'.

Jeff Hurst

During my working life I have been led by others, have had leadership done to me, have done leadership to others and have led others. For 24 years in the Army I experienced many leaders first-hand. They came from different countries, different cultures, had different upbringings, and very different educational backgrounds. They were trained at great public expense and all had an understanding of theories, such as those of Maslow, McGregor and Adair. My experience is that much of the leadership in the Army is centred on the needs of the task, some on the needs of the group and a little on the needs of the individual.

Despite the diversity of individual leaders all had one thing in common — authority. The whole basis on which the military functions is unquestioning loyalty of the followers to the leaders, a soldier has no choice but to follow their leader, the consequences of not following are severe. No military leader has a democratic legitimacy to take the lead; however, some create legitimacy because of their skill, personality, character traits, personal integrity and application of training. All have legitimacy because of their appointment, power and status, and all have ultimate authority with recourse to severe sanctions.

For the last 10 years I have been working in the third sector, the term used, in my view, to describe every type of organisation that is not in the private or public sector. I began working in the third sector as a regional manager for a national registered charity, which had 300 staff, working in 16 different locations across England and Scotland delivering services to 3000 service users. For the last 4 years, I have been the Chief Executive of a small registered charity that is also a company limited by guarantee as well as a social enterprise. It has 28 staff working in 4 different sites in a city delivering services to 600 service users. Similar to the Army — providing that I act within the direction given to me by the Board of Trustees and within the provisions of the legislation that governs businesses and charities — I have, by virtue of my position, complete authority over the staff and volunteers, but does that make me a leader and do the workforce follow my lead?

In both my military and third sector careers, the leaders and the workforce have been united in the pursuit of a single cause with everyone focused on the organisational objectives. The objectives of both the military and charity are focused on people. In the Army, it was peacekeeping, protection, removing the threat of mutual destruction, the removal of dictators to restore civilised society and creation of freedom for individuals within a democracy. In the charity it is protecting individuals, improving the conditions of the people living in the most disadvantaged communities and creating independence and freedom within a democracy.

The real difference between the two has been the leadership culture. In the Army, there are clear symbols of power and status associated with positions of leadership. Leaders are segregated and live, socialise, and even eat separately from their followers. There is a process of recruitment, selection, training and testing leaders that is based on educational attainment, social status and financial independence.

Within small charities, leaders often emerge from within and the functions of leadership are not solely vested within the managerial framework or organisational hierarchy. Strategy is set by trustees and senior managers to meet the organisation's mission and is often decided following wide stakeholder consultation, which is usually conducted by the staff. The managerial tasks and actions to achieve the strategy are often decided in consultation with the workforce and where possible, the service users. They are also often created in dialogue with the donors and funders of the charity, as often grant-making charitable trusts require clearly defined outputs and outcomes to be achieved by their investment. This distribution of leadership tasks enables charities to get a wide range of views. It enables communication with those responsible for the delivery of the mission, to ensure they understand the mission and their contribution to delivering it, as well as ensuring that they have the skills and abilities to deliver it.

In the Army, soldiers are prepared to follow their leader even if it means death but this leadership is reinforced with authority, discipline and significant consequences. So why do others follow? In charities, the workforce is likely to have a shared values base that is aligned to the organisational values, culture and mission. The following values are high on the list: trust, respect, transparency, integrity, fairness and equality. It is vital that leaders consistently act and behave in accordance with those values and create a culture to enable the workforce to do the same.

I firmly believe that most people are capable of great things. To do so they need the following: (i) the opportunity, (ii) resources and (iii) support. To me leadership means creating a supportive, values-based culture that is clearly articulated and acted upon. It is essential to allow, with boundaries, individuals freedom of action to achieve the mission in the best possible way for the service user and the member of staff. I draw my leadership inspiration from a quote by General Patton. *Never tell people how to do things, tell them what to do and they will surprise you with their ingenuity.*

Leadership also means clearly identifying and setting the desired levels of standards. For me that means setting the bar as high as possible and achieving as much as you can. If you don't quite clear the bar that is OK, as long as everyone knows that. This approach generally produces better standards than setting the bar too low and achieving it easily.

In my experience, the best leaders are those who consciously take the time and effort to understand the motivation and behavioural drivers of those they lead and ensure that they provide them with the opportunities, resources and the support they need in order to enable them to do the best they can.

The current economic and social climate provides significant challenge for leaders across all sectors.

For the *public sector* this includes:

- Rebuilding trust and faith in political democracy, politicians as people, and political parties as organisations
- Rebuilding trust and faith in public institutions, which following many public enquiries, have been exposed as being poorly led with police forces found to be institutionally racist, hospitals putting management targets before patient care, and departments incapable of procuring equipment or services and having no concept of balanced budgets
- Delivering large and complex change programmes in short time spans involving large numbers of job losses
- Leading and managing services in decline, doing more with less and maintaining quality
- Significant loss of organisational memory and knowledge

For the *private sector* the challenges include:

- Creating an alternative market system than the current one based on maximising profits, creating wealth and a style of business leadership that appears only to be self-serving
- Realising that rather than just creating financial value, business can create or destroy social value
- Setting and delivering strategic objectives in a complex and fast changing external environment that seems to function on the edge of chaos

For the *third sector* the challenges are:

- Creating sustainable business models to deliver increased levels of services with less funding and resources. This will involve the design and application of new organisational structures and financial engineering to enable third sector organisations to generate earned incomes. Traditional sources of income are changing and decreasing including; diminishing public sector grants; individual donations are becoming harder to generate; charitable incomes from assets are reduced by low interest rates; and low returns on investments
- Charities will be required to be more business like yet many people choose to work in the sector because it is not a business culture. Wages in the third sector are generally lower but the conditions of service and environment or more people focused

- Delivering innovation and change and managing new and unknown risks that challenge the charities, values and culture
- Doing all of the above within the existing capacity

Within the third sector, there is pressure from political sources for the sector to create innovative solutions to fix the broken society. The sector has historically been seen as a place where innovative solutions to difficult problems have been born. This is largely due to the lack of bureaucratic constraint, the democratic and distributive nature of its leadership, and the desire to overcome barriers to service delivery. Funding is often linked to innovation and yet as the sector is required to innovate it often means losing what already works well in favour of a little or an untried way of working.

In the United Kingdom there has been a drive towards volunteering and seeing volunteers as a way to increase third sector capacity. There is, however, a naivety and misunderstanding as to the value volunteers bring. Volunteers need managing, training, supervising, yet cannot be accountable or responsible for their actions within the workplace. They require a different kind of leadership — after all, their commitment is voluntary and their motivation for volunteering is likely to be different to paid employees. I am not suggesting that volunteers are of no value or do not have their place but they are not employees and should not be treated as such.

Funders are now requiring third sector organisations to collaborate with each other and with organisations from other sectors to deliver savings and create additional value. So just who should we align ourselves with in collaboration — competitors or complementary organisations? What form should this collaboration take — a new business model of an alliance based on shared risk and reward or a traditional imbalanced partnership using prime and sub-contractors where the least powerful partner eventually gets shafted?

The third sector will be required to deliver more services to more people who have greater needs but with less available resources. The effect on staff and the impact on delivery and sustainability are likely to be considerable. Staff, in most third sector organisations, will rarely say 'no', and will go the extra mile often at their own expense. That will require leading them effectively and ensuring they do not overpromise what they cannot deliver.

It is likely that there will be mergers of third sector organisations caused by a lack of finance or by the need for larger contracting to deliver social care services and achieve economies of scale. The organisations proposing to merge may serve the needs of the same cohort of service users but have different organisational cultures and values. This will test leadership in many ways some of which are likely to be new such as making roles redundant, TUPE (Transfer of Undertakings — Protection of Employment), culture change, standardisation and imposing new brand identity and values.

Achieving this is likely to require additional investment to build organisational capacity, deliver leadership training across all levels of management, and will require a different set of skills and focus of the Board of Trustees. And herein lies the leadership challenges for the Chief Executive Officers:

- Generating income that will not be spent delivering front-line services to spend on unproven and high-risk changes with unknown outcomes when it is likely that organisations will be spending reserves to meet the demand for services
- Competing for contracts and commissions with the very organisations that you are required to collaborate with
- Up skilling to deliver these new dimensions while maintaining existing levels of service delivery
- Working collaboratively within different cultures
- Taking the whole organisation and the service users on the journey

Andy Kerr

Leadership is a hugely rewarding role to play. It is a privilege to be leader, it comes with huge responsibilities and should be enjoyed, tempered and tested but most of all it should be embraced and enjoyed. I have played a variety of leadership roles as a student, as a local political leader, as a business leader, as a national political leader, and now as a leader in the third sector. I have worked with, met and viewed from afar many great and some very poor leaders, some with training and others without and all have made an impression positive or negative, many to copy and some to not.

I am a trait theorist in that there are, I believe, certain leadership traits which we have and that with supported learning, we can develop those traits into leadership skills. In addition, there is a set of behaviours that we expect to see in our own leaders and learning by example can support new and better leadership behaviours. I believe strongly that managers can develop into leaders but that the two roles of managers and leaders are massively different. A leader lays out the vision and direction. The manager plans and allocates, while the leader aligns and communicates. The manager organises, controls and monitors, while the leader motivates and inspires. The purpose of the leader is change and the purpose of the manager is order and consistency.

Leadership means three things to me:

1. *To support or change the culture as required. It is the role of the leader to mould a positive and creative culture.*

At *Sense Scotland* I defined the culture that I want to engender. This is a culture which is open, creative, inclusive, trustworthy, challenging, involved team working and treating everyone with respect. To achieve this I have set out my ambitions as a leader which are: to inspire, to enable, to realise a shared ambition, to communicate, to represent the values, to make decisions in partnership and to build trust. I regularly test the impact of my approach with 360-degree appraisal, employee surveys, and heart to heart discussions.

2. *Challenge the approach and seek opportunities, take risks and let others do the same.*

We have open discussions about the culture of the organisation, warts and all. We have set up an investment fund for staff to take risks on the projects which they think will work. We are training all our managers and supervisors in our Sense Scotland Business School. The senior management team is now known as the leadership team and we are trying to embody and live to a new set of values.

3. *Have empathy, using your natural personality, self-awareness and social skills to be part of the life of your staff.*

Appreciate who you are, be authentic, use the strengths that you have, be aware of your weaknesses and talk about them. I meddle, I swear and I have a bad memory and I tell people and I am not proud. As a leader, I supplement my natural style with the training and skills I have acquired and the learning from the feedback I have received.

I fear that in many organisations mediocrity floats to the top and there is a lack of measured risk taking. We do not teach, support and mentor leaders. We are culturally held back by our attitudes towards leadership. The challenge is to start talking about it, living it and changing behaviours. We need to ask the following questions and address them. Do those who have been fortunate enough to get some training get mentored and supported to implement what they have learnt? Do behaviours really change? Does the corporate culture allow change to happen? How do we recognise good leadership? I suspect we could do better in all these aspects.

Is it the case that we have run out of room to float ideas, to not just think about new ways but actually to deliver? Politicians, public, private, and third sector leaders have a veracious media to contend with. Politicians and officials have very narrow windows of opportunity to really change things, we now have almost an annual cycle of elections which forces playing safe and not upsetting any group or individual. The advent of 'retail politics' where the agenda is about instant gratification — in return for votes — makes reform and real change, when it is really necessary, very difficult. It is really possible to lead or even for ideas to be given a proper hearing?

There is a preference for the safe ground to the radical, due to protectionism of roles and status. The senior manager who has made it or the professional classes who find it so easy to protect themselves at the cost of others. We need to create space for radical thinking in the sector which allows ideas to grow and develop which are not attacked or undermined by vested interests. We need to challenge the views held about the sector, many of them based on fear and self-protectionism and respond publicly to some of the outrageous demands being made on us. We need to build our own confidence to speak collectively and be assertive.

Above all I believe that leaders are required to leave a legacy of not just a succession strategy but also of having created, developed and supported new leaders. That is what we are doing at Sense Scotland. Our Business School provides leadership development programmes. Our supervisors (about 140), who are about 15% of our staff, are being exposed to new ways of working and thinking about how to be a leader. They will be our leaders of tomorrow, along with other employees who have the capability to lead. Leadership is not a qualification, but a set of values and approaches, inherent and/or trained. It creates values and communities. Leadership is also about human and community capital, as well as business and organisational success.

Elaine Tait

After an eclectic career working in many different sectors, I can only marvel at the similarity of leaders who have influenced and nurtured me over the years. It goes without saying that leaders should be strategic, creative and inspirational. I have taken the opportunity here to reflect particularly on the behaviours displayed by all leaders who have influenced me for the better and the worse. I, therefore, caution readers to be alert for nostalgia and selective amnesia in my five observations on leadership and its future. In my working life, I have been fortunate to learn from some highly effective leaders, but I have also had extremely uncomfortable encounters and coped with some rather volatile working relationships.

My first observation is that you do not need to be liked as a leader; indeed an injection of healthy tension brings an edge to the team, feeds competition and fosters innovation. But the balance is critical. Place too much store on individualism and the team implodes, create an atmosphere of fear and individuals retreat, single out people for blame and you are lost. This applies universally in my experience, and the 'dog eat dog' culture in commerce is equally alive in the rarefied university sector or the NHS where avoidance of blame can replace profit as a source of motivation. Leaders need to earn respect but they do not need to be liked.

My second observation is that effective leaders learn fast to delegate and live with the consequences. This is, perhaps, the hardest lesson for aspiring junior managers. Leaders must be intuitive, know their people, establish mutual trust, empower their teams and give them the confidence to take risks. However, responsibility without authority or with constant overruling is hugely damaging. Squeezed middle managers experience this often and are seen, with some justification, as the block in the system with no authority to take decisions and no status as a result. In my experience, the NHS struggles particularly here with managers who neither speak the same language nor share common targets with their clinical colleagues; both are striving to do their best but inevitably clash with difficult consequences — the mid Staffordshire hospital scandal serves as a very real and recent example.

The immortal words of Corporal Jones *Don't panic* (in the TV programme 'Dad's Army') give me my third observation that truly exceptional leaders stay the course and do it quietly with confidence and support for their teams. Textbooks abound with high profile examples of political leaders, sports captains and military men but the 'no panic' rule applies at all levels. I have been fortunate to learn from many, such as: a CEO under threat of dismissal who refused to release information given under guarantees of confidentiality; a district general hospital manager under siege from the media in the aftermath of the Dunblane shootings; and a ward sister standing firm against a fierce assault during an episode of a galloping hospital infection. In all cases, these people were crystal clear about their priorities, made absolutely no fuss and reassured their trembling teams.

Learning to control your workload is my fourth observation. A leader giving the impression of an unsustainable workload and who is at their desk all hours of the day and night with little or no time for unimportant issues or people creates barriers, dictates the working culture and inhibits others with potential. The sage advice of Dame Rennie Fritchie of *When stressed, only do what only you can do* has stayed with me for 25 years and saved my teams and me on a good number of occasions. I remember well being intimidated by receiving emails from government ministers at 03.00 in the morning and fearing criticism for leaving on time to collect my children from nursery. I can think of no better way of deterring those seeking a reasonable work life balance, from aspiring to leadership roles today, than continuing to applaud an unmanageable workload.

Being visible is my fifth and final observation and unless carefully managed, advances in communications technology may be the incremental enemy of leadership. Leaders are by definition ridiculously busy and creating time for 'walking the shop' is difficult and can generate alarm if irregular or unannounced. The CEO who made a concerted effort to hold meetings in other peoples offices, the hospital manager who ate in the staff canteen, and the Director of Public Health who played in goal, even though badly, for the staff team took the temperature of their organisations, detected stress, and bolstered morale. The visibility or otherwise of leaders influences the culture of their organisation. However, there is a cautionary note to this, as it needs to be played carefully lest informality is misinterpreted as a lack of authority — it is a critical balance. Information and communication technology make virtual visibility easier and actual visibility more challenging. The future will decide which is the more critical.

This takes me neatly to brief comments on where leadership in the NHS is heading at a time of financial constraint amidst a plethora of leadership courses, curricula and rhetoric. I am not convinced you can teach leadership but it can and is learned through experience and mentorship. Most doctors can give you any number of senior, often long retired, famous names who inspired them as juniors and who, in turn, they aspire to emulate. This is rarely true of non-clinical managers and they need some champions. The NHS faces unimaginable management challenges to cope with rising public expectations and falling budgets. It is all too tempting to control by central policy edict, guidelines and targets or to distract from these challenges by yet more structural change. If local NHS services are to deliver for patients and staff, managers must have delegated responsibility at all levels and the authority to manage in line with local needs. Senior managers must have greater confidence in their job security and must foster improved understanding between clinical and non-clinical staff. The status of managers must be raised. I remember well the time when I was embarrassed to admit at dinner parties that I was a hospital manager — this must change.

Finally, consider the now retired Sir Alex Ferguson, who against all the odds enjoyed a 26-year term of office. He was not always liked but he was respected by players and opponents, lived and breathed Manchester United, undoubtedly produced results and yet still found time to go horse racing. Can he teach us something about leadership?

4.8.4.   *Mutual and Cooperative*

Mike Grigor

Throughout my career I have come across a large variety of leaders at varying levels of seniority, who I reported to, worked with, or had dealings with. Now I have the opportunity to consider if they were good managers or good leaders? My initial thoughts when starting work were that my managers were also my leaders. Looking back now, although I respected them, they were task orientated, good at what they did, and ensured that all tasks were done correctly and on time. Both were good at doing things right; however, they were very much managers not leaders.

Throughout my early career in banking, I have worked with a large number of good managers and less what I would call strong leaders. I think this was due to banking being a very risk adverse industry, where the main focus was on policy and procedures and where any little mistake would be highlighted and staff held accountable. It was very much a conservative approach with a view of getting things right first time with strict procedures and rules. This led to an environment where management was recognised as the norm, ahead of innovation and leadership characteristics. In my view, leadership in the bank was respected but not inspirational. Throughout time the culture of the bank changed and the areas where leadership became more apparent were the newly created business functions, where there was far more focus on business development and growing the business. These were areas where there was no micromanagement. Two-way interaction was encouraged and there was delegation of authority for managers to manage their own local business. Strong and regular communication was encouraged at all levels, recognition of success was evident, while still ensuring high compliance was adhered to, with ownership at all levels. Staff bought into the vision and strived to contribute. Strong leadership in these new business areas did not require day-to-day management, but an awareness of what was happening and what actions required to be taken, when and by whom. There was also an acknowledgement that staffs have different skill sets and that it was important to provide them with the opportunity to flourish in areas where they had key strengths. The leadership characteristics that became evident were strategy, direction, drive, focus and innovation. However control, policies and management were still evident.

As a sales culture began to be embraced by the bank, there emerged a new breed of leadership, where driving profit and sales were seen as success. This led, on occasions, to management by fear, micromanagement of figures, and a focus on results driven business where growth in profit was king. To me this was not leadership, as it did not involve the buy-in from staff at all levels. This was sales management without the controls in place.

As stated earlier, leadership drives the business, while acknowledging the controls and management required. In converse to this, there are still areas within the bank, where management rather than leadership is more evident. For example, in risk and project management, micromanagement is still evident from the top down. There are, of course, exceptions to this, where leaders are identifying and driving the change via sponsorship and can be seen to lead the business through transformational change.

Leadership is not task orientated, but about the understanding of what needs to be done to drive an organisation or a business forward. It is about gaining buy-in from staff to a shared vision. It is about providing staff with the opportunity to grow within their own role and feel that they are able to contribute to the business. It is not about micromanagement.

Leadership to me is a simple concept. It is about gaining the respect of peers and staff and creating a vision and getting buy-in to the vision from the staff to take it forward. It is about creating a desire to succeed among all colleagues by ensuring they can see where they fit in and contribute to the wider picture. It is about creating an environment where staff believe in what you are striving to achieve, while giving them the opportunity to grow and flourish in their own careers.

Looking at leadership with the third sector, there are similarities to what changes occurred in banking 20 years ago, when banking started to move towards a sales culture, with a more pro-active promotion of products to their customers. At the time in banks, the management was very much focused on processes and procedures and customers were dealt with on a reactive basis. Until recently, the third sector relied very much on a low risk, grant backed operating model, where the majority of senior management had worked within

172 of 256 172 Public and Third Sector Leadership: Experience Speaks

the sector for many years. This is changing in two ways: first, the focus is moving away from being solely reliant on grant funding, to a focus on contracts and also on earned income via trading; second, due to the impact of the recession creating a new resource pool from private sector redundancies, there are leaders from this sector moving into the third sector and bringing an external perspective to leadership to the sector. Such new leaders in the third sector are facing challenges in introducing change and implementing new ways of working, which in a large number of circumstances are required, in order, to allow organisations to survive and grow. It is about establishing the new direction of their organisation and taking their staff and trustees on that journey, which may be an uncertain path to the one they have previously been on. As with the issues encountered in the banking sector, where leadership was often achieved via a fear factor and micromanagement and driven by profits over process, history has told us that this is a dangerous path to follow. Strong leadership is about setting the vision, creating buy-in from staff and stakeholders, and driving the organisation forward, balanced with an understanding of the risk implications of growth and change, while still maintaining the core values of the organisation.

Stephen Mann

Some real paradoxes are emerging in leadership. Despite all the books written on leadership and the investment in leadership training in recent years, there has not been the sea change or collective raising of capability one might have naturally expected as a result. Demand is outstripping supply which suggests that either more or different leadership is needed in today's work environments, or that much of the investment and insight has been wasted. The inconvenient truth is that no one seems to be asking why there seems little real evidence of increased or improved delivery even as the clamour for more and better leadership gets louder. Leadership remains in scarce supply despite high and increased demand. Inevitably, many people believe they possess the skills but do not know what leadership is, while others are unaware of their potential to be much more effective leaders.

Perceptions of leadership are often based on key events, interventions or stories that are told which create some mythology around it. The focus on symbolic moments, however, tends to underplay more rounded and balanced assessments of what makes good leaders. Similarly, an emphasis on particular leadership skill sets or attributes ignores the fact that an intelligently applied blend of skills is essential to achieve the alchemic force of leadership required for sustainable change. Rather than simply using the best and worst examples of leadership as pointers and reference points, it might be better to focus more on how leaders can become more consistently effective.

Leaders are increasingly unable to rely on having any direct personal impact to create these key moments which in turn help create symbolic leadership. In bigger, more complex, multi-location or multi-national organisations, the natural starting point is also more remote. It is easier for senior people to gain a sense of comfort by this distance and once surrounded by the apparatchik outlook and trappings that go with the job, they simply are known as the face on the intranet page. It is hardly, therefore, a surprise that many leaders are unconnected with their organisation and their colleagues.

Leadership is often confused with ego. Self-centred leadership, however, is not authentic nor does it attract followership. Ego combined with the widely used and frequently favoured alpha style is also seen as the basis for effective leadership. An approach based on sound and fury will get you noticed and resonates with people who see a mirror of their own style but who themselves may not be exemplars of leadership. I have not seen many people like this who are effective leaders. When moments of truth occur, they often revert to their predominant personality type rather than use strategic leadership skills, avoiding the risks or discomfort that are essential to their further development or which would make them so much more effective.

Leadership is different to management but a good leader needs to be good at both. Textbook philosophy draws the distinction between them but unhelpfully suggests that leadership skills are somewhat magical or otherwise charismatic at the expense of other, more predictable and practical traits. Good leaders need to understand the importance of processes, capabilities, performance management frameworks, and above all consistency. Given the uncertainties, contradictions and the complexities now involved in exercising judgement, leaders need keen sensing skills — founded on emotional intelligence along with a wider ability to see patterns and their consequences. Good strategic judgement is an essential capability of leadership.

Leadership is how you make things happen successfully on a sustainable and repeatable basis. It needs to be delivered authentically and with skill. An essential element is to act as a sense maker for others, gaining trust and engagement through shaping and sharing context, explaining why actions are required, and motivating through demonstrating progress against the bigger picture.

Delivering change through leadership is now much more complex. Traditional command and control approaches can be important in crises or intense periods of change but they are no longer a basis for delivering sustainable change. With the breakdown of traditional hierarchical structures and authorities there is little natural tribal loyalty upwards with communities of interest being formed at very local levels in organisations. These communities or loose collectives cannot simply be told what to do anymore. Consistently bringing the best out of people requires different and much more subtle approaches to engaging them. Good leadership can be learned to some extent but sensing skills and emotional intelligence are required to be really effective. Sensing is more innate and if someone possesses it they will have the capability to learn and grow.

The more senior you become the less you know for certain and a range of skills (technical, political, strategic and cultural) is now needed to understand situations and their implications and outcomes. Leadership is inevitably contextual and what good leaders have is an ability to understand what is required from multi-layered environments and act both effectively and appropriately. Leadership also requires an essential innate restlessness to continually change and challenge yourself. Even the strongest leaders struggle with repeatable transformations, which reinforces that leadership is primarily contextual. Typically, people underestimate the resistance to change and/or how long it takes. This resistance is not always overt but it is often easier if it is. Good leaders are aware of the temptation to compromise early or compromise on the wrong things, which creates the illusion of progress but reduces the potential of what can be achieved.

Leaders also need to be clear on what they will be judged by and by whom. There is no right answer and leaders probably don't get to decide anyway but being aware is important. Many people overlook the basic legacy of leaving their organisation in a better shape with some choices available as a consequence of their time as its steward.

We are in the midst of major structural changes, creating new paradigms which are both unknown and uncertain. The old frameworks and order no longer apply in the way they did and the challenge for leaders is to create a meaningful sense of purpose. Doing this in an environment where across all sectors and geographies there is little additional funding or growth available, requires recognition of new realities which are quite different to what many leaders grew up with.

The practical challenge is how we need to manage and make progress against short-term outcomes while transitioning our organisations to meet the new realities. In many cases, the new realities do not offer the promise of sunny uplands in the future. It is important for leaders to avoid confusing survival of their organisation with real strategy. They need to be clear about the choices being taken and their consequences and communicate them well. A strategy without consequences is a poor strategy. In this context, communicating and developing a shared sense of purpose with authenticity is an essential leadership skill.

The current environment also requires courage and persistence. The resistance to change and the pull to maintain the *status quo* are significant even when all the rational arguments scream the need to act and act quickly. Leaders need to build enough of a coalition of interest to give themselves sufficient space to create the change and establish sufficient momentum so that progress eventually becomes sustaining.

The key challenge is how to transition to new and different business models when the rules of the game and traditional consensus are established in past models which have been shown to be lacking, but not always recognised as such. The paradox is that in a world where the need for what we do has never been greater, the levels of trust are so low. This is reinforced by the fact that leadership in many organisations is often focused on survival and not strategy. Leading the transition of any business in the absence of any real growth is the new environmental paradigm. Strategic leadership and sense-making in a world with many more paradoxes, contradictions and uncertainties will be at the heart of meeting this challenge.

4.8.5. *Social Enterprise*

David Cook

For the past 22 years, I have been privileged to lead an arts organisation operating across Scotland, on its long and sometimes convoluted journey from near collapse to sustainability. When I joined, it was a small but important charity on which many people relied but which was very dependent on revenue funding and deeply in debt. Now it is a substantial social enterprise which no longer requires revenue grant funding but creates its own income through public and private capital investment. We have doubled in size in the last 5 years and are becoming more ambitious year-on-year, looking for and seizing opportunities to support more people in more ways and to increase both our cultural and social impact as well as our financial sustainability. It has been a journey characterised by an evolution of language as much as by the development of the organisation itself. I have moved from describing myself as an arts manager to social entrepreneur: someone more outwardly concerned with the wider impacts in society and more interested in achieving these through enterprise and trading rather than subsidy. All new terminology requires acclimatisation, and in the same way that many artists grapple with the burden of that label, it can take time to become comfortable with words like 'leadership' and thinking of oneself as a leader, without sounding or feeling pompous. Leadership is a loaded word, one that seems to bring wider responsibilities, but there is definitely a mode of operating that is beyond just managing.

It is often stated that leading is about creating and communicating a vision then persuading others to get behind it, but we do not have to buy into the myth that leaders have to be charismatic figureheads, born to lead, and constantly generating unique ideas in their sleep. Even in the cultural sector where they are prized above all else, ideas are not enough. The world is littered with unimplemented ideas. Leadership is mostly about making ideas happen. And they do not all have to be original ideas. Creative leaders are often inspired by and synthesise previously disparate existing ideas into something new.

Being able to communicate and inspire are both important and if you are lucky to be born with these gifts, so much the better. Most of us, however, find by trial and error how to express ourselves coherently, how to influence others thinking, and how to harness our innate enthusiasm and positivity to inspire our co-workers, colleagues and supporters. Leadership is about behaviours, not traits, and we can all develop new and effective behaviours. Leadership can be learnt, but perhaps only in practice.

Peter Drucker said that to be a leader, you have to have followers. According to this definition if no one follows, you are not a leader. So, what makes people follow? First, courage — a quiet confidence in one's internal voice. There are always negative people trying to stop you from realising your ambitions, often for their own personal reasons. Leaders have the courage to stand by their beliefs and stand up to those who undermine ideas, change and vision. Second, at the risk of sounding trite, leaders understand their own values, and insist on unwavering compliance with these values from others. If people don't know what you believe in, they will not follow you. This is especially important in values-driven enterprises in the third sector, where colleagues and supporters need to believe deeply in the cause, or collective action fails. Finally, it's about being relentless. A leader delivers, every time, working calmly through seemingly intractable problems. He or she does not give up and does not let others give up.

Mostly, it's about delivery. For example, it is not possible to be an aspiring writer. A writer is someone who writes. As novelist Chuck Wendig put it, *aspiring is a meaningless null state that romanticizes not writing.* In the same way, it is not really possible to be an aspiring leader. A leader is someone who leads. It is a state of being defined in its doing. So, just do it.

Though it is often cited, the greatest practical challenge is not the pace of change. Good leaders love change. Nor is it technology or globalisation because if you are willing to engage with it, it is a fascinatingly big world out there. The biggest challenge has to be the legacy we are leaving for the younger generation. Young, intelligent people today struggle to get any work experience, never mind pay. The abandonment of free tertiary education, the transposition from the United States of unpaid internships, and the dearth of meaningful employment for anyone under 25 has to be sorted. Today's leaders need to show young people, who will be our successors, what it means to lead, and we need to give them the opportunities to do it for themselves. The huge disparities in wealth distribution, which are growing fast in western economies even in recession, and the consequent fracturing of social capital, are also a blight that has to be addressed. Otherwise, the benefits of any economic growth we can achieve together might just be washed away by social collapse.

It is a tough time for leaders. Many of society's leaders, such as our politicians, bankers and journalists have let us down and people have lost faith. To call yourself a leader and put yourself forward to address a challenge, run an enterprise or otherwise take charge of others is often to be seen as having suspect motives. Perhaps the biggest challenge we have is to restore some of that lost faith in the notion of leadership itself.

In the third sector, we still need a great shift in mindset. Too many people continue to rail against the slow death of grant funding, rather than looking for new and more financially sustainable operating methodologies, whether through a lack of foresight or an unwillingness to accept reality. More specifically, unless cultural organisations find ways to leverage their ideas, their intellectual property, and the unfailingly innovative thinking of the artist into financial returns, many of them will perish. Doing this, while staying true to ethical and artistic values is not easy. Neither is it impossible. But standing in the gloaming raging at the fading sun is deceitful.

The third sector as a whole also needs to redefine its mechanics of govern-ance. Dynamic, socially impactful entrepreneurship in the sector is hampered by a reliance on the clunky and outmoded charitable limited company where leadership has to be ceded, sometimes ineffectively. At best, this dilutes its impact. At worst, it diverts energies and resources away from the mission, sometimes handing responsibilities to people who do not share the sector's values. If we want the sector to thrive, we need to find new corporate struc-tures which liberate the innovators while still protecting the public interest.

Leadership is changing, and through the impact of technology becoming more *distributed*, more plural. Third sector leadership has a huge part to play in encouraging this plurality, helping our communities and our people, parti-cularly our creative and our young people, realise their potential. Never has this been more needed in such times of economic and social challenge. In an ever-globalising world economy, our voices need to be heard and it is up to us to make sure this happens.

Mike Finlayson

I was born in the fifties when Churchill was the leadership icon. When I started work in the 1970s, most of the bosses had either been in the World War II or had done National Service and virtually all were men. Great leaders were 'Churchillian' — strong and indomitable. This culture invariably shaped my early leadership style. I suppose I became a proper leader when I was appointed director of a department store in my late twenties. If leadership was a product of age and experience, I had neither at that time. Over the next three decades I led a variety of organisations in the private and third sectors. Over time, my attitude towards leadership and my practice of it changed.

The *Oxford English Dictionary* defines leadership as 'the person who leads or commands a group, organisation, or country'. The key word is perhaps 'commands', implying control. In this definition leadership is interpreted as being about big things, like organisations and countries I am not sure when the definition was last revised, not in the last thirty years I suspect. This was the definition I grew up with. By contrast, 'Wikipedia' defines leadership as 'the process of social influence in which one person enlists the aid and support of others in the accomplishment of a common task'. This definition is laden with active words, but the key ones for me are 'enlists' and 'influences'. The reference to 'one person' suggests leadership cannot be shared, which is implicit in the Oxford version. Apart from this, the contrast with the Oxford version is stark. Both definitions are products of their time.

Psychometric tests suggest my natural style is more akin to the Oxford Dictionary version, but despite occasional lapses, I am I believe more 'Wikipedian'. I think that this is a consequence of social change, my exposure to the culture of organisations I have worked in, and training over the years. Perhaps it is enlightenment but I think that it is zeitgeist, which determines how leadership is defined and practiced. The Wikipedia definition feels right.

It feels more moral and overall more likely to be effective in the world today. I have a niggling feeling, however, that whilst this is what we say we want, when times are tough we tend to crave the comfort and security of direction which, at times, is appropriate. Perhaps the practice of leadership is about what is appropriate under the circumstances, the skill to adopt, the right approach, the wisdom to recognise when to apply it and the humility to eschew it when it is not needed or wanted. It may also be about being willing to share it, something neither definition implies.

In the first decade of the 21st century, the global financial crisis and the Arab Spring exposed a catastrophic failure in leadership. Today leadership is in crisis. The myth of omnipotent leaders has been shattered. Mubarak, Assad, Gaddafi and others have faced the wrath of the masses. Wall Street's 'masters of the universe' have been exposed as mere humans, albeit greedy ones. People throughout the world are fed up with the greed, corruption and arrogance of leaders. Just when leadership is needed most, trust and confidence are ebbing away. The emperor is losing his clothes and a dangerous vacuum is emerging. History, once again is repeating itself. Ironically, it is during these times that people demand strong leadership — ideally, the proverbial 'benevolent dictator'. In response to this demand, articulate, strong leaders emerge who appear to have the solution. Invariably, they tell the masses what they want to hear and point to the failure of incumbent leaders. I confess to doing this myself when taking over the leadership of organisations. This appears to be true for the recruitment of leaders in all sectors — when times are tough, you need tough leaders. Talking about Churchill, Clement Attlee quoted from Macbeth: *He was a fine captain in a storm.* I would guess that during recent storms being tough is considered a pre-requisite. The challenge for Europe, indeed the world, is surely to avoid extremism. The same must, in general, be true for institutions.

Clearly politicians are not the only leaders. Leaders permeate all sectors of society and operate at all levels. Invariably, their first responsibility is to their prime stakeholder and not wider society. I think that this is a subtle but critical differentiating factor. Without accountability beyond the prime stakeholder, accepting a wider social responsibility is a matter of discretion, which the private sector, in particular, is perceived to have abandoned. This is also a charge increasingly levelled at the public sector which is perceived to exist for its own benefit and not the public it is there to serve. When the pressure is on, people and institutions tend to look after themselves first. In a complex and interdependent society, I believe what should drive all leaders is the pursuit of social capital. Well-run institutions that make a positive contribution to society invariably build social capital which benefits all.

Traditional sectors are breaking down and demarcation lines, financial, structural and cultural are becoming increasingly diffuse. Businesses are putting on the sheep's clothing of the third sector. The third sector is putting on the wolf's clothing of the private sector. The public sector seems undecided about what to wear and is trying on both but neither seems to suit.

I feel that leaders need to think about and understand what is happening in the wider society, how it may affect them, and what they can do to shape the future. They should think beyond their immediate sphere of influence, beyond today and over the horizon.

If leaders in the third sector have to adopt business practices to achieve social purpose, which seems to be the reality of the world we now inhabit, they need to understand how the private sector works, not just the nuts and bolts, but its mentality and culture. They also need to engage with, and influence, the public sector on different terms, not as passive recipients of funding or sub-contractors, but as partners for public good. Leaders in the public sector need to understand social value and the impact it has on present and future costs and on social cohesion. A point well made in the 'Christie Report', commissioned by the Scottish Government to look into the future of public service provision. They too need to re-examine their relationship with the third sector. Economist Will Hutton, Director of the Work Foundation, suggested in *The State We Are In* and *New China, New Crisis* that an economy can only be sustained if sufficient social capital exists to underpin it. If this is true, then business leaders have to understand the role which the third and public sectors play in building and sustaining social capital and accept their responsibility to contribute to it.

I think that the greatest challenge for leaders is not just to react to fast-moving economic, social and cultural change, but to understand it, not just from a narrow sectorial perspective, but holistically, then armed with this understanding to rise above the confusion and help to shape it. This is perhaps the supreme example of the 'common task' referred to in the Wikipedia definition, which of course comes from the people.

Martin Stepek

My experience of leadership started on the day I was conceived. That is how it is when you are born into a family business. In my case, my parents were not only my mum and dad but also co-owners of a substantial electrical retail business and my dad was the Managing Director. So in the family home, conversations about entrepreneurship, leadership, business worries, and so on were the norm as was being press-ganged into working in the business at weekends and school holidays.

My dad is Polish and was taken with his family to the Soviet GULAG in 1940 as a political/class enemy. His mother died of starvation as a result. My mother, a Scot, was born into a mining family and her father died when she was eight years old, so the family of twelve children was raised by my widowed grandmother through the Great Depression and World War II. My parents' tragic early years nurtured a culture of deep ethical values of compassion, self-reliance and honesty in me.

Despite my best efforts to avoid it, I found myself drawn into the family business after my student days and quickly became a company director, ultimately co-owning and leading the business from 1987 to 2002. For my siblings and me, leadership was about *values* and *relationships*. We tried to nurture our people as people, not employees, in the firm belief that this would benefit everyone in the system and ultimately the business itself. We tried our best to be the example of the values we believed in — the values of our parents.

Since 2002, I have developed a portfolio career, the largest part of which is my role as CEO of a social enterprise and charity — the Scottish Family Business Association — which I co-founded in 2005. This organisation brings together world leading understanding and best practices unique to the challenging business model where family members work in or own a business together. Leading a charity is very different to leading a business, especially in terms of fundraising, but the principles of expounding vision, values and the primacy of nurturing people are the same.

In the late 1990s, I developed a deep interest in the concept and practice of mindfulness, which is now evident in the field of leadership. Mindfulness derives from Buddhist meditation and is highly rated for the treatment of depression, anxiety and stress. Scientific and medical research shows that it develops greater levels of clarity of mind, calmness and concentration, whilst affording a more open and compassionate perspective on issues. To my mind, these are absolutely critical mental and emotional intellectual faculties of good leadership but difficult to develop by normal learning methods, so mindfulness meditation has proven to be a very effective set of practices. With mindfulness centres at Oxford University and mindfulness leadership programmes taught at Harvard and delivered in-house at Google, it is fast becoming recognised across the globe.

My practice of mindfulness has added a deep dimension to my perception of leadership. I believe you can only ever lead yourself and that leadership is an entirely inner matter. The more you nurture those qualities of calmness, clarity of mind, core ethics and openness to new thinking — what Zen describes as an 'empty mind' (the expert's mind sees few options, the beginner's mind sees all) — the more believable you will be to people. The more authentic you will be when you communicate and the simpler but deeper your key vision and messages will be. So instead of trying to develop your external skills, such as public speaking, managing-by-walking-about, in-house newsletter statements, and so on, focus on building your inner qualities and trust that the external results will come.

I believe that these qualities, which are the finest inner human aspects of our nature, are becoming even more necessary due to the economic recession and the destruction of trust in our political and corporate systems. Particularly within Britain but applicable globally, the scandals, mismanagement and unethical leadership surrounding so many of our key pillars of society demands a new vision and a new generation of leaders who can restore the trust of citizens in these vital institutions and sectors.

We need a combination of *ethical*, clear-sighted leaders together with new thinking on how to practically sustain the material and health benefits derived from capitalism, without the destructive effects on mental health, a sense of community and our natural environments. To achieve this requires a major paradigm shift, a cultural evolution, which can only be achieved by visionary leadership. Ironically the trend is towards greater nationalism and splintering of old, often imperially created nations, into a greater number of smaller states. This serves only to enhance the 'act locally' half of the Green adage but misses the 'think globally' half. With the European Union struggling with its monetary union project, as a result of a lack of political union to manage it, the international leadership structures required to handle the major economic and environmental issues of our day seem sadly lacking.

Perhaps though this absence of formal political leadership creates a gap into which civic society can step and play a crucial role. Rather than the somewhat scattergun approach of the anti-capitalist movement generally and the Occupy protests more recently, a combination of ethical business and social enterprise-led movements can make more headway. The social enterprise sector is a great contributor to the economy and employment in every country around the world. My business has been working with the cooperative sector and other social enterprises to try to attain greater *collaboration*, mutual support, and ultimately a vision of a shared ethical body of enterprise. In order to challenge and create an alternative to the values-free, self-gratifying, short-termist corporate world model of the economy, we have to, at present, endure. This, in my view, is what leadership ultimately means, the successful improvement of our society and world for the benefit of all.

4.9. Key Themes from the Reflections

The collection of views expressed in this chapter provides us with a rare insight into the experience and perceptions of leaders in the third sector on leadership and the challenges which they face. An overview of the key points made by each of the contributors can be found in Table 4.2. In this section, we will summarise briefly the key themes which emerge from each of the questions which have been addressed in the reflections above.

4.9.1. Experience

In terms of understanding where the experience of leadership comes from for leaders in the third sector, it seems to be from work itself. Initially, individuals have learnt as followers through observing and working with leaders and then as leaders themselves. John Lauder's comments sum up where the experience of many of the contributors has come from: *My experience of leadership comes partly from being led by others in my earlier career, observing both good and bad practice and considering how best to apply the former and avoid the latter when I got a chance to lead an organisation.* Experience has been gained from 'poor' leaders about what not to do and also

Table 4.2: Essay summaries — Experience, perception, means, challenges and sector.

Name	Experience	Perception	Means	Challenges	Sector
Bishop	• Through studying leadership • Leading projects	• Leadership is 95% a privilege and 5% undesirable	• An opportunity to create, innovate, develop and ultimately change something	• Lack of economic growth • Old systems failing	• Knowing where, how and when to grow and who to grow with
Elliot	• Leadership roles	• Distinction of leadership behind the scenes and in public sphere	• Supporting people — giving them confidence and opportunities to speak	• Connecting with non-financial resources	• Connecting with non-financial resources
Lauder	• Being led bothers • Observing good and bad practice • Attending leadership courses	• Leadership is about establishing clarity of purpose and agreeing a common mission and approach	• Listening • Being confident • Ensuring the mission is taking is understood • Being followed • Being prepared to front the organisation but not take the credit	• Climate change	• To keep a clear focus on the vision, mission, aims and objectives • To develop alliances and partnerships
Paterson	• Being exposed to different leaders • Being in leadership roles • Leading change programmes	• For the organisation, within the organisation and beyond the organisation	• Creating a strategic plan and implementing it • Transformational approach — motivating others • Emotional Intelligence • Challenging assumptions • Stakeholder engagement	• Poverty • Focus on measurements and outcomes	• Delivering services which improve experiences and outcomes • Collaboration and partnerships

Taylor	• As a manager in the commercial sector • Through promotions	• Divided perception — one the one hand cynics, play power games, rarely liked • On the other hand, those who think deeply, are courageous, dream, innovate and nurture creativity, take risks	• Engagement of people through intellect, imagination and heart • Excitement, vision and passion	• Adapting to changes in the environment while retaining focus on the mission • Adapting to new markets and technologies	• Adoption of a consumer-centric mindset • Leaders to speak out and be noticed
Ashcroft	• Started as a follower • Moving through series of management then leadership roles • Having a mentor	• It fits the needs of the organisation • Understanding and responding to internal and external challenges	• Having a clear goal or aim • Creating a burning platform	• Economic pressures to focus on efficiency and cost management • Demographic change	• Constraints on public funding • Need to attract new funding • Increasing regulation • Increased transparency through social media
MacLeod	• Leadership roles in the voluntary and public sectors • Being inspired by others	• Lead people not systems • It is about change, growth and evolution	• Keep a clear focus on the vision, mission and aims and monitor progress • Taking risks • Having conversations • Turn the talk of values into distinct actions		• Changing the culture in order for the sector to be recognised as a key player • Having the right capabilities, skills and potential

Table 4.2: (Continued)

Name	Experience	Perception	Means	Challenges	Sector
Mould	• Various leadership roles in different sectors • Insight into politicians as leaders • Working with leaders	• Having strong values • Faith • Humility • Personal morality • Teamwork • Persistence • Having your feet on the ground	• Leaders embody what they are about • Resilience • Staying in touch — listening and observing	• Recession • Austerity	• Honing the personal qualities of leadership
Nicolas	• In community roles in France • Leading projects in the United Kingdom	• A role played by highly committed, creative, hard-working individuals	• Leaders act on behalf of the community	• Funding	• Identifying leadership potential to bring about change • Balancing immediate needs of the community with long-term visions
Schwarz	• In community development both in Africa and in the United Kingdom	• Living the values, vision and mission	• Trusting, encouraging and supporting people • Balancing needs of individual with needs of organisation	• How to get value for less cost	• Sticking to the values, vision and mission • Maintaining independence from government

Collier	• Leading small- and medium-sized organisations	• Leadership is the process of gathering all stakeholders around a collective understanding of the endeavour • Creating a compelling story to motive stakeholders	• Gain commitment to the purpose of the organisation • Communication • Coalition building • Building and motivating people • Being visible • Encouraging others to take responsibility	• Limited growth — period of stagnation • Reduction in living standards • Divisions between countries, rich and poor • Creating consensus on issues such as climate change, energy and ageing population • Investing in the infrastructure for innovation to flourish	• Keeping the belief in the special nature of the sector • Legitimacy • Authenticity • Civic leadership • Sectoral cultural dissonance • Innovation
Harris	• Learning on the job • Learning from other leaders	• Having a clear vision which can be articulated	• Clear vision • Employ the right people • Apply the spirit not the letter of the law • Greater empowerment of colleagues • Ambitious for the company first and foremost	• Lack of government commitment to the sector	• Managing operations — not compromising on quality • Amount of change • Attempting to be leaner and respond to cuts

Table 4.2: (*Continued*)

Name	Experience	Perception	Means	Challenges	Sector
			• Understand the company's risk profile • Don't focus on the potential financial impact of any decisions • Be outward facing • Understand the competition • Always feel passionate about what you do		• Stretching managers to the limit
Hurst	• Being led by others • Having leadership done to him • Leading others	• In the army the leadership culture is clear symbols and status • Leaders are segregated and live, socialise and eat separately • In charities leaders often emerge from within — leadership is distributed	• Creating a supportive, values-based culture that is clearly articulated and acted upon • Clarifying, identifying and setting the desired levels of standards • Take time to understand the motivation and behavioural drivers of others	• Creating a sustainable business model to deliver increased levels of service with less funding and resources	• Pressure to create innovative solutions to fix the broken society • Managing and training volunteers • Collaboration with other organisations across the sector to deliver savings and create additional value • Deliver more services to more people who have greater needs but with fewer resources

Kerr	• Variety of leadership roles • Observing other leaders	• Leaders need certain traits • Managers can develop into leaders • Leadership and management are very different • Purpose of leader is change	• To support or change the culture as required • To challenge the approach and seek opportunities, take risks and let others do the same • To have empathy • Be authentic	• Lack of risk taking • Lack of training, supporting and mentoring leaders	• To create space for radical thinking • To challenge views held about the sector • Respond to demands made on the sector • Build confidence and speak collectively • Rising public expectations • Falling budgets • Need for greater confidence in job security • Need to raise status of managers • Moving from a reliance on grant funding to one a focus on contracts • Introducing change
Tait	• Learning from other leaders • Learn to control your workload • Being visible	• Need to be liked to be a leader — need to earn respect • Effective leaders learn fast to delegate	• Leaders must be intuitive • Learn to control your workload • Be visible		
Grigor	• Working with and observing other leaders • Working in a changing culture	• Understanding what needs to be done to drive an organisation forward • Gaining buy-in from staff • Providing staff with the opportunity to grow	• Gaining respect • Creating a vision • Getting buy-in to the vision • Creating a desire to succeed • Creating an environment where staff belief what you are striving to achieve		

Table 4.2: (Continued)

Name	Experience	Perception	Means	Challenges	Sector
Mann	• Leadership is often confused with ego • Leadership is different to management • Leaders need sensing skills — founded on emotional intelligence	• It is how you make things happen on a sustainable and repeatable basis	• To act as a sense maker • Delivering change • Requires an essential innate restlessness to continually change and challenge yourself • Being clear on what you will be judged by and by whom • Courage and persistence	• Structural change • Little additional funding or growth	• How to transition to new and different business models • Low levels of trust
Cook	• Leading an arts organisation	• Making ideas happen • Being able to communicate and inspire	• Having followers • Courage • Understanding their own values • Being relentless	• The legacy we are leaving for the younger generation	• Looking for new, financial sustainable operating methodologies • Redefining the mechanics of governance
Finlayson	• From great leaders such as Churchill • Leading a variety of organisations	• What is appropriate under the circumstances, the right skill to	• Influencing • Supporting others	• The pursuit of social capital	• Leaders understanding what is happening in the wider society

in the public and third sectors	adopt the right approach, the wisdom to recognise when to apply it and the humility to eschew it		• Understanding social value and the impact it has • Relationship with government • To understand economic, social and cultural change • Need to develop ethical leaders
Stepek	• Running a family business • Practicing mindfulness	• The successful improvement of our society for the benefit of all	• Building your inner qualities	• Restoring the trust of citizens in institutions and sectors

from 'great' inspirational role models about what to do. In the words of Rory MacLeod, *In work settings, there were leaders everywhere, above, beside, and below me. The effective ones, in the minority, quietly but significantly stood out. Others simply quoted rules and systems. One learns from this, from immersing and being hands on with tasks, learning to be reflective, visionary and honest. To see yourself and your behaviours, and your actions, as others see you.* David Cook supports the view that leadership can only be learnt in practice. Similarly, Edel Harris emphasises that it is not the qualifications or the accolades of leaders who have inspired her, but their 'behaviours', such as honesty and integrity. A few of the contributors believe that leadership can be taught; however, all tend to agree that although you can teach leadership, it can and is learned through experience and mentorship.

From learning about leadership through practice, the leaders in the sector have identified what they think qualifies as good leadership. This includes: delegating, providing a vision, being visible and supporting people. In the words of Jeff Hurst, *the best leaders are those who consciously take the time and effort to understand the motivation and behavioural drivers of those they lead and ensure that they provide them with the opportunities, resources and the support they need in order to enable them to do the best they can.*

So leadership, for leaders in the third sector, is developed through experience — learning from others and doing leadership — and cemented in place by reflective practice.

4.9.2. *Perceptions*

Perceptions about leadership are mixed depending on an individual's experience of leadership. Richard Taylor points out that his perception is divided as he still comes across what he terms, *those increasingly redundant types who cynically exercise control over others through high-handed interventions … while there are others who not only think deeply about what they do, but care about how they do it … they understand their own limitations and those of others.*

Perceptions appear to change and evolve as a result of experience. John Lauder, for example, notes that his perception of leadership has changed over time and for him leadership is now about establishing clarity of purpose and agreeing a common mission and approach and then making sure that it is driven forward. Jeff Hurst also emphasises that his perception has evolved about the importance of leadership and it is now about creating a clear purpose, which has come from his experience first in the military and then in the third sector.

There is a common perception that leadership is about developing and implementing a clear vision, which involves balancing the immediate needs of the community with the long-term vision of the organisation. The vision needs to take into account the values and mission of the third sector organisations and stay true to their *raison d'etre.* Bernard Collier points out that, *leadership is about sticking to the core purpose and mission of the sector and working with all stakeholders whether internal or external to get commitment to it.* Steven Paterson eloquently describes this as

leadership being for the organisation, within the organisation and beyond the organisation. Various contributors highlight different parts of this: Verene Nicolas, for
example, focuses on leadership beyond the organisation and says that leaders in the
sector achieve the core purpose of their organisation by acting on behalf of the community with deep concerns for the dignity and well-being of the people.

So it would seem that the perception of leadership appears to change as individuals move from followers to leaders. As this happens, individuals become more
focused on the mission of the organisation and develop a stronger perception that
leadership is about creating a vision and gaining commitment to it from internal
and external stakeholders to the organisation.

4.9.3. What Leadership Means

Leadership means many things to the leaders in the third sector. We will discuss
three themes which emerge from the reflections in terms of the meaning of leadership: leadership is different from management; leadership is an approach; and leadership is about personal qualities.

Leadership is different from management
Leadership is seen as being different from management, in that leadership is about
having a vision and strong values to support the vision. Edel Harris points out that,
*compared to management, leadership is about vision — they [leaders] see a journey's
end before others have even thought about packing a case.* A leader creates a vision
and direction, while a manager plans, allocates, organises and gets the best out of
people to achieve goals and targets. For Andy Kerr, the difference is that the purpose of the leader is change, while the purpose of the manager is order and consistency. While for Mann, although he recognises that there are differences, he feels
that a leader needs to be good at both management and leadership. Mann criticises
the often magical portrayal of leaders in textbooks, compared to managers and
emphasises that a leader has to have management skills as well.

Leadership is an approach
Leadership means a specific approach. Kerr points out that, *Leadership is not a qualification, but a set of values and approaches, inherent and/or trained. It creates values
and communities.* The specific approach required by leadership is identified through
the various reflections in this chapter as:

• *Supporting people.* Leaders need to ensure that permanent staff, as well as volunteers, are managed and trained to cope with the changes. They also need to ensure
  that morale and motivation does not suffer
• *Ensuring the reputation of the organisation.* Leaders have to stand by their vision
  and even when times are tough make sure that the business values are not
  compromised.

- *Ensuring that ethical obligations are adhered to.* Leaders need to find ways to leverage their ideas and their intellectual property into financial returns, while staying true to ethical values, in order to retain the foundations on which the sector is built.

So, leadership means an approach which is strongly build on the mission, ethics, reputation and people within the organisation.

Leadership is about personal qualities

Leadership means the personal qualities which individuals bring to the role. The importance of the personal qualities of leadership is emphasised throughout the essays. Numerous personal qualities are cited by the contributors including: influencing, motivating, inspiring, being visible, listening, observing, empowering others, having conversations with people, being authentic, resilient, empathetic, courageous, gaining respect, trust and credibility, and having a strong set of values, Chris Mould emphasises that *good leaders have strong values and they have thought about those values deeply. They know how their values apply in all sorts of contexts such as making decisions about money, assessing strategic business opportunities, deciding whom their organisation should partner with and dealing with challenging people problems.*

Stephen Mann says that the qualities are based on *how you make things happen successfully on a sustainable and repeatable basis. It needs to be delivered authentically and with skill. An essential element is to act as a sense maker for others, gaining trust and engagement through shaping and sharing context, explaining why actions are required, and motivating through demonstrating progress against the bigger picture.*

Mann points out that to achieve this, leaders need sensing skills and emotional intelligence. While Martin Stepek takes this a step further and talks about the critical mental and emotional intellect of leadership being linked to 'mindfulness' which he defines as clarity of mind, core ethics and openness to new thinking, which in turn creates authenticity. As Chris Mould says, *developing and honing the personal qualities of leadership is where the difference between success and failure will always reside.*

Such personal qualities are vital for creating what is of a growing importance across the sector — *collaborative* leadership. At its most basic, collaborative leadership means delivering results across boundaries. For Verene Nicolas, it is about anchoring the leadership role in an intention to serve the community and nurture cultures of trust. It is, however, wider than this — the views in this chapter show that collaboration is about working across not just the third sector but also across the public and the private sectors. Collaboration is seen as being vital for dealing with current and future challenges.

4.9.4. Challenges

The leadership challenges affecting the United Kingdom and Europe are complex and predominantly external to organisations. Here we have grouped them under global, political, economic, social and reputational challenges.

Global

Globalisation can be understood as the process of intensifying social and economic transactions (Scherer, Palazzo, & Matten, 2009, p. 327). It is accompanied by a dissolving relevance of territorially bound social, economic and political activities, and a stronger worldwide interconnection of organisations (Crane & Matten, 2007). As a result, leaders are having to work across increasing global boundaries to address global issues. As Bernard Collier points out in his narrative, there is a need to create consensus on a number of areas including: climate change; energy policy; and the growing competitive challenge from the BRIC (Brazil, India, Russia, China) countries as well as the CIVETs (Colombia, Indonesia, Vietnam, Egypt, Turkey, South Africa). The awareness among leaders of global risks such as environmental hazards, worldwide diseases, and epidemics is fostering cross-border coordination of nation-state activities and the incorporation of non-state organisations such as NGOs and third sector organisations into the decision-making processes in relation to the factors of globalisation (Scherer & Palazzo, 2008).

Coinciding with globalisation is the process of an increasingly connected global society that is more sensitive to social and environmental violations, as well as the growth of non-governmental organisations that gather and reinforce particular interests (Den Hond & De Bakker, 2007). As a consequence, organisations are being monitored more closely by a diverse group of stakeholders, who are increasing the pressure to legitimise organisational conduct (Palazzo & Scherer, 2008). Stakeholder management is, thus, becoming a vital aspect of the agenda for organisations (Patzer & Voegtlin, 2013).

Political

The political challenges are mentioned in a number of the narratives. Andy Kerr points out that *Politicians, public, private and third sector leaders have a veracious media to contend with, politicians and officials have very narrow windows of opportunity to really change things, we now have almost an annual cycle of elections which forces playing safe and not upsetting any group or individual. The advent of 'retail politics' where the agenda is about instant gratification in return for votes makes reform and real change, when it is really necessary, very difficult.* This is reiterated by Edel Harris who says that she is worried that the UK Government has not woken up to the fact that the numbers of vulnerable, disabled and older people are increasing while at the same time there is a race to the bottom in terms of what public commissioners will pay for care services. Harris concludes that there is a need to see strong political leadership and ask ourselves what sort of society we want to live in. The absence of formal political leadership is also mentioned by Martin Stepek. He refers to the European Union which he sees as struggling with its monetary union project, as a result of a lack of political union to manage it. Stepek further states that *the international leadership structures required to handle the major economic and environmental issues of our day seem sadly lacking.*

Economic

The impact of the economic recession and the eschewing years of austerity is a key challenge. The financial crisis requires leadership which entails leaders focusing on several specific actions including making decisions and taking action under pressure and clarifying and communicating decisions to internal and external stakeholders, as well as the media. Leaders are also having to inspire their staff to do what needs to be done which has been described as, transforming the crisis into a challenge (Bass & Riggio, 2006). They also have to set an example in their behaviour for as Murphy (2003) says in his article about crisis management, a crisis does not make character — it reveals character.

For leaders in the third sector dealing with the financial crisis is not about returning to the so-called glory days; rather as Gary Bishop says, what is needed is fresh thinking which learns from the success and failures of the past and creates a new future. To do this, Harris, says that there needs to be a vision and business values which are not compromised even when times are tough. As Bernard Collier advises that, *Leaders will need to find a balance between supporting those disadvantaged by the financial depression, while investing in the infrastructure for innovation to flourish.*

Social

Demographic changes are becoming a serious challenge, particularly the increases in longevity and the consequences this has for society, the economy, and local communities across Europe and more widely. For leaders, Jane Ashcroft says that this means leading an ever more diverse team and meeting the expectations and needs of an ageing workforce with the changing expectations of Generation Y and the new millennials. Social factors also comprise of an increasingly mobile workforce, as well as an on-going individualisation of personal lifestyles (Scherer et al., 2009). This means that organisational leadership is having to review its policies and procedures for recruitment, selection, retention and promotion.

Reputation building

Rebuilding the reputation and trust of leadership after the debacle of the economic crisis is a key challenge. As David Cook points out, it is a tough time for *many of society's leaders, such as our politicians, bankers and journalists, have let us down and people have lost faith. To call yourself a leader and put yourself forward to address a challenge, run an enterprise or otherwise take charge of others is often to be seen as having suspect motives. Perhaps the biggest challenge we have is to restore some of that lost faith in the notion of leadership itself.* This is reiterated by Martin Stepek who says that the scandals, mismanagement and unethical leadership surrounding so many of the key pillars of society demand a new vision and a new generation of leaders who can restore the trust of citizens in these vital institutions and sectors. As a result of these demands, organisations are increasingly being confronted by stakeholders who want to see an enhanced awareness for corporate social responsibility. If organisations disregard such stakeholder demands, it can have severe effects on their reputation and licence to operate (Patzer & Voegtlin, 2013).

Such challenges, as outlined above, put pressure on organisations to continually change and adapt in unstable environments. As Graetz (2000, p. 550) acknowledges, *against a backdrop of increasing globalization, deregulation, the rapid pace of technological innovation, a growing knowledge workforce, and shifting social and demographic trends, few would dispute that the primary task for management today is the leadership of organisational change.*

Patzer and Voegtlin (2013) point out that such challenges cannot be countered solely by organisational solutions, as there is a need for flexibility to address unforeseen events. Instead, they suggest that leaders need to use their positional power and discretion, to act in a timely manner to new situations and challenges, to engage in active stakeholder dialogue and to implement solutions, and to take responsibility to improve their reputational conduct.

4.9.5. Sector

The individual reflections in this chapter highlight a number of sector-specific challenges (including those already mentioned). The main ones are: defining the role of the sector, increasing collaboration across sectors, improving the quality of services provided, creating a sustainable business model, delivering innovation and change, and the crisis of leadership. We discuss each of these briefly.

Defining the role of the sector

As result of the changing external environment and a reduction in funding in the sector, there is on-going debate about the role of the sector. Many leaders, such as Collier are adamant that the special nature of the sector needs to be retained. While others (such as Pam Schwarz and John Lauder) question whether the values, vision and mission can be adhered to and ask whether this is the right time to review the fundamental foundations and move on to agree new alliances and partnerships. Knowing when, how, and where to grow and critically who to grow with are all central challenges.

Increasing collaboration

Collaboration with other organisations across the sector to deliver savings and create additional value is a key challenge. Funders are now requiring third sector organisations to collaborate with each other and with organisations from other sectors to deliver savings and create additional value. So leaders are asking who they should align themselves with in collaboration — competitors or complementary organisations — and what form this collaboration should take. Jeff Hurst questions whether it should be an alliance based on shared risk and reward or a partnership using prime and sub-contractors. Steven Paterson says that collaborative and partnership working is a challenge but one which offers potential solutions: *Organisations have to find a balance of preserving their own place in the sector while being confident enough to share knowledge and information for wider benefit.* There is recognition that it should be possible to benefit from collaborative working as long as the time is taken to identify who organisations should therefore align themselves with in collaboration and what form the collaborations should take.

Creating a sustainable business model

Creating a sustainable business model to deliver increased levels of services with less funding and resources is a key challenge. Traditional sources of income are changing and decreasing, including diminishing grants. Individual donations are also becoming harder to generate, charitable incomes from assets are reducing due to low interest rates and low returns on investments. The key challenge is how to transition to new and different business models when the 'rules of the game' and traditional consensus are established in past models which have been shown to be lacking, but not always recognised as such. The paradox is that in a world where the need for what the third sector does has never been greater, the levels of funding are so low. This is reinforced by the fact that leadership in many organisations is often focused on survival and not strategy. Stephen Mann concludes that, *leading the transition of any business in the absence of any real growth is the new environmental paradigm. Strategic leadership and sense making in a world with many more paradoxes, contradictions and uncertainties will be at the heart of meeting this challenge.*

So a new business model will need to involve the design and application of new organisational structures and governance to enable third sector organisations to generate earned incomes.

Delivering innovation and change

Delivering and implementing innovation and change is a challenge for the sector. Given that for the vast majority of the sector there are not enough resources to fund services, leaders need to find new ways of providing services. Bernard Collier points out that the sector will need to find new organisational models, which use technology and utilise volunteers more in a way that enables them to support beneficiaries. As Gary Bishop offers, there is the opportunity to create, to innovate, to develop and ultimately to make changes. This will involve, according to Andy Kerr *changing or moulding the culture so that it is positive and creative.* David Cook, however, is mindful that, *dynamic, socially impactful entrepreneurship in the sector is hampered* and to make it happen, he says that there is a need to *liberate innovators.*

4.10.   The Crisis of Leadership

Whether the contributors say it overtly or not, there is an underlying sense that leadership in the sector is in crisis. Traditional sectors are breaking down and demarcation lines (financial, structural and cultural) are becoming increasingly diffuse. Mike Finlayson describes it as, *businesses putting on the sheep's clothing of the third sector and the third sector putting on the wolf's clothing of the private sector, while the public sector seems undecided about what to wear and is trying on both.* To address this, Finlayson says that within the third sector, *leaders need to think about and understand what is happening in the wider society, how it may affect them and what they can do to shape the future. They should think beyond their immediate sphere of influence, beyond today and over the horizon.* If leaders in the third sector have to adopt business practices to achieve social purpose, they need to understand how the private sector works. They also need to engage with and influence the public sector on different terms, not as passive recipients of funding or sub-contractors, but as partners.

In the third sector, leaders appear to be confronted with challenges which they are not yet fully equipped for, either organisationally or individually. This has interesting parallels with the public sector (see Chapter 3). The traditional approach to leadership is outdated to the changing context in which the sector is operating. This has led to a call for a radical rethink of the role of leadership in the sector.

4.11. Tri-Sector Leadership

The critical challenges are increasingly requiring leaders in the third sector to collaborate with the private and public sectors to create solutions. Hank Rubin (2009) has written that collaboration is a purposeful relationship in which all parties strategically choose to cooperate in order to accomplish a shared outcome. In his book *Collaborative Leadership: Developing Effective Partnerships for Communities and Schools*, Rubin asks *Who is a collaborative leader?* His answer is that you are a collaborative leader once you have accepted responsibility for building, or helping to ensure the success of, a heterogeneous team to accomplish a shared purpose.

Archer and Cameron (2009) build on this approach in their book *Collaborative Leadership: How to Succeed in an Interconnected World*. The authors identify the basic task of the collaborative leader as the delivery of results across boundaries between different organisations. They say that getting value from difference is at the heart of the collaborative leader's task and that they have to learn to share control and to trust a partner to deliver, even though that partner may operate very differently from themselves.

In an issue of the *Harvard Business Review*, Lovegrove and Thomas (2013) examine the careers of leaders who have been successful in addressing complex challenges requiring collaboration across a wide range of stakeholders. In this article (Lovegrove & Thomas, 2013), Harvard Kennedy School professor Joseph Nye says these are people who have the ability to engage and collaborate across the private, public and social (third) sectors. Lovegrove and Thomas (2013) call this tri-sector leaders: these are people who can bridge the chasms of culture, incentives and purpose that separate the three sectors. Lovegrove and Thomas (2013) offer further that tri-sector leaders are distinguished as much by mindset as by experience. The skills these leaders require to work across sectors are:

• *Balancing competing motives.* Tri-sector leaders need a strong sense of mission (similar to the leaders in the third sector) and want to work on a large scale. They are able to find ways to pursue overlapping and potentially conflicting professional goals

- *Acquiring transferable skills.* When leaders move between sectors, they acquire a growing array of tools and tactics, and strengthen their ability to work across boundaries
- *Developing contextual intelligence.* Lovegrove and Thomas (2013) observe that tri-sector leaders must not only see parallels between sectors but also accurately assess differences in context and translate across them. This ability to understand how different organisations and bureaucracies work, they say is contextual intelligence
- *Forging an intellectual thread.* Many tri-sector leaders need to develop subject matter expertise in a particular area. Developing and applying an intellectual thread across the sectors, gives leaders the capacity to understand underlying principles and to transcend some of the constraints
- *Building integrated networks.* Since hiring managers rarely look outside their own sectors for talent, those with tri-sector careers rely on their integrated, cross-sector networks to build leadership teams and to convene the diverse groups that can address and resolve tri-sector issues
- *Maintaining a prepared mindset.* Lovegrove and Thomas say many tri-sector leaders speak of the need to prepare financially so that they can afford to say yes when the president calls. They also need to be ready and willing to deviate significantly from the familiar road to embrace opportunities

This approach to tri-sector capabilities is perhaps something that leaders in the third sector need to consider, especially as they are under increasing pressure to collaborate across the public and private sectors. Such an approach will provide them with the opportunity to develop the capabilities they require to address the complex challenges they are facing, as well as to develop and grow the sector.

4.12.   Summary

In summary, this chapter provides an overview of the shape of leadership in the third sector, and the general environment and the challenges they face. We find leaders are operating in a sector that that is sensitive to social, economic and political change and is still in a state of flux as its workforce and services respond to the drivers for change. This is placing significant pressure on leaders who have to navigate the external environment, while attending to internal organisational issues including ensuring a consistent pipeline of funding, retaining independence, and the core mission of the sector.

The unique views expressed by the narratives in this chapter provide a deeper insight into leadership in the third sector, than has previously existed. The views are valuable for a number of reasons including:

- They help to extend the knowledge and views of leadership in a way that acknowledges the uniqueness of the sector

- They are a starting point to understand better the challenges faced by leaders in the sector
- They serve as an illustration of the benefit of approaching leadership through the eyes of those practicing leadership

Perhaps the greatest challenge the leaders in the third sector face today is how to transform and survive amid constant turbulence and disruption. There are numerous examples of companies in other sectors, like Border Books, Woolworths and Kodak, who failed to recognise the need to change and suffered as a result. The challenge for leaders in the third sector, which is facing real threats, is to keep up with the pace of change, let alone get ahead of it. At the same time, the political, economic, social and financial stakes are rising. The mission and values drive organisations in the sector, which is admirable, yet they consider their strategies only rarely. Today, any organisation that is not rethinking its direction, at least every few years, as well as adjusting to constantly changing contexts, and then quickly making operational changes is putting itself at risk. As the leaders in the third sector can attest, the tension between needing to stay ahead of an increasingly tough environment and continuing to deliver services can be overwhelming. As leaders, they cannot ignore the daily demands of running their institutions, which many of them strive to do exceedingly well. However, what they also need to do is to identify the most important hazards and opportunities early enough and formulate creative strategic initiatives and implement them quickly, in order to ensure the sustained survival of their organisations, and the unique services they provide.

There is much to be proud of in the third sector, as evidenced in the reflections. These leaders: understand and accept their social and environmental responsibilities; demonstrate integrity and a dedication to the espoused beliefs and values of their organisations; and their moral courage and ethical standards are strong. That being said, the role of leadership in the third sector needs to be reassessed if it is to weather the storm of austerity and cope with a sea of change.

References

Alcock, P. (2010). A strategic unity: Defining the third sector in the UK. *Voluntary Sector Review, 1*(1), 5–24.

Alcock, P., & Kendall, J. (2011). Constituting the third sector: Processes of decontestation and contention under the UK Labour governments in England. *Voluntas: International Journal of Voluntary and Nonprofit Organisations, 22*(3), 450–469.

Angelou, M. (2013). Life's work: An interview with Maya Angelou by Alison Beard. *Harvard Business Review, 91*(5), 152.

Archer, D., & Cameron, A. (2009). *Collaborative leadership: How to succeed in an interconnected world.* London: Routledge.

Bass, B. M., & Riggio, R. E. (2006). *Transformational leadership.* London: Taylor & Francis.

Billis, D. (Ed.). (2010). *Hybrid organisations and the third sector: Challenges for practice, theory and policy.* Basingstoke: Palgrave Macmillan.

Boal, K. B., & Hooijberg, R. (2000). Strategic leadership research: Moving on. *Leadership Quarterly, 11*, 515−549.

Buffett, W. (2003). *Omaha World Herald,* 27 April, p. 3.

Clark, J. (2007). *Voluntary sector skills survey.* London: NCVO.

Clore Duffield Foundation. (2007). *Proposal to create a Clore leadership programme for the third sector.* A context paper commissioned by the Clore Duffield Foundation in Spring 2007. Retrieved from http://www.cloresocialleadership.org.uk/media/files/11/CSLP

Cormack, J., & Stanton, M. (2003). *Passionate leadership: The characteristics of outstanding leaders in the voluntary sector — What sector leaders think initial research findings.* Hay Management Group for ACEVO.

Crane, A., & Matten, D. (2007). *Business ethics: Managing corporate citizenship and sustainability in the age of globalization.* Oxford: Oxford University Press.

De Hoogh, A. H., Den Hartog, D. N., Koopman, P. L., Thierry, H., Van den Berg, P. T., Van der Weide, J. G., & Wilderom, C. P. (2005). Leader motives, charismatic leadership, and subordinates' work attitude in the profit and voluntary sector. *The Leadership Quarterly, 16*(1), 17−38.

Deakin, N. (1996). The devils in the detail: Some reflections on contracting for social care by voluntary organisations. *Social Policy & Administration, 30*(1), 20−38.

Den Hond, F., & De Bakker, F. G. (2007). Ideologically motivated activism: How activist groups influence corporate social change activities. *Academy of Management Review, 32*(3), 901−924.

Diefenbach, T. (2013). Incompetent or immoral leadership? In R. T. By & B. Burnes (Eds.), *Organisational change, leadership and ethics* (pp. 149−170). London: Routledge.

Dunphy, D., & Benn, S. (2013). Leadership for sustainable futures. In R. T. By & B. Burnes (Eds.), *Organisational change, leadership and ethics* (pp. 196−251). London: Routledge.

Edwards, M. (2009). *Civil society* (2nd ed.). Cambridge: Polity Press.

Evers, A., & Laville, J. L. (Eds.). (2004). *The third sector in Europe.* London: Edward Elgar Publishing.

Finance Hub. (2008, March). *The decline of local authority grants for the third sector: Fact or fiction?* London: Finance Hub.

Finkelstein, S., Hambrick, D. C., & Cannella, A. A. Jr. (2009). *Strategic leadership: Theory and research on executives, top management teams, and boards.* Oxford: Oxford University Press.

Graetz, F. (2000). Strategic change leadership. *Management decision, 38*(8), 550−564.

Hailey, J., & James, R. (2004). Trees die from the top: International perspectives on NGO leadership development. *Voluntas: International Journal of Voluntary and Nonprofit Organisations, 15*(4), 343−353.

Halfpenny, P., & Reid, M. (2002). Research on the voluntary sector: An overview. *Policy & Politics, 30*(4), 533−550.

Hamel, G. (2009). Moonshots for management: What great challenges must we tackle to reinvent management and make it more relevant to a volatile world? *Harvard Business Review,* (February), 91−98.

Harris, B. (2010). Voluntary action and the state in historical perspective. *Voluntary Sector Review, 1*(1), 25−40.

Hesselbein, F. (2002). *Hesselbein on leadership.* San Francisco, CA: Jossey-Bass.

Hodges, J. (2011). The role of the CEO and leadership branding: Credibility not celebrity. In R. Burke, G. Martin, & C. G. Cooper (Eds.), *Corporate reputation: Managing opportunities and threats* (pp. 181−220). London: Gower.

Hodges, J., & Martin, G. (2012). Can leadership identity reconstruction help resolve the integration-responsiveness problem in multinational enterprises? A case study of leadership branding. *International Journal of Human Resource Management, 23*(18), 3794–3812.

Hopkins, L. (2010). *Mapping the third sector: A context for social leadership.* London: The Work Foundation.

Hudson, M. (2011). *Managing without profit: Leadership, management and governance of third sector organisations.* London: Directory of Social Change.

IBM. (2010). *Global CEO survey.* New York, NY: IBM.

Kay, R. (1996). What kind of leadership do voluntary organisations need? In D. Billis & M. Harris (Eds.), *Voluntary agencies: Challenges of organisation and management* (pp. 130–148). Basingstoke: Palgrave Macmillan.

Kirchner, A. (2006). Value-based leadership: A third sector view. *British Journal of Leadership in Public Services, 2*(4), 30–33.

Kirchner, A. (2007). A leadership model for export. *International Journal of Leadership in Public Services, 3*(3), 49–55.

Knoke, D., & Prensky, D. (1984). What relevance do organisation theories have for voluntary organisations? *Social Science Quarterly, 65,* 3–20.

Lovegrove, N., & Thomas, M. (2013). Triple-strength leadership. *Harvard Business Review, 91*(9), 47–56.

Macmillan, R. (2010). *The third sector delivering public services: An evidence review.* Working Paper No. 20. University of Birmingham, Birmingham, UK.

Mendonca, M. (2001). Preparing for ethical leadership in organisations. *Canadian Journal of Administrative Science, 18*(4), 266–276.

Mulgan, G. (2007). *Social innovation: What it is, why it matters and how it can be accelerated.* London: Young Foundation.

Murphy, S. K. (2003). Crisis management demystified: Here's how to prevent a crisis from ruining your institution's reputation. *University Business, 6*(2), 36–37.

NAVCA. (2011). *Social value: Briefing 1 — Introduction to social value.* Sheffield: NAVCA. Retrieved from http://www.navca.org.uk/socialvaluebriefings. Accessed on 11 November 2011.

NCVO. (2012). *The UK civil society almanac.* London: NCVO. Retrieved from www.ncvo-vol.org.uk/almanac

O'Boyle, A. (2010). *'If not now, then when?' The report of the pilot group of NCVO Leadership 20:20.* London: NCVO.

Osborne, S., Chew, C., & McLaughlin, K. (2008). The innovative capacity of voluntary organisations and the provision of public services: A longitudinal approach. *Public Management Review* (Special Issue on Innovation in Public Services), *10*(1), 51–70.

Palazzo, G., & Scherer, A. G. (2008). The future of global corporate citizenship: Toward a theory of the firm as a political actor. In A. G. Scherer & G. Palazzo (Eds.), *Handbook of research on global corporate citizenship* (pp. 577–590). Cheltenham: Edward Elgar Publishing.

Paton, R., & Brewster, R. (2008, 20–22 November). Making deeper sense in the midst of great busyness: A study of and with third sector CEOs' paper given at the 37th Annual Conference of ARNOVA, Philadelphia, PA, USA.

Patzer, M., & Voegtlin, C. (2013). Leadership ethics and organisational change: Sketching the field. In R. T. By & B. Burnes (Eds.), *Organisational change, leadership and ethics* (pp. 10–34). London: Routledge.

Pearce, C. L., & Conger, J. A. (2003). *Shared leadership: Reframing the hows and whys of leadership.* Thousand Oaks, CA: Sage.

Plummer, J. (2009). How infighting sank the Third Sector Leadership Centre. *Third Sector*, 23rd March, 2009.

Reid, B., & Pearson, G. (2011, May). *Developing leadership in the social sector: Year 1 evaluation of the Clore social leadership programme*. London: Clore Social Leadership Programme/Work Foundation.

Rubin, H. (Ed.). (2009). *Collaborative leadership: Developing effective partnerships for communities and schools*. London: Sage.

Scherer, A. G., & Palazzo, G. (2008). Globalization and corporate social responsibility. In A. Crane, A. McWilliams, D. Matten, J. Moon, & D. Siegel (Eds.), *The Oxford handbook of corporate social responsibility* (pp. 413–431). Oxford: Oxford University Press.

Scherer, A. G., Palazzo, G., & Matten, D. (2009). Globalization as a challenge for business responsibilities. *Business Ethics Quarterly, 19*(3), 327–347.

Schmeuker, K., & Johnson, M. (2009). *All Inclusive? Third sector involvement in regional and sub-regional policy making*. Newcastle: IPPR. Retrieved from http://www.ippr.org/images/media/files/publication/2011/05/all_inclusive_1711.pdf

Schwabenland, C. (2012). *Stories visions and values in voluntary organisations*. Hampshire: Ashgate Publishing.

Spangenberg, H., & Theron, C. C. (2005). Promoting ethical follower behaviour through leadership of ethics: The development of the ethical leadership inventory (ELI). *South African Journal of Business Management, 36*(2), 1–18.

Statement of Recommended Practice. (2005). Charities Commission, UK. Retrieved from http://www.CharitiesCommission.gov.uk

Thach, E., & Thompson, K. J. (2007). Trading places: Examining leadership competencies between for-profit vs. public and non-profit leaders. *Leadership & Organisation Development Journal, 28*, 356–375.

Tierney, T. J. (2006). Understanding the nonprofit sector's leadership deficit. *Leader to Leader, 1*, 13S–19S.

Trevino, L. K., & Brown, M. E. (2004). Managing to be ethical: Debunking five business ethics myths. *Academy of Management Executive, 18*, 69–81.

Venter, K., & Sung, J. (2009). *Do skills matter? A literature review on skills and workforce development in the third sector*. Skills — Third Sector. Retrieved from http://www.skills-thirdsector.org.uk/documents/STS_Do_Skills_Matter_Report.pdf

Wheatley, M., & Frieze, D. (2011). *Walk out walk on, a learning journey into communities daring to live the future now*. San Francisco, CA: Berrett-Koehler.

Wilderom, C. P. M., & Miner, J. B. (1991). Defining voluntary groups and agencies within organisational science. *Organisation Science, 2*, 366–377.

Wilding, K. (2010). Voluntary organisations and the recession. *Voluntary Sector Review, 1*(1), 97–101.

Wolfenden Committee. (1978). *The future of voluntary organisations*. Croom Helm: London.

Chapter 5

Conclusion

In writing this book, our aim is to advance further, knowledge of leadership in the public and third sectors in the United Kingdom. This aim was originally driven by an identified need to fill the gap in the literature on leadership in these sectors, but also by a desire to give people in these sectors the opportunity to voice their opinions about their experience of leadership, their perceptions and understanding of leadership, in addition to the challenges that they face on a daily basis and indeed, the challenges that they expect to face in the years ahead.

5.1. Summary of Current Leadership Thinking

Leadership is a subject that has generated significant interest among scholars and practitioners alike. However, almost everyone who thinks, studies, writes or practices leadership interprets it differently.

In short, leadership is a complex phenomenon that touches on many organisational, social and personal processes (Bolden, 2004). It depends on a process of social influence, whereby people are inspired to work towards group goals, not through coercion, but through personal motivation.

In terms of an objective overview of leadership, there are many different perspectives and lenses to look at leadership from and/or through. In this book, we adopt the lens of the leadership philosophy in studying leadership. The most prevalent leadership philosophies, in the first part of this century, include: adaptive leadership, authentic leadership, distributed leadership, ethical leadership, servant leadership and shared leadership. Leadership philosophies focus on what kind of leadership one should offer — they contain values-based ideas of how a leader should be and act, and the sources of a leader's power. A philosophy also provides us with far more and deeper references to society, politics and civilisation than models or styles.

5.2. Public Sector Summary

In the public sector in the United Kingdom today, significant challenges are present, and will continue to be present in the years ahead, including: continual demands to modernise; higher expectations on the part of the general public and consumers who expect public services to keep up with private ones; a greater focus on connectedness; increased opportunities and requirements for partnership working both across the public sector and with private and third sector organisations; more personalisation of services; pressures to harness new technology and deliver government services electronically; and to deliver improved services through a motivated workforce in an age of austerity.

We offer, however, that the main challenge facing the public sector in the United Kingdom is that of leadership. In this regard, the challenge requires a new way of thinking about leadership in the sector.

A leadership challenge in the public sector appears to be the shift away from traditional technical or operational roles to more collaborative, networked leadership roles. These roles imply the need for greater political awareness, more collaborative and engaging behaviour, and exceptional influencing skills.

Looking at the available literature, it would seem that we are certainly moving away from the 'heroic individual' model and towards a more distributed, collective and empowered approach where the relationship between leaders and followers (or constituents, colleagues, collaborators) is most important. Leadership, then, is about making it possible for everyone in the organisation — or within a network of organisations — to contribute. Leslie and Canwell (2010) suggest that senior public sector leaders will need to demonstrate four key leadership capabilities:

1. Developing the insights necessary for successful change within complex systems
2. Building the cognitive skills to manage effectively in demanding environments
3. Demonstrating the emotional intelligence to motivate their people
4. Building leadership at all levels of the organisation, by developing capability and ensuring that overly complex structures do not impede the ability of individuals across the organisation to exercise leadership

We suggest, then, that with budgets being radically reduced — while citizens' expectations continue to rise — public sector leaders will be challenged to demonstrate a set of capabilities that may not be familiar to the leaders at either central or local levels.

Turning to current leadership thinking within the sector, we are reminded of some of the key areas of interest, which were identified in Chapter 3:

- The criticism of individuality in leadership
- The importance of collective endeavour — where individuals can contribute to the establishment and development of a common purpose (vision)
- Leadership as one of the key cornerstones of innovation, because it plays an important role in changing the status quo
- The potential for leadership is broader than has been thought hitherto
- The importance of collective leadership in collaborative advantage and trust

From the individual reflections in Chapter 3, and in terms of leadership philosophies, we see evidence of leadership adaption, leadership authenticity, leadership distribution, leadership ethics, leadership serving and leadership sharing. In addition, the importance of putting the *follower* at the centre of leadership is clearly centre stage. In terms of self-awareness and insight, we also note the honesty and acceptance by many of the contributors — especially in relation to their limitations and an understanding (thereof) — of their desire to learn and develop their leadership skills further.

More generally, we note that the act of doing is very important in leadership, particularly drawing on soft skills. We argue, with some conviction, therefore, of the importance of putting the verb back into leadership. Finally, we restate the importance of intellect that leadership demands.

We also suggest that the reflections, offered by the public sector leaders, complement and support current leadership theory and thinking particularly around the areas of collaboration, collective endeavour, relationships between leaders and followers and the importance of networks, insight, cognitive skills, emotional intelligence and capability. In addition, we judge that the authors' reflections will help scholars and theorists develop and advance further theory in this sector, particularly revisiting and 'surfacing' the leadership philosophies that will be required to meet the many general and sector-specific challenges.

5.3. Third Sector Summary

The third sector, which is understood broadly in this book as the vast array of charities, voluntary organisations, community groups, cooperatives, mutuals and social enterprises, finds itself in a time of significant change. During the past ten to fifteen years it has, amongst other things, grown in size — in part through public funding, contracting for service delivery, and investment in support infrastructure. The sector has also: gained a much higher profile in public policy and the media; become the subject of much greater policy attention, with cross-party political support; and at the same time, engaged in various debates around independence, values, ethos, professionalism, effectiveness, and accountability. Such change has had a significant impact on the role and responsibilities of leaders within the sector. Yet, as mentioned in Chapter 4, research on leadership in the sector is relatively embryonic. The vast majority of the literature on leadership assumes that leadership occurs in the private and public sectors. The little literature that does exist on the third sector tends to focus on the role and characteristics of Chief Executives in relatively large professional voluntary organisations. Little attention has been given to leadership in the third sector as a whole, or in its sub-sectors, such as the charity sector or new and growing movements within the sector, such as 'social enterprise'. This is one of the reasons why, in this book, we sought the views of leaders from a cross section of organisations. The reflections from the

206 Public and Third Sector Leadership: Experience Speaks

leaders in the sector make a start at understanding what leadership means and the context in which it is operating. It opens the way for more specific research across the sector of both a quantitative and qualitative nature, inductive and deductive. Moreover, from a practical point of view, we hope that it will encourage leaders from other sub-sectors in the third sector to voice their views on leadership and the challenges that they are facing in order to identify opportunities for sharing and learning together.

5.4. Public versus Third

5.4.1. Similarities

The reflections in this book emphasise a number of similarities between third and public sector leadership. Both sectors are experiencing a radical shift in their political and economic environment. Since 2007—2008, they have been operating under the shadow of austerity, first with the double threat of recession — in the form of increased demand for services against resources — and secondly, in seeking to understand and negotiate a changing political and ideological climate following the outcome of the 2010 General Election. The focus in both sectors has shifted towards an emphasis on survival and resilience, along with an intensified need for collaboration and increasingly desperate attempts to demonstrate value for money. It is possible, therefore, that both sectors are undergoing a significant transformation in their shape, their role and their relationship with the state.

The major shakeup of both sectors is accompanied by a rapidly escalating complexity and one that will only increase in the near future. Part of the increasing complexity faced by leaders is (and will continue to be) the broader task of meeting the demands of a wider range of stakeholders than they have traditionally been used to. The complexity of this task is amplified by a further similarity, the increasing speed of change which leaders in both sectors are facing. It has been triggered by a reduction in government resources and the need to generate more funding from other sources.

To address the decline in resources as well as an increase in demand, leaders in these sectors are being forced to work together and build alliances. Collaboration within, and across sectors, offers an opportunity for leaders to work flexibly and deliver enhanced benefits to their stakeholders. Collaborative working is likely to become an increasingly central feature of the work of leaders in both sectors as it will enable them to continue to meet and enhance their objectives in an era of ever complex needs and scant resources. For collaboration to take place, it needs innovation and to be driven by leaders with the right commitment, attitudes and capabilities. Yet in both sectors, there appears to be a leadership deficit in the capabilities required.

Leaders in the public and third sectors need to develop new capabilities to cope with increasing changes. The third sector — we contend — will be expected to provide more public services in the future, while the public sector is faced with providing more with less. Both sectors require more investment in developing their leaders in order to cope with the demands that are, and will be, placed upon them. The challenge of the present and the future then is, and will be, to build a cadre of leaders across the sectors with the skills to collectively accomplish what is needed for each sector to survive and thrive.

So is leadership similar in the third and public sectors? There are similarities in that the majority of leaders have gained their experience of leadership from work itself. Leaders from both sectors perceive leadership as being authentic — being true to themselves and to their followers. There are also commonalities in that leadership is seen as providing direction, communicating, collaborating and building trust. Common across both sectors are the concerns about how they will, on the one hand, meet increasingly diverse stakeholder demands with, on the other hand, less resources. Within this setting, there is a need to engage in proactive stakeholder management to secure their legitimacy and their licence to operate in a changing society.

5.4.2. Differences

In 'scoping' this chapter, we considered that there would be a difference in the experience, perception and enactment of leadership in the public and third sectors. On reflection, however, and in looking again at Chapters 3 and 4, we are not sure if there is a marked difference at all between experience, perception and meaning. The context, at present, may be different but as has been stated throughout this book, we are witnessing more *blurring of boundaries* between these sectors in the United Kingdom.

5.4.3. Challenges Across the Sectors

In Chapter 3 we established that the public sector challenges included:

- Having meeting spaces and *head space* allowing for a sharing of values and aspirations
- Being allowed to deliberate, to be allowed not to understand, and trying to make sense of change and what it means
- Helping people develop, learn and enhance their skills
- Understanding the importance of valuing, supporting and resourcing
- Empowering and team membership
- Awareness and understanding of the importance of leader—follower relationships
- Leading without authority and leading diversity
- The importance of flexibility and agility
- Managing and understanding complexity
- Galvanising effort and spirit
- Problems with hierarchical leadership
- The need for critical thinking
- The importance of the role of leadership and innovation

In Chapter 4, we established that the main sectoral challenges were: defining the role of the sector; improving the quality of services; creating a sustainable business model; and delivering innovation and change.

We could spend time trying to explain, and elaborate on, any difference between the sectors in terms of challenges. We, suggest, however, that the differences, if any, are minimal.

Perhaps the only real difference is defining the role of the sector, as offered by the analysis of the third sector. But as was seen in Chapter 3, this is also an issue in the public sector. The recent report, 'Why the NHS needs to partner with the private and voluntary sectors' (Wells, 2013), is a case in point.

It would appear, then, that it is not the differences in the sectors that are worthy of comment, but rather the similarities, and a recognition of these similarities, that demands greater focus and attention.

In summary, then, these sectors are no longer discrete. These authors in the public and third sectors have commented on their experiences of leadership, their perceptions of leadership, leadership meaning (as they see it), leadership challenges (general) and leadership challenges (specific). We contend — and believe that the reader will also share this view — that their reflections are broadly similar.

We are left wondering, then, how we develop leadership to meet the current and future challenges in both sectors as they continue to overlap and perhaps, merge.

5.5.   Leadership across the Sectors

The changing business environment, with an increasing focus on growth, volatility and complexity, along with a decrease in resources requires a significant change in thinking about leadership in the public and third sectors, as is evident by the reflections in this book. The increasing complexity of the work environment means that leaders in the public and third sectors are unable to possess all the necessary expertise to perform all the required leadership functions effectively. Against this background, there is seen to be a need to move away from the dominance of viewing leadership roles and individual leadership as synonymous constructs (Avolio, Jung, Murry, & Sivasbramaniam, 1996; Bass & Bass, 2009) to considering leadership as a more fluid construct (Hiller, Day, & Vance, 2006). This thinking has led to the emergence of a model that is more appropriate to the increasingly complex environment in which leaders from the public and third sector are now operating — the concept of tri-sector leadership (Lovegrove & Thomas, 2013), which we outline in Chapter 4. The recognition of the value and relevance of such a model will help create a leadership identity across the sectors.[1] This is not to suggest that the use of

---

1. This view is echoed elsewhere; for example, Forth Sector Development Limited (2012, p. 4) in their paper, *Leadership in the New Order* discuss the *4th sector* and suggest that the boundaries between the private, public and third sector are blurred and indeed overlap.

one single dominant model is what is required and should replace all other models. Rather it is about replacing simplistic models with frameworks for thinking about leadership in specific sectors. In exploring this idea, Avolio, Walumbwa, and Weber (2009) suggest that leadership is a complex phenomenon that has to include considerations of contextual issues and challenges. It is important, however, to consider whether or not situational models may need to include some other components (Higgs, 2003). Avolio et al. (2009) and Walumbwa, Lawler, and Avolio (2007) suggest that there is a need to ensure that leadership is executed in an authentic manner within any framework.

In the context of the public and third sectors Avolio et al. (2009) state that the concept of authenticity and authentic leadership would appear to be essential. The key components of authentic leadership include: self-awareness; self-regulation; relational transparency; and a clear moral compass. Such a framework places an ethical component at the heart of leadership in the sectors (By & Burnes, 2013). In addition to the comments by these scholars, this book offers that we also need adaptive, distributed, ethical, servant and shared leadership. We do consider that there are flavours of these philosophies throughout the individual reflections in this book.

The environment is changing and the public and third sectors must also change if they are to have a sustainable future. For leaders in both sectors, this implies a new conceptualization of leadership. To be able to react adequately to the diverse demands of multiple stakeholder groups, leadership within the sectors needs a theoretical foundation that can guide leaders and provide an orientation in dealing with the complex dilemmas they are facing. It needs to enable them to produce decisions, satisfy a majority of stakeholders and provide a framework for leadership in the sectors.

5.6. Limitations

The public and third sectors in the United Kingdom are of considerable size (absolute and relative), are complex, complicated and growing. It would be difficult even in many volumes to capture and understand the many issues that these sectors present — we do hope that the reader will understand that there is only so much that we can cover in one volume. In addition, the sectors are changing rapidly: this book is cross-sectional research undertaken during 2013. It represents the views of the authors and contributors during this time period only.

That being said, while it is possible to argue that our sample is not representative of the larger population of current personnel in the public and third sectors, this sample is large in the context of previous research on public and third sector leadership. Moreover, few studies have actually utilised this methodology with such a diverse and eclectic sample. Of note, access to this sample has provided an unparalleled opportunity to enhance our understanding of leadership within this contemporary setting. In terms of the book's aim, we are also not aware of other such books that try to explore and understand the reflections from as many individuals that are contained within this volume.

5.7. Future Research

The emerging themes from our review of the literature and the individual reflections appear to highlight a need for a more differentiated research agenda for leadership in the public and third sectors, involving comparisons between the sectors and across different geographies.

A number of key research gaps and priorities have, therefore, been identified. Four research questions are outlined below. Of note, and at the time of writing, we consider that little research attention has been given to these areas.

1. What is the most relevant leadership framework?

   There is a need to investigate new and relevant leadership frameworks for the sectors. In Chapter 2, we referred to the New Public Leadership framework, proposed by Brookes and Grint (2010) which they say should include: a form of collective leadership; context; type and scale of problem; collaborative advantage; performance and public value; and reflecting trust. We ask, however, if we have already moved beyond New Public Leadership. We think so and we think that this book demonstrates this. Is there a case, therefore, to consider the concept of tri-sector leadership across the public, third and private sectors? Otiso (2003) points out the benefits of tri-sector partnerships as enabling participants to transcend sectoral limitations. The opposing strengths of these sectors prove that not only can none single-handedly satisfy the demands and needs of stakeholders, but that they must partner for success. Otiso (2003, p. 227) concludes that:

   > Tri-sector partnerships foster success by utilizing mutual strengths and skills, promoting community participation, local capacity-building, self-help and empowerment, efficient resource mobilization, and diffusion of best practices.

2. What constitutes leadership effectiveness in the public and third sectors?

   Studies on leadership effectiveness typically seek either to specify the individual qualities of 'heroic' leaders or, increasingly, to highlight the collective and collaborative nature of 'post-heroic' leadership (see Chapter 2). While these discourses are frequently seen as dichotomous and competing, the reflections in this book show that leaders often value practices that combine a number of elements. Collinson and Collinson (2009) in a study in Higher Education found that leaders in the sector tended to prefer subtle and versatile practices that they term 'blended leadership' — an approach that values, for example, both ethical and collaborative, or distributed and authentic. While Riggio and Reichard (2008) describe a framework for conceptualising the role of emotional and social skills in effective leadership.

As yet, there is no clear picture about what constitutes leadership effectiveness in the sectors. Further research is clearly required. Could it perhaps be the concept of *intellectual leadership*, which may include:

- Developing the insights necessary for successful change within complex systems at the organisational level
- Building the cognitive skills to manage effectively in demanding environments
- Demonstrating the emotional intelligence to motivate their people
- Building leadership at all levels of the organisation, by developing capability and ensuring that overly complex structures do not impede the ability of individuals across the organisation to exercise leadership

In addition, we consider that there is no escaping the comment made by David Cook, when he says: *The biggest challenge has to be the legacy we are leaving for the younger generation.* Although outside the scope of this book, this concern and discourse does not appear in current leadership literature. More generally, we note the concerns of the World Economic Forum, who in their '2014 Global Risk Report' (section 2.3 Generation Lost?, p. 33) state:

> In many countries, dramatically high unemployment is frustrating young people's efforts to earn, generate savings, gain professional experience and build careers. Traditional higher education is ever more expensive and its payoff more doubtful. These issues need to be addressed inclusively on local, national and global levels to minimize the risks of a breakdown in social cohesion and enduring loss of human and economic potential.

As authors, we do not have an immediate solutions for this; that being said, we do judge that a significant outcome of this book is to surface such issues.

3. How can the leadership deficit be solved?

This challenge is complicated by the very nature of the sectors. Unlike businesses, they cannot address the leadership deficit by 'growing their own' supply of future leaders. Successful companies routinely invest enormous amounts of money and time attracting talented junior managers and developing them into leadership candidates. They recognise that competency in developing talent is a potent form of competitive advantage. Most third sector organisations (even the larger ones) are too small, however, to provide meaningful career development opportunities for next-generation leaders. Nor can they afford to make the investment in recruitment, retention and development, particularly in an environment that tends to view such expenditures as a wasteful overhead.

To accomplish their missions, organisations in the public and third sectors need both financial capital and human capital. But whereas financial shortfalls are easily measured, simply communicated and impossible to avoid, leadership shortfalls can be hard to calibrate, awkward to discuss and tempting to avoid. This is what makes the emerging leadership deficit so dangerous. What if we fail to understand and acknowledge the escalating need for new leaders? What if, in aggregate, we under-invest in building leadership capacity and fail to create a mix of rewards that will attract and motivate talented managers? What if we cannot overcome the barriers and fragmentation that are likely to impede the flow and mobility of capable executives into and within the sector?

The first imperative — for individual organisations and the sectors overall — is to acknowledge and understand the enormity of the problem. In particular, business and strategic planning skills appear to be missing, especially in the third sector. Chapman, Brown, Crow, and Ward (2006, p. 6) state:

> Many small and medium sized [organisations] lack capacity and capability in terms of business planning and strategic planning because they have inadequate governance structures in place to provide the support the organisation needs. As a result organisations run on a hand to mouth basis in the belief that a new funding source will come along soon; and, of course, there is plenty of evidence to suggest that in the past, this is precisely what has happened .... This research casts serious doubt about the preparedness of the [third sector] as a whole for change and instead suggests that the general sense of optimism about sustainability in the longer term may be misplaced.

This concern about misplaced optimism, lack of awareness, and vision is echoed in other research. Packwood (2007, p. 36) offers:

> Some [third sector] organisations reasoned that they spend so much time struggling for survival that they have very little time or energy to develop leadership skills, or to undertake the research needed to gain a clear picture of what is coming round the corner.

There are calls for a more differentiated support response for both sectors in commissioning and procurement, and particularly a concern for more in-depth and tailored training. The Charity Commission reiterated this as a recommendation from its study of public service delivery (2007, p. 23):

> There is clearly a need for increased support to locally-based, lower-income charities that want to get involved in delivering public services but which currently lack the capacity to do so. There is government recognition that there is also a need to build the capacity of parts of the public sector to work in true partnership with charities and the wider third sector. The government may also wish to consider what can be done to ensure that smaller and more local organisations have

access to appropriate capacity building opportunities. Potential barriers created by current frameworks for commissioning services, procurement and contracting, funding and monitoring need to be fully investigated, understood and addressed.

The second imperative is to make this challenge a top priority, in governance, in planning and in day-to-day decision making. Ignoring the issue, or behaving as though it were a long-term problem to be solved by future generations, will almost certainly exacerbate the depth and breadth of the crisis.

Closing the gap will require action, as well as a willingness to innovate, experiment and take risks at both an organisational and a sector level. In individual organisations, board members and senior managers must all commit to build strong and enduring leadership teams. At a sector-wide level, there is a need to collaborate to nurture the flow and development of a cadre of leadership talent. In this context, three imperatives are salient: invest in leadership capacity; refine management rewards to retain and attract top talent; and expand recruiting horizons while fostering individual career mobility. To address the leadership shortfall, much greater attention to building leadership capacity and capability is needed — and that will require a shift in investment.

4. What are the constructs of political and philanthropic leadership?

If we consider that the third sector is moving further into an era where its role and influence will increase significantly, and the reliance of the public on its actions will grow, the delicate balance to be struck between doing good through the state and doing good through private means will come under increasing stress (Lenkowsky, 2010). Although this book has commented upon public and third sector leadership, and indeed, their similarities, the role of the private funder — philanthropy — has, not hitherto, been considered. Future research may want to consider this type of leadership.

5.8. Endnote

The world in which the public and third sectors operate is changing, and the leadership in these sectors also must change if they are to have a sustainable future. However, at the time of writing, there is still too little known about leadership in the sectors and the lack of a valid context-specific leadership framework for these sectors not only in the United Kingdom and Europe but also elsewhere in the world.

This book has provided a much needed and overdue space for the voices of leaders within the public and third sectors in the United Kingdom to be heard. Our hope is that this is just the start of approaching leadership through the eyes of those practicing leadership in these sectors across the globe.

References

Avolio, B. J., Jung, D. I., Murry, W., & Sivasbramaniam, N. (1996). Building highly developed teams: Focusing on shared leadership process, efficacy, trust, and performance. *Advances in Interdisciplinary Studies on Work Teams, 3,* 173−209.

Avolio, B. J., Walumbwa, F. O., & Weber, T. J. (2009). Leadership: Current theories, research, and future directions. *Annual Review of Psychology, 60,* 421−449.

Bass, B. M., & Bass, R. (2009). *The Bass handbook of leadership: Theory, research, and managerial applications.* New York, NY: Simon and Schuster.

Bolden, R. (2004). *What is leadership.* Research Report 1. Centre for Leadership Studies, University of Exeter.

Brookes, S., & Grint, K. (Eds.). (2010). *The new public leadership challenge.* Palgrave Macmillan: London.

By, R. T., & Burnes, B. (Eds.). (2013). *Organisational change, leadership and ethics.* Oxon: Routledge.

Chapman, T., Brown, J., Crow, R., & Ward, J. (2006, March). *Facing the future: A study of the impact of a changing funding environment on the voluntary and community sector in the North East of England.* Middlesbrough: Social Futures Institute, Teesside University.

Charity Commission. (2007, February). Stand and deliver: The future for charities delivering public services. Charity Commission, London, RS15.

Collinson, D., & Collinson, M. (2009). Blended leadership: Employee perspectives on effective leadership in the UK further education sector. *Leadership, 5*(3), 365−380.

Forth Sector Development Limited. (2012). *Leadership in the new order.* Discussion paper. Forth Sector Development Ltd. Retrieved from http://www.forthsector.org.uk

Higgs, M. (2003). How can we make sense of leadership in the 21st century. *Leadership and Organization Development Journal, 24*(5), 273−284.

Hiller, N. J., Day, D. V., & Vance, R. J. (2006). Collective enactment of leadership roles and team effectiveness: A field study. *The Leadership Quarterly, 17*(4), 387−397.

Lenkowsky, L. (2010). The politics of doing good. In J. L. Perry (Ed.), *The Jossey-Bass reader on nonprofit and public leadership.* San Francisco, CA: Jossey-Bass.

Leslie, K., & Canwell, A. (2010). Leadership at all levels: Leading public sector organisations in an age of austerity. *European Management Journal, 28*(4), 297−305.

Lovegrove, N., & Thomas, M. (2013). Triple-strength leadership. *Harvard Business Review, 91*(9), 46−56.

Otiso, K. M. (2003). State, voluntary and private sector partnerships for slum upgrading and basic service delivery in Nairobi City, Kenya. *Cities, 20*(4), 221−229.

Packwood, D. (2007). *Commissioning, contracting and service delivery of children's services in the voluntary and community sector.* London: VCS Engage.

Riggio, R. E., & Reichard, R. J. (2008). The emotional and social intelligences of effective leadership: An emotional and social skill approach. *Journal of Managerial Psychology, 23*(2), 169−185.

Walumbwa, F. O., Lawler, J. J., & Avolio, B. J. (2007). Leadership, individual differences, and work-related attitudes: A cross-culture investigation. *Applied Psychology, 56*(2), 212−230.

Wells, W. (2013). Why the NHS needs to partner with the private and voluntary sectors. *The Guardian,* 4 December.

Epilogue

When I think about what makes a good or effective leader, the first thing that springs to my mind is what does 'good' or 'effective' mean? Is it someone who grows the organisation? Meets the goals? Is a jolly nice human being or a bit of a ruthless high-achiever? Who is the real judge of who is a good leader and what good leadership looks like? And that's why I think books such as this are so important. They make you think hard, about leadership in general, but more importantly, about what leadership means to you.

Some would argue that success for leaders is measured by their achieving some objective or some result. But here's the thing about leadership: there is always a new challenge, aim, goal. You may achieve something and celebrate for a while — but then what? Is it about more? Bigger? Better? When we examine successful leaders it becomes clear that they are not necessarily the ones who 'won' all the time or who always achieved their aim. And there are some individuals who undoubtedly achieved political, financial or professional 'success' but who we might not to consider to be good leaders.

It seems to me that 'followers' (for want of a better term) tend to measure good leadership in terms of how the leader's behaviour impacted on them; affected how they felt and thought about the work and more importantly, about themselves. Indeed success in leadership terms seems to me to be more about what others think, not what you think.

A board of trustees might perceive their CEO as a 'good' leader because he/she made a tough decision to lose some staff and as a result kept the charity financially viable. But I'm fairly sure that at least some of the staff affected wouldn't make the same analysis.

A local councillor might perceive a senior civil servant as a good leader because he or she managed to make a public service more efficient by reducing some of it. But it's entirely possible that the local community might perceive the civil servant as a poor leader for not standing up to the local councillor and fighting their corner.

Ultimately it's human beings who make the judgement about the quality of an individual's leadership. And their judgement entirely depends upon their context, values and perceptions. We evaluate those who are leading us differently to how we evaluate historical leaders. As Tony Blair once famously said about the Iraq war 'History will be my judge'. Many of my colleagues in the sector would choke on their tea if they heard me say that, although I profoundly disagreed with Margaret Thatcher's policies, I would nonetheless argue she was, on occasion, an exceptional leader. I think the Dalai Lama is an inspirational, kind and wise man. I'm not convinced about the effectiveness of his leadership. Am I right about either of these two people? Of course not. But then neither are those who would argue the opposite.

And that's the point about leadership for me, which is so well reflected in this book. Organisations aren't in and of themselves complex: people are. Products, services, systems, processes, all of these can be broken down into relatively simple analyses of cause and effect, and the relationships between them can be mapped and visualised diagrammatically through simple flowcharts.

But people can't. And that's why great leadership can be so hard to define and indeed, replicate. Years of scientists and psychologists studying the nature of humanity and consciousness can't fully explain why people behave the way they do. The scientific method means that you can replicate an outcome by reproducing the exact circumstances that produced it in the first place. You can theorise about why a certain event happens and this theory can be tested by experiment and observation and proved to be right or wrong depending on whether or not your predicted outcome happens.

But with people, even with simple experiments, minimal variables and highly tuned approaches, the outcome is always unpredictable at the level of the individual. You can say on average what might happen or is likely to, but you can never be absolutely sure because the range of variables that influence human behaviour and thinking is so vast that to date it simply cannot be fully understood.

So what does this mean in terms of leadership and effectiveness? Well it means that leadership can rarely be simply about replicating a piece of behaviour that you observed in some other leader that seemed to produce the results you want in your own organisation. All leaders, whether they are coming from a position of formal authority, or not, will have different people in a different context with a different history. We have to find our own way. But we will find it better if we listen and learn from others.

And as this book shows, attempting to find a model of leadership that 'works' for all leaders in all contexts is very difficult. If it was simple then everyone would attend the same leadership training course and be able to produce outstanding results all the time. And successful leaders would be successful all the time at everything — yet that is so clearly not the case.

So is good leadership then about achieving a certain pre-determined outcome? I'm not sure it is. Because even if you can identify a precise set of leadership behaviours that will help to achieve your goal, what you can't do is predict accurately what is going to happen in the external environment, or how human beings might react, that might affect your ability to reach your destination.

So, perhaps being effective as a leader means to be sensitive to and aware of the moment and the context that you are in and have the behavioural flexibility to respond to circumstances as they occur. Precisely because the world is inherently unpredictable.

I have come to believe, from my own experience, and from the research in this book, that success in leadership is not about the goal you achieved or the destination you reached, but how you negotiated the path.

Debra Tyler
Chief Executive
Directory of Social Change